THE COMPLETE GUIDE TO
Walking
IN Canada

THE COMPLETE GUIDE TO
Walking
IN Canada

INCLUDES
Day-hiking & Backpacking

ELLIOTT KATZ

FIREFLY BOOKS

A FIREFLY BOOK

Published by Firefly Books Ltd. 2001

First Printing 2001

U.S. Cataloging-in-Publication Data is available.

National Library of Canada Cataloguing in Publication Data
Katz, Elliott
  The complete guide to walking in Canada : includes day hiking
& back-packing

2nd ed.
Includes index.
ISBN 1-55209-370-0

1. Walking – Canada – Guidebooks.   2. Trails – Canada – Guidebooks.
3. National parks and reserves – Canada – Guidebooks.   I. Title.

GV199.44C2K39 2001   917.104   C99-931951-5

Published in Canada in 2001 by
Firefly Books Ltd.
3680 Victoria Park Avenue
Willowdale, Ontario, Canada   M2H 3K1

Published in the United States in 2001 by
Firefly Books (U.S.) Inc.
P.O. Box 1338, Ellicott Station
Buffalo, New York, USA   14205

Design by Interrobang Graphic Design Inc.
Printed and bound in Canada by Friesens, Altona, Manitoba

*The Publisher acknowledges the financial support of the Government of Canada through
the Book Publishing Industry Development Program for its publishing activities.*

Dedication

To Leah and Sarah

When you walk, it shall guide you.
Ethics of the Fathers 6:9

Raise now your eyes and look from where you are:
northward, southward, eastward and westward…
Arise, walk about the land through its length and breadth.
Genesis 13: 15, 17

Preface

You start walking a trail into a natural area—you're discovering another world. Canada's magnificent natural areas are best experienced on foot. Even in popular areas, nature paths often let you escape the tourist crowds. At Moraine Lake near Lake Louise in the Rockies—one of Canada's most popular tourist areas—I began walking three kilometres along the serene lake's edge and I was free of the tour bus crowds and savoring the freedom of the hills. The peace was overwhelming—I heard total silence as I hiked self-sufficient through the wilderness.

You can use this guide to explore trails of all types—interpretive trails including paths that are accessible for wheelchairs and strollers, day-hikes, and backpacking treks. Over the past few years, a variety of new trails have been built—long-distance trails for backpackers, and self-guiding interpretive trails for families and individuals who want to learn about the environment they're walking through. Walking in Canada means discovering trails in and near many cities as well as in less populated places.

To walk in the wilderness is to experience nature directly. The opportunities are as diverse as is Canada's geography. Pick up this book and discover:

- surf-washed beaches of Vancouver Island's west coast, where whales swim offshore
- the route followed by the Klondikers of 1898 over the Chilkoot Pass
- the lush Coast Mountains, lofty Selkirks and majestic Rockies
- prairie trails used by native peoples and fur traders
- rugged Lake Superior shores and Killarney's turquoise lakes that inspired Group of Seven artists
- nature trails along a creek through a forest a few minutes from the center of Toronto

- a Quebec autumn forest ablaze with color
- red cliffs and river meadows of Nova Scotia's Cape Breton Highlands
- fiords and windswept treeless barrens of Newfoundland

The book is divided into two main parts. Part One covers such how-to basics as equipment, food and cooking gear, routefinding, hiking with children, hiking in winter, and what to do about insects. Part Two — covering all of Canada's provinces and territories and organized west to east—is a comprehensive guide to trails in Canada. Walks are usually interpretive nature trails, where there often are signs or a brochure that explain the phenomena being observed. Also included are short walks, up to two hours long. Day-hikes are trails that take anywhere from several hours to a full day, but are not meant as overnight backpacking trips. Backpacking trips are those suitable for overnight or longer and include backcountry campsites or shelters.

Descriptions include information on length of trails, highlights, topography, forest cover, and wildlife and birdlife. Each description offers addresses for more information, including a website address whenever possible.

Over the years, Canada's trails have let me escape from the hectic city to the serene natural beauty with which Canada has been abundantly blessed. I hope you use this guidebook as a way to discover more trails that lead to special places and experiences.

Contents

part one

Getting Ready

1

Walking's Magnificent Benefits

► Walk—it makes you feel good and lets you savor our wilderness.

► Set realistic goals.

If someone tells you take a walk—do it for the magnificent physical and spiritual benefits. Walking is as natural to the body as breathing, but too many of us have taken it for granted.

Walking Is Good Exercise

Walking can help your heart and circulation. When you are sedentary, blood collects in the lower part of your body, depriving the brain and upper body of blood. The heart muscle works harder to maintain circulation.

When you walk, the muscles of the feet, calves and thighs give the blood an extra push that lessens the load on the heart and helps to lower blood pressure. Walking also aids the respiratory system and digestion.

Hiking helps you sleep better. Charles Dickens cured his insomnia with nightly walks. If you're inactive, when you go to bed your mind is tired but your body isn't. After a day of walking, your body is truly tired and sleep comes easily. A walk in unpolluted air puts color in your face. Walking helps burn extra calories.

Walking Makes You Feel Good

"Unhappy businessmen, I am convinced," wrote the philosopher Bertrand Russell, "would increase their happiness more by walking six miles every day than by any conceivable change of philosophy."

When the mind is tense, angry or feels a painful emotion, the muscles in the body become tense, which can cause headaches, backaches, high blood pressure and insomnia. Walking at a steady pace releases the tension in your muscles, relieves the physical pain and causes the mind to relax.

Walking in nature clears the head. It kickstarts your mind to come up with ideas and solutions to problems. Plato expounded his philosophy while walking in an olive grove. It was during a walk in a February snowstorm that Pierre Elliott Trudeau decided to retire as Prime Minister.

Pace and Rhythm

Walking is the symphony of mind and body. Good rhythm is as important in walking as it is in music. Disjointed stop-and-go city walking is often exhausting, but you can hike at a steady tempo for several hours without becoming tired.

When starting out, amble down the trail at an *adagio* (leisurely) tempo. As the muscles loosen, speed increases and you gradually work up to an *andante* (moderate) pace. When walking on flat ground the tempo can often be brought up to a brisk *allegro con alma* (with spirit, soulfully) without getting out of breath. Sing a song (in your head or aloud) to keep a steady rhythm while walking: a march for a sprightly step to cover distance, or a long ballad for leisurely rambles.

Novice hikers often keep an erratic pace. They race down the trail in the morning, soon tiring. Like the fabled tortoise who beat the hare, the hiker who keeps a steady pace will cover a greater distance and be less tired at day's end than the Speedy Gonzales who makes several jackrabbit starts and soon drops from exhaustion.

Set Realistic Goals

It's better to underestimate the distance you'll walk than to try to go too far. When planning a trip, take several factors into account.

YOUR PHYSICAL CONDITION ▶ If you're out of shape, you may find 25 km on the first day a little too ambitious. As you walk your muscles tone up, and you'll gradually find yourself able to walk farther and faster and be less tired at the end of the day.

TERRAIN ▶ A rigorous 2 km climb over a mountain pass takes a lot more out of you and a lot more time than a 5 km ramble through gently rolling fields.

WEATHER ▶ Walking on warm days over dry trails is faster and easier than slogging through ankle-deep mud.

TIMING ▶ Times given in guidebooks are usually an average for experienced hikers under good conditions. If you've just come from the city, you might double the given times for the first day or so until you know how your hiking times compare with the guidebook's.

YOUR GOAL ▶ If your main interest is nature, you may stop often to look at a plant or flower, identify an animal's tracks, marvel at the flight of geese or gaze at mountain vistas, and will likely cover just a few kilometres a day. Or you may like to cover more distance and then relax at mountain summits, lookouts or waterfalls.

RESTING ▶ Plan for rest stops when deciding your trip's distance.

Walking Uphill and Downhill

UPHILL ▶ Approach hills with slow, short steps and avoid long strides. As the grade gets steeper, slow your pace but keep the rhythm steady. Keep your energy output at a comfortable level. Frequent rests may become necessary.

Slowly but surely you reach the top. Once there you'll most likely be faced with a downhill stretch. You may find going downhill is actually more tiring than going uphill.

DOWNHILL ▶ Hiking down a hill, especially with the extra weight of a full pack, requires that you expend energy to hold yourself back against the force of gravity. Going downhill may be easier on the heart and lungs than an uphill climb, but it is harder on the knees, ankles and feet. When faced with a stretch of downhill, shorten your stride and slow down to reduce the wear on these vital parts of your walking equipment. Make sure your boots are laced tightly to reduce the chance of blisters forming from your feet sliding forward in your boots.

Rest Stops

After reaching a mountain summit, waterfall, alpine meadow, stream or other scenic spot, take a rest. Adjust your boots and clothing, then have something to eat and drink.

Many hikers average a rest stop about once an hour. If you need to rest very often, try walking more slowly.

2

The Right Equipment

- ► Wear lightweight trail shoes or medium-weight hiking boots. Break them in before you head out.

- ► Use a pack that fits you and is the size needed for the trips you take.

- ► Get a sleeping bag that will keep you warm in the coldest weather you expect to encounter, but don't get more bag than you need—it's extra weight.

- ► Dressing in layers is the lightweight efficient way to be comfortable in a variety of conditions.

- ► Use a lightweight tent to keep you warm, dry and free of biting insects—and to provide privacy.

Modern Equipment Makes Hiking Easier

WHAT YOU NEED DEPENDS ON YOUR OUTINGS ▶ For a day-hike, you need hiking shoes and a daypack with food and extra clothes. An overnight or longer backpacking trip involves a sleeping bag, backpack and tent. The wrong equipment can mean a miserable trip.

When shopping for equipment, keep in mind the duration of your trip and the weather conditions you're likely to encounter.

IT DOESN'T HAVE TO BE EXPENSIVE ▶ You can equip yourself well with moderately priced gear. Quality brands reduce the chance of problems with poor workmanship. Cheap equipment may be uncomfortable—you'll probably soon replace it.

Think about each purchase carefully. Consider alternatives. Decide if you really need the item. You can reduce the cost of outfitting a family with growing children by sharing among several hiking families.

The Feet: Boots and Shoes

Hiking is miserable when your boots are torturing your feet!

Hiking shoes are good for most day outings and most hiking trails where you won't have to deal with snow or wet conditions. Hiking shoes are flexible, comfortable and easy to break in. They have less padding and reinforcing than boots, but provide some support and protection.

Medium-weight hiking boots are best for all-round backpacking on rocky and muddy trails and the occasional snowfield. They weigh 1.2 to 2 kg (2½ to 4½ pounds) a pair. The sole—less flexible than on trail shoes—provides protection from rocks. The boot's padded and more rigid upper portion provides more support.

Heavyweight mountaineering boots are too much boot for backpacking. Some hikers mistakenly think extra cost and bigger boots make for better hiking. The boots' stiff soles are meant for climbing and take forever to break in. Remember, a pound on the feet is like five pounds on the back.

Prevent Painful Blisters—Get the Right Fit

On an average day's walk you may lift and pound your feet onto the ground more than ten thousand times. If your heel chafes, it can create a painful blister that may keep you off your feet for several days.

Visit a hiking equipment shop that has several lines of footwear. Wear your hiking socks. Try as many pairs as you can until you find the right fit.

Hiking shoes can be fitted in the same way as regular shoes. Be more careful with boots because there is a greater chance of chafing. A boot must be long enough so that when it's laced snugly your toes do not hit the front while walking downhill. This can cause sore and blistered feet.

TIPS *for fitting boots*

- *General rule for boots.* Stand in the unlaced boot. Push your foot to the front. The length is about right if you can insert one finger down behind the heel.

- *Test for length.* Slide your foot back and lace the boot tightly. Make sure there is room for your feet to swell—as they will after a long trek—and for a second pair of socks. You should be able to wiggle and curl your toes. The ball of the foot should be comfortably snug and should not roll around when you stand on the edge of the sole.

- *Another test for length.* Lace the boots tightly. Slide your foot forward as if you're walking downhill with a heavy pack. Your toes should not push against the front. If they do, or if your toes feel pinched, the boot is too short or too narrow.

- *Walk with the boots.* If your heels move loosely up and down, the boot is too long or too wide at the heel. There is often slight lifting of the heel, which won't chafe your foot. Too much lifting can result in a painful blister.

- *Take time finding the best fit.* Be sure the boots you buy are a comfortable fit.

- *When a boot feels right.* Once the boot feels right, try a size smaller and a size larger. If you're not satisfied with any boot in a shop, try another store. Be sure you have the right fit before you buy, since many shops will not exchange boots once you've worn them outside. Your first hiking trip with new boots is not the time to find out if they fit.

Give Children Hiking or Running Shoes

Since children quickly outgrow footwear, outfitting them with hiking shoes or high-topped running shoes is a good route. Buying boots every year can be expensive. To save money, pass down boots and hiking shoes to younger children and trade with other families.

Break in New Footwear with Long Walks

To avoid chafing and blisters, start breaking in new shoes or boots before you go hiking. This is especially important before going backpacking. The pack's extra weight increases the pressure on your feet, resulting in blisters.

TIPS *for breaking in boots*

- After buying the boots, check the fit at home by wearing them indoors.

- Then go on longer walks outside. Be sure to wear hiking socks.

- Always check that the tongue is straight. Leather has a memory, and the tongue will stay in the same position once the boot is broken in.

Hiking shoes are usually broken in relatively quickly, but boots take 50 to 100 km of walking. Boots stretch slightly with use and conform to your feet. While the leather is still stiff, watch for tender spots or blisters on your feet. When the boots are broken in, blisters are less likely to form.

Look After Your Boots

Treat leather boots regularly with a dressing to preserve the leather and help keep water out. A silicone wax waterproofing protects the leather without softening it the way oil and grease waterproof dressing may.

TIPS *for maintaining boots* _____

- Mud can dry out leather. Always clean mud and dirt from your boots when you return from a trip, and treat them with water-proofing.
- Apply dressing only to clean, dry boots.
- Brush off loose mud, and wash off the ground-in dirt. Let boots dry before applying waterproof dressing.
- After you've cleaned and treated your boots, store them in a cool, dry place.

Always dry boots at room temperature. If your boots get soaked, stuff them with newspaper and let them dry slowly in a cool, well-ventilated room. Never try to dry boots near a fire, heating duct or oven. Direct heat cracks leather and loosens the glue that holds the soles to the uppers.

Hiking Can Be Hard on the Feet

This is especially true if you're carrying a heavy backpack. At the end of the hiking day, slip on a pair of sneakers or other lightweight shoes to give your feet a rest from your hiking boots.

TIPS *for preventing blisters*_____

- Keep your toenails short. This helps prevent a toenail from rubbing the skin of the next toe.
- In hot weather, stop often and wash or air your feet.
- If parts of your feet are prone to blistering, protect them with tape or moleskin.

If you feel a hot spot on your foot, stop immediately and cover the chafed area with moleskin or molefoam. Pull up your socks, remove pebbles, tighten laces or make other adjustments to prevent more hot spots.

If a blister develops, cover it with moleskin. Always carry moleskin or molefoam with you on a backpacking trip.

Self-sufficient with a Pack on Your Back

Natives, explorers and fur traders were the first to roam North America with packs on their backs. Natives hauled heavy loads with pack boards strapped to their shoulders. *Voyageur* fur traders adapted native pack boards to carry loads of furs over portages.

To hike self-sufficient in the wilderness, you need to carry food and equipment in a pack that leaves your arms and head free.

Today's hiking equipment lets us carry supplies and equipment more comfortably than ever before. Because we walk upright we don't carry the weight on our backs like a pack animal. Older packs hung the weight from the shoulders and pulled away from the back. This put pressure on the spine and strain on the back muscles. Modern packs with hip belts transfer the weight to the hips, making a big difference in comfort.

HIP BELT SAFETY ▶ To take as much weight as possible off your shoulders, keep the belt tight. A hip belt with a quick-release buckle lets you dump the pack quickly in case you fall. This helps prevent the pack's weight from hurting you. For safety, unbuckle the belt before crossing streams or walking on logs or over slippery terrain. If you fall while fording a river and the belt is around your hips, the pack's weight can hold you face down in the water.

Daypacks for Exploring

For day-hiking you can use a daypack, belt pouch or fanny pack. Belt pouches and fanny packs can carry lunch, water bottle, map, guide-book and compass. They're light enough to carry on trips where you set up a base camp and go exploring by day.

Daypacks are larger and have room for a sweater, jacket and poncho. They can comfortably carry small loads. A waist belt keeps the pack close to your back and prevents it from shifting and throwing you off balance—something you'll appreciate when skiing or bicycling.

Frame Packs—Internal and External

INTERNAL FRAME PACKS CAN BE CONVERTED TO LUGGAGE ▶ Unlike the older rucksacks, which pulled on the shoulders, modern internal frame packs have more comfortable suspension systems and hold the weight close to your center of gravity. Full-size packs tend to be narrower and not as high as external frame packs, making it easier to hike through thick bush. Some internal frame packs can be converted from backpack to luggage for easy handling at a hotel or airplane, an advantage if you're combining hiking and traveling.

EXTERNAL FRAME PACKS CARRY WEIGHT HIGH ▶ External frame backpacks have the advantage of carrying the weight high, close to your back and near your center of gravity. The rigid frame efficiently transfers the weight to the hip belt. With the hip belt and shoulder straps done up tightly, more than 75 percent of the weight should be carried by your hips, and the remainder on your back and shoulders.

Backpacks come in different sizes of frames for different sizes of people. Be sure to get a comfortable fit that won't hit your thighs.

Most packs made by quality manufacturers incorporate good quality frames and comfortable suspension systems. If you can't afford one of these packs and have to settle for an economy model with a straight frame and simple web belt that does not transfer weight to the hips, you can usually purchase a hip belt separately and attach it to the pack in place of the web belt.

Packbags with Side Pockets

Most bags are made of waterproof coated nylon. This material usually keeps contents dry unless the pack is dropped in water. In very wet weather protect the bag with plastic—a large garbage bag should last a few days.

On an external frame pack, the bag extends for three-quarters of the length of the frame. At the bottom you can strap on your sleeping bag and pad. A packbag that, in effect, is one undivided large pocket opening from the top is good for carrying bulky items. The packbag divided horizontally into two pockets, with zipper access to the lower pocket, is more popular since it's easier to reach equipment at the bottom of the pack.

Big side pockets are handy for items that you want to reach quickly such as water bottle, trail snacks, rain gear, moleskin and toilet paper —and to stow sweaters you've shed while walking. Zippers on all pockets and compartments should be strong, dependable and covered with rain flaps. Most top-loading packs have a map pocket on the storm flap.

Buy the size of bag needed for the length of the trips you plan to take. A bag that is too large is extra weight and may tempt you to fill it up with unnecessary "just might come in useful" gadgets. A packbag's capacity is often indicated in cubic centimetres or inches. Bags suitable for general backpacking of up to a week or ten days average from 24,600 to 65,550 cm³ (1,500 to 4,000 cubic inches). Expedition bags are up to 82,000 cm³ (5,000 cubic inches).

Children's Packs—Making Kids Feel Involved

Children old enough to walk independently usually want a pack of their own so that they can feel like a full participant in the hike. A day-pack is a good first pack.

A child's fully loaded pack should not weigh more than one-quarter the child's weight. A pack stuffed with a sleeping bag or down-filled clothing appears large in size without being heavy. Buy a pack that will be comfortable—avoid cheap, poorly constructed packs that may cause misery and discourage kids from going hiking again.

When you feel a child is strong enough, you can buy a small back-pack designed for children.

Load Your Pack for Comfort and Balance

Stow heavy items such as cookware, stove, food and tent high in the bag and close to your back. This arrangement puts the pack's center of gravity high. It also keeps most of the pack's weight pushing downward on your hips and not pulling on your shoulders. Lighter equipment—such as sleeping bags and clothes—should go at the bottom of the pack.

For ski-touring and cross-country travel through thick bush, keep the center of gravity low. This makes it easier to keep your balance.

Keep items in the same place each time you pack. It makes finding small items easier, especially in the dark.

Avoid Miserable Nights— Get a Good Sleeping Bag

After a full day on the trail, nothing is worse than a miserable night shivering in a sleeping bag you thought would keep you warm. You can always tell who was cold at night. They were up at dawn, gathered wood and started a fire to warm up. Lacking re-energizing sleep, they then plod along the trail with no enthusiasm.

A sleeping bag that will keep you warm at the coldest temperatures you're likely to encounter, given the region and time of year, is a necessity, not a luxury. Don't scrimp on a bag, or you'll curse yourself on a cold night. But don't go overboard and buy a super deluxe expedition bag rated to −40°C (−40°F) if the coldest time of year you plan to camp in is late fall and early spring when there is only an occasional night below freezing. An expedition bag is extra expense, extra weight, and plain uncomfortable since it is just too hot. If you do take up winter camping then you'll need another bag, or you can use your regular sleeping bag with a second one.

Manufacturers produce a variety of sleeping bags with different insulation, construction and shape. Making a choice isn't all that difficult. Choose a bag with the appropriate temperature rating, check that the manufacturer is reputable, and shop at a reliable hiking store where the staff knows the equipment.

SLEEPING BAGS DON'T PRODUCE ANY HEAT ON THEIR OWN ▶ They conserve your body heat, trapping it in the dead air space created by the bag's insulation and preventing that body heat from being carried away by wind or absorbed into the cold ground. The total thickness of the sleeping bag's insulation is known as the bag's loft. It's a fairly good indicator of a bag's temperature range—and a good criterion for comparing insulating qualities of several sleeping bags.

A sleeping bag with 15 cm (6 inches) of loft has 7.5 cm (3 inches) of insulation around the body. When shopping, you'll probably find bags with 15 cm (6 inches) of loft rated to approximately −7°C (20°F). This rating takes into account wind, dampness and a person's metabolism and allows for the comfort desired by most hikers. Given the difference in hikers and conditions, use temperature ratings to compare sleeping bags made by the same manufacturer.

The type of insulation influences the price and weight of the bag. Any material that keeps air from circulating away from your body is an insulator. It is the thickness of the insulation, not the weight or type, that determines the degree of warmth. For backpacking, a sleeping bag must be lightweight and pack to a small size for carrying. Goose down, duck down and polyester fills meet these requirements.

Fills: Down versus Polyester

You're looking for insulation fills that are lightweight, warm and small to pack, which means natural down or synthetic polyester. Down is the fluff that grows close to the skin of waterfowl. It traps air more efficiently and provides more loft for its weight than other materials. It also allows moisture given off by the body to pass through. The average person gives off about half a litre (one pint) of vapor at night. If that vapor is accumulated in the sleeping bag, the insulation would be less effective. Down bags also stuff small for carrying. Goose down and duck down are considered of similar quality. As with other natural products, quality varies.

Polyester also keeps you warm when wet and is now a popular alternative to down. A synthetic-filled bag doesn't absorb water directly into the structure, so if it's wet it will still keep you warm. It can dry from your body heat alone. If a polyester bag becomes soaked, wring it out and you'll sleep warmer in it than in a wet down bag. When down gets wet, it loses almost all its loft. Sleeping in a wet down bag can be colder, giving polyester the advantage if you're using a tarp or other minimal shelter in rainy areas. Compared with down, polyester compresses less underneath your body weight, so it provides some insulation beneath you. Polyester also costs less. But down is lighter for the same amount of warmth and packs smaller than a polyester bag of the same weight.

Once you decide between down or polyester and determine the temperature range you want, other differences in sleeping bags aren't earth-shattering.

Fabric

The sleeping bag's fabric lets moisture pass through. Almost all sleeping bags are made of rip-stop nylon or taffeta nylon. Both materials are light, strong and wind resistant, and they allow vapor to pass through. When you get into your bag the nylon may feel cold, but it quickly warms from your body heat.

Differential Cut: Preventing Cold Spots

Many sleeping bags have a differential cut—the inner shell is smaller than the outer shell. This allows the fill to loft more evenly around the bag and helps prevent cold spots when your knees or elbows press the inner shell against the outer shell.

Baffles: Keeping Down from Shifting

Sleeping-bag makers use several methods to keep down distributed evenly around you and prevent the down from shifting and lumping up in certain spots—such as the bottom—leaving other areas without insulation. The simplest and least expensive method is sewn-through construction, in which the inner and outer shells are sewn directly together. The problem with this method is that each seam has no insulation and is a cold spot.

To eliminate these cold spots, most down bags are constructed with vertical baffles to prevent the down from moving and to allow the down to loft. Baffles are usually made of light nylon material and connect the inner and outer shells around the bag.

Three patterns of baffles are square box, slant box and overlapping V-tubes. Square-box construction, the simplest, is a series of straight walls separating the down. Slant-box construction, the most common, uses longer offset baffles that partially overlap each other. It's considered better than square box as it allows the down to expand more. Overlapping V-tubes are small triangular compartments that interlock. This pattern is more efficient but requires about twice the amount of baffling material, making the bag heavier and more expensive.

Polyester comes in rolls of batting and does not have a shifting problem. Inexpensive synthetic-filled bags use sewn-through batting construction and are only suitable for warm weather camping. Better quality bags use double-quilted (also known as laminated) construction. This consists of two sewn-through batts with the seams staggered so that one batt's thin area is covered by the thick part of the other.

Zippers: Controlling Ventilation

Zippers provide ease in getting in and out of the bag and help control ventilation. Nylon zippers are self-lubricating, do not freeze up, and are lighter than metal.

JOINING TWO SLEEPING BAGS ▶ Sleeping bags with full length and across-the-foot zippers can be joined together if the zippers (as well as the occupants) are compatible. To join sleeping bags with zippers only on the side, one right-hand and one left-hand zipper is required. If you want to be able to snuggle, buy sleeping bags made by the same manufacturer to be sure they have the same zipper type and size. The zipper of a quality sleeping bag is covered by a tube that will keep out cold drafts.

Choosing the Style You Need

MUMMY BAGS ▶ The most common bag for backpacking, the snug-fitting mummy bag is light and warm.

BARREL BAGS ▶ Also called the semi-mummy, a barrel bag has more room around the shoulders and hips, letting you move your elbows and knees while sleeping. The barrel bag is preferred by hikers who may feel claustrophobic in a mummy bag.

HOODS ▶ A hood prevents heat loss from your head. Because an unprotected head can lose a lot of heat, the mummy and the barrel bag have built-in hoods. On warm nights the hood can be left flat; on cold nights, the draw cord is pulled tightly with only your nose exposed. If your nose is cold, breathe through a sweater. Don't breathe through your bag, since it will absorb moisture.

RECTANGULAR SLEEPING BAGS ▶ These are heavier than, but not as warm as, mummy bags and are suited only for short summer trips.

Children's Sleeping Bags

A baby or toddler can snuggle in their parents' sleeping bags. When kids get bigger, this arrangement becomes impractical. Several manufacturers make sleeping bags specifically for children. Synthetic-filled bags with a flannel liner are best for possible bed-wetters. For an economical sleeping bag, shorten an old bag to the required length.

Keep Sleeping Bags Dry

Don't lay the bag directly on the ground where it can absorb moisture. Put a waterproof layer such as groundsheet or tent floor between the sleeping bag and the ground. In the morning, open the bag and air it. Let it dry in the sun to remove any body moisture.

Sparks from a campfire can melt holes in the sleeping bag's shell fabric. Keep your sleeping bag a good distance from the fire. If you do get a hole in your sleeping bag, immediately patch it with tape to prevent losing any down.

STUFF SACKS ▶ Although the material is treated to make it waterproof, the stuff sack should be lined with a plastic bag—just to be sure of absolute protection in a downpour. Storing a bag in a stuff sack for a long time can cause down to lose its resiliency. Store unstuffed bags in a dry place where they can remain lofted.

Insulation and Sleeping Bag Covers

SLEEPING PADS INSULATE YOU FROM THE COLD GROUND ▶ When you're in a sleeping bag and feel cold, much of the cold is from the ground and not the air. The solution? Insulation. A foam pad is usually sufficient for summer conditions, though it provides minimal comfort. Self-inflating foam mattresses are generally warmer and more comfortable than foam pads. They're also more expensive.

SLEEPING BAG COVERS PROTECT YOU FROM WIND AND MOISTURE ▶ Covers protect the bag from wind and moisture. They're generally used for extra protection when you're sleeping under a tarp or in a snow shelter. The top of the cover is breathable rip-stop or nylon taffeta and the bottom is coated with waterproof nylon that serves as a groundsheet.

Sleeping in a Hammock

If you don't like sleeping on the hard ground, bring a lightweight backpacking hammock made of nylon netting. Hammocks are especially handy when you're sleeping on rocky hills. Just find two trees spaced the correct distance, and tie one end of the hammock to each tree. If there's a chance of rain, rig a tarp over the hammock. And if you're hiking in buggy country, look around for army surplus jungle hammocks, which are enclosed with mosquito netting.

Clothing: The Layered Look

It isn't necessary to spend a fortune on hiking clothes. You can probably find most of the clothes you need for summer trips among the clothes you already own. Thrift shops may also offer bargains on durable outdoor clothing.

The type of clothing to bring depends on where you're hiking and the time of year. During Canada's warm summer days you can hike in shorts and a T-shirt. Evenings are cool and you'll need long pants, a long-sleeved shirt, and a sweater or light jacket for warmth and protection against biting insects, which feast on hikers in early evening.

Weather on a hike can range from sweltering, humid days in thick forest to cold rain on a windy mountaintop. To keep weight down, bring the least amount of clothing that will keep you warm (or cool) in the conditions you'll encounter. The most efficient system is layers of light clothing, rather than heavy clothing.

You can then add or remove layers as the weather and your activities change. When you're moving and producing heat, you'll want to roll up sleeves, undo the collar and change into shorts. When you stop, you'll probably feel like slipping on a sweater or windbreaker and putting on a pair of long pants.

Bring Hats—for Cold, Sun and Rain

Unlike the rest of the body, the flow of blood to the brain is constant regardless of changes in air temperature. The head radiates more heat than the rest of the body. Up to 50 percent of your body heat can be lost through an uncovered head and neck. If the head and neck are cold, the feet and hands will also be cold.

A wool hat, balaclava, tuque or watch cap keeps you warm. Uncovering your head will cool you. A hat helps you regulate your body heat quickly. It can save you the trouble of taking your pack off and removing a sweater, and then reversing the process as the weather cools.

In hot weather, an uncovered head under scorching sun can make you dizzy and lead to heat stroke. A cotton hat keeps the sun off your head and provides ventilation. Sun hats with wide brims keep the sun out of your eyes and off your ears and nose. Bandanas are versatile and can be used as sun hats and to protect the back of the neck from sunburn.

Socks—for Protecting Your Feet

Proper socks reduce friction between boot and foot, cushion feet from the pounding of walking, keep feet warm and absorb moisture. Socks made mostly of wool are best for hiking. Wool wicks sweat away from the foot to keep it relatively dry. Socks should be higher than boots. To last longer, socks should be reinforced with nylon at the heels and toes, or be a cotton and nylon blend. A common blend is 80 percent wool, 20 percent nylon.

Some hikers wear light socks under heavy socks. The lighter inner sock eliminates the itchy feeling of the heavy wool. Other hikers wear two medium-weight socks. Experiment and use the combination that suits you.

DRYING WET SOCKS ▶ Drying wet socks over a fire is time consuming and often burns holes and chars socks. To dry wet socks over a fire, put them a safe distance from the flame and check them regularly.

Placing wet socks in your sleeping bag and letting your body heat dry them is another way to dry socks. It's effective, but don't do more than two socks at a time or the dampness will make you cold in your bag.

Dry wet socks in the sun by spreading them on rocks or tying them to the outside of your pack.

KEEPING FEET DRY ▶ If you're slogging through wet and muddy terrain and don't want small lakes in your socks, there is a way to attain a semblance of dryness. Place a plastic bag between the inner and outer socks, or over the outside layer. Fold the bag carefully to avoid wrinkles that may press into your foot. Your feet will remain warm and dry except for perspiration, most of which will be absorbed by the inner layer of socks.

Underwear

Cotton underwear is best for summer. Cotton absorbs sweat; nylon doesn't and becomes clammy. A cotton T-shirt doubles as an undershirt on cool days. For cold weather, you'll want long bottoms and long-sleeved tops. Two types of underwear are popular with cold-weather hikers. Thermal underwear is made of wool with a nylon outer layer and a cotton inner layer. Fishnet underwear (made of wool-nylon or cotton-polyester blends) provides insulating dead-air space when worn under a shirt. It also lets perspiration evaporate.

Wear Loose-Fitting Pants

Pants of cotton denim, corduroy or hard-finish wool are suited for hiking. Avoid cuffed or flared pants—they can catch on rocks or underbrush and trip you. Pants with tight hips or knees make walking more tiring. Many hikers always wear shorts for the freedom of movement and ventilation. In cool weather, you can add more layers to the upper part of your body; add the heat generated by walking, and your legs will be warm. In wet weather, long pants become heavy with water and more energy is required to lift each leg. When you're wearing shorts in the rain, your legs will be warm as long as you're moving. And you'll have a dry, warm pair of pants in your pack to slip into at camp.

Wear long pants on cool evenings and cold rest days. They'll protect you from biting insects, poison ivy and poison oak, and when you're traveling in rough thick bush, so you won't scratch your legs.

When hiking in winter or in wet chilly areas such as British Columbia's coastal rainforests where you're guaranteed to get sopping wet at least once during your trip, bring wool pants. They can keep you warm when you're wet.

To keep your pants up you'll need a belt or suspenders. If the pack's padded hip belt presses into your skin, you may prefer suspenders.

The First Layers—Shirts and Sweaters

The layer system is applied to the chest area which, after the head, is most important to regulating body heat.

THE FIRST LAYER IS USUALLY A COTTON T-SHIRT ▶ If it's a hot day that's probably all you need on your torso. Cotton absorbs perspiration without feeling clammy. If the weather is hot and humid, wear a T-shirt to prevent sunburn.

THE SECOND LAYER IS A SHIRT ▶ It could be a cotton-flannel, chamois or light wool shirt with long sleeves and long tail. The long sleeves protect the arms from insects. When you get warm you can roll up the sleeves, unbutton the front and pull out the tail. Then, when it cools, you roll down the sleeves, button up the front and tuck in the tail.

THE THIRD LAYER IS A MEDIUM-WEIGHT SWEATER ▶ This is more versatile than a heavy sweater. Pullover sweaters with crew necks are good. Turtleneck sweaters may be too hot on the back of the neck. V-neck sweaters won't protect the top of your chest. Wool keeps you warm when wet, making a wool sweater a necessity.

The Next Layer—Shell Clothing

Shirt and sweater layers create dead-air space, which is what keeps you warm. An outer layer of a wind parka helps prevent the wind from penetrating and cooling that dead-air space.

Wind clothing is usually windproof and water repellant—meaning it sheds some rain or snow. And it's breathable—it lets your body moisture out. Moisture that can't escape condenses, and you're drenched in perspiration.

Nylon wind parkas are the lightest. Nylon wind pants are useful when you're hiking in windy, exposed areas. Until recently, wind clothing couldn't be waterproof and breathable. Gore-Tex laminate solved this problem. It's both waterproof and breathable, making it comfortable in a wider range of conditions.

One style of wind parka features a two-way nylon zipper covered with a storm flap with snaps. The zipper should reach to the chin, and the hood should have a drawstring to adjust the opening around the face. The parka should also have a drawstring at the waist, and an elastic or Velcro closing on the cuffs. The pullover style of wind shell, known as an anorak, doesn't have as good ventilation as the open front design.

Wind parkas usually abound in patch pockets—two cargo pockets, slash pockets for hands and two breast pockets, most with Velcro-closed storm flaps.

Ponchos and Other Rain Gear

USE A PONCHO TO COVER YOU AND YOUR PACK ▶ When you're hiking in a downpour, a poncho provides good ventilation and reduces condensation inside because it's open on the sides. The hood keeps rain from running down your neck.

Some ponchos have sleeve extensions to help keep your arms dry. Ponchos of coated nylon are the lightest. The cheap vinyl-plastic type of poncho tears easily.

In a pinch, ponchos can also serve as groundsheets, but try to avoid this use. They tear easily, and wear on the material makes it less waterproof.

RAIN JACKETS AND CAGOULES ▶ A nylon-coated rain jacket should not have any seams directly over the top of the shoulder. If the zipper in the jacket is left open, it provides some ventilation. For strenuous hiking, however, rain jackets tend to be too hot. A cagoule is like a waterproof, loose-fitting anorak that reaches to the knees. It's good protection against rain but has little ventilation.

RAIN PANTS ▶ Waterproof rain pants have little ventilation. Mainly they're comfortable for standing around camp. They are handy if you're walking through thick underbrush that has just received a heavy rainfall—so long as you can ventilate the upper part of your body to compensate for the lack of ventilation to the lower part. A better solution is to walk in short pants.

Mittens for Chilly Days

Wool mittens are good to have on chilly days in the mountains during early spring or late fall. They're essential for winter trips. Mittens are warmer than gloves because they keep the fingers together.

Insulated Clothing as the Outer Layer

For more warmth on cool Canadian mornings and evenings, or for treks on tundra or windy alpine ridges, most hikers carry a down or synthetic-filled jacket or vest. Down is warmer and packs smaller than the synthetic polyester fills, but when down is wet it loses a lot of its insulating value. Down is mostly suitable for cold, dry conditions.

It's preferable to wear synthetic-filled clothing on trips in wet areas. Polyester fleece keeps you warm when it's wet outside, and it dries quickly with body heat. Although this material doesn't pack as small as down, on summer trips there should be enough room for it in the pack.

A down-insulated sweater has long sleeves, reaches the hips, is lighter and takes up less space than a wool sweater. Insulated jackets and parkas extend over the hips and contain more insulation than a sweater to keep you warm at colder temperatures. Vests keep the torso warm and are for temperatures that don't require a jacket or for when you're engaged in a vigorous activity. They allow unrestricted arm movement, which is especially appreciated in cross-country skiing.

A Complete Change of Children's Clothing

Always bring at least one complete change of clothing for each child and a good supply of extra socks. Some of the children's clothing should be in bright colors; if kids wander off, they'll be easier to find. It may be difficult to find rain pants and other gear in children's sizes. If you're so inclined, making kids' hiking clothes is relatively simple and will save a lot of money.

Carry Your Shelter— or Sleep Under the Stars

Much of Canada gets rain or is plagued by bloodthirsty mosquitoes and blackflies that make it unpleasant—if not downright miserable—to sleep outdoors unprotected. You can't always depend on cabins or shelters, since they may be full when you arrive. Tents provide that little haven from the elements.

There are, however, a few places in Canada where you can backpack without carrying some sort of shelter – that is, if sleeping under the stars is your thing.

Tarps for Solo Hikers

If you hike alone and find a tent too heavy or more shelter than you need, a tarp may be better suited to your needs.

Tarp shelters can be used in different situations. Although they protect against wind and rain, they don't do the job as well as a tent. And mosquitoes are still free to bite the parts of your body sticking out of the sleeping bag. A tarp measuring 2 by 2.5 metres (6 by 8 feet) is about right for one person. A small floorless tent of bug netting can protect you from bugs. A rain-fly from a double-wall, two-person backpacking tent makes a good tarp for one person. Good quality nylon tarps are usually made of urethane-coated rip-stop. For ease in setting up, they generally have grommets around the edge and other strategic points.

Devices for attaching a cord to tarps include a ring and ball—which work along the same principle as a garter. Or you could tie off a small stone. Use strong lightweight cord such as braided white 0.5 cm (⅛ inch) nylon of 250 kg (550 pound) test strength.

Dry, Private, and Bug-Free—the Perfect Tent

Though tarps save weight, they don't protect you completely from the elements. In a windy rainstorm, you and your equipment would probably get drenched. Get a roomy tent if you hike in areas where it often rains continuously for several days. You'll appreciate the space to dress and store gear without going stir-crazy. A tent with good insect netting will provide the bug-free environment needed to preserve sanity.

Another advantage of a closed tent is privacy. Campsites on popular trails can be very crowded. The privacy of your own tent is appreciated. If you're planning to set up a base camp and take day-hikes, you can keep your gear inside the tent.

A three-season tent should keep you dry, comfortable and warm. Before buying a tent, decide what you need. Some people buy more tent than they require and pay for it not only in higher costs but added weight. A four-season tent with snow flaps and frost liner is just not needed for summer backpacking.

Don't carry more than 1.5 kg (3 pounds) of tent per person. A two-person tent should weigh about 3 kg (6 pounds). Anything weighing much more is too heavy.

Things to look for in a backpacking tent include a waterproof floor that extends up the sidewalls for several centimetres to keep out ground moisture, and insect netting on all doors and vents. If you want to keep your gear inside the tent, there must be enough room. If you keep your pack outside, you can cover it with your poncho.

Most backpacking tents are made of nylon. Most single-wall waterproof nylon tents will keep out most of the rain. Since the inside of the tent is warmer than the outside, moisture from your breath and body, which cannot penetrate the waterproof single wall, will condense on the inside of the tent. Good tents use a double-wall construction that has a coated nylon fly over an inner tent of breathable nylon. The fly keeps the rain out and the inner tent allows moisture to escape. If you already have a single-wall tent you can add a rain-fly to it. A fly also keeps the tent cooler on hot days. If you plan to do most of your camping below the timberline, this is the type of tent you need.

Again, the rule for other equipment applies to tents also. Don't buy more than you need; it will just be an unnecessary expense and add extra weight.

3

Eating Well on the Trail: Food and Cooking Gear

- ► Carbohydrates are quick-energy foods.
- ► Fat provides heat energy.
- ► Protein produces energy that lasts longer.
- ► Water is the heaviest ingredient in food, so plan a menu using food that is dried or normally low in water.
- ► Campfires are fun to sit around, but for cooking it's more efficient to use a lightweight stove.

Hiking Burns Calories

You need to eat tasty energy-boosting food for physical well-being and to be in good spirits.

Day Trips

Pack some sandwiches, fresh vegetables and fruit, cheese and quick energy trail snacks. Make it a picnic outing. Since you're carrying only one or two meals, weight is not as crucial. Just remember that big jugs of juice are heavy.

Backpacking Trips

On overnight or weekend trips, you can carry fresh vegetables and fruit, canned food and other relatively heavy food without much discomfort. On a trip longer than three or four days, choose food for its light weight, bulk, nutrition, cooking time and taste

Bring Food You Like

A person of average weight and metabolism burns about 3,500 calories a day while hiking—though everyone has different energy needs, and a general rule cannot be applied. Bring food you like and determine your needs from experience. How you feel is the best measure of how well you are eating.

Carbohydrates, Fat, Protein and Salt

CARBOHYDRATES—FOR QUICK ENERGY ▶ Snacks consumed during rest stops on the trail should be high in carbohydrates. Dried fruits, chocolate, candy and other sweet foods are high in sugar—one type of carbohydrate—and are favorite trail snacks. The starch in bread, rice, peas, corn and potatoes is another common type of carbohydrate.

FAT—FOR HEAT ENERGY ▶ Found in meat, margarine and nuts, fat is another source of calories. The body stores fat and can convert it into heat energy very quickly when needed. On cold days, especially on winter trips, add extra margarine to your morning oatmeal for the extra heat it will provide.

PROTEIN—FOR LONG-LASTING ENERGY ▶ Protein, found in meat, fish, eggs, milk and cheese, consumes calories in its conversion into energy.

SALT—TO PREVENT DEHYDRATION ▶ Salt is needed in your food to prevent dehydration. Your body releases salt in perspiration and urine. When you exert yourself hiking and perspire more than usual, you lose more salt which needs to be replaced.

Food Planning

Water—the Heaviest Ingredient

On trips longer than five days, food is probably the heaviest part of your outfit. Water weighs one kilogram per litre (8 pounds per gallon). By using foods that are mainly low in water, such as dehydrated and freeze-dried foods, and other foods that are normally low in water, you can plan for about one-half to one kilogram (about 1¼ to 2¼ pounds) of food per person per day.

Simple Meals Mean More Time Hiking

BREAKFAST ▶ Instant oatmeal and granola are quick and filling. On rest days, you can spend the morning frying pancakes.

LUNCH ▶ Lunch is usually a short stop on the trail, so make it simple and quick to prepare. Instant soup and sandwiches of salami, cheese, peanut butter or honey are filling and provide energy for the afternoon's hike.

SUPPER ▶ Cooking time can be a little longer; a half-hour wait is reasonable. Any longer and famished hikers may rebel. Cooking for a shorter time conserves fuel, an important consideration on long trips.

New Foods and Old Favorites

Food tastes better in the outdoors. Foods that didn't appeal to you at home may be delicious in the backcountry. When planning a trip's menu try new foods, but be sure to carry favorites, too. Bring some herbs and spices to make prepackaged dinners more exciting.

Tasty Lightweight Food in Your Supermarket

Before going to a hiking gear shop for prepackaged backpacking dinners, check supermarkets and health food stores for foods that are lightweight and may be lower cost. You can put together complete menus with supermarket food, though they may be heavier and bulkier than freeze-dried food.

It's more difficult with supermarket food than with prepackaged freeze-dried food to calculate the amount you'll need. Experience is the best guide. Figure out the amounts needed for each meal and portion pack in plastic bags.

BREAKFAST IDEAS ▶ Granola, instant oatmeal, cream of wheat, pancake mix with raisins and other dried fruit, powdered milk and fruit juice crystals are suitable.

LUNCH IDEAS ▶ Use rye, pumpernickel or other heavy bread, crackers, margarine, cheese, salami, sausage, beef jerky, sardines, tuna, salmon, kippers, corned beef, peanut butter, jam, honey and instant soups.

SUPPER IDEAS ▶ Make meals with dried soup, bouillon cubes, spaghetti or other pasta, bulgur or other grains, instant potatoes, canned meat and fish, and dried vegetable flakes. Also suitable are many of the instant meals made by adding hot water. Add life to one-pot suppers with seasonings such as curry, chili powder, onion flakes, and green-pepper and red-pepper flakes.

HOT DRINKS ▶ Coffee, cocoa and tea with sugar and powdered milk are lightweight.

Dehydrated Food—Dried with Hot Air

Dehydration has been a natural way of preserving food since people started to store food. The process removes 80 to 97 percent of the food's moisture, shrinks the food and significantly reduces its weight.

Dried fruit, beef jerky and dried vegetable flakes are some of the foods produced by hot-air drying. Dried fruit can be eaten as is, but you may want to soak some overnight and add it to your morning oatmeal. Dehydrated vegetables should be soaked until almost completely rehydrated. Soaking time depends on the type and size of the vegetables. If they require more than 15 to 30 minutes, place them in a small container of water several hours before mealtime, and then tuck the container into your pack. The same method works to reduce the cooking time of dried beans.

Hot-air drying is a relatively simple and inexpensive process. You can buy home food dehydrators in some housewares stores. Home-dried foods are free of the preservatives added to improve the appearance of commercially prepared food.

Freeze-Dried Foods—A Wide Variety

Many of the prepackaged foods sold in hiking equipment shops have been freeze-dried. Freeze-drying is more expensive than the hot-air method, but tends to retain more flavor. Cooked or raw food, depending on the type, is frozen in a vacuum at a very low temperature, down to −45°C (−50°F). Freeze-drying preserves the original color, nutritional value and shape of the food. The product is porous, enabling quick rehydration.

If you buy freeze-dried food, there is a big selection. Freeze-dried food can be purchased as complete meals or in separate portions of meat, vegetables and fruit. Because of the high cost of freeze-drying, manufacturers have concentrated on products with high food value, such as meat, poultry and fish. Most freeze-dried food will be palatable if the instructions for preparing it are strictly followed. Some items require cooking; for others, you just add hot water. The suggested number of servings marked on each package tends to be optimistic. A dinner intended for four servings will usually satisfy only two or three hungry hikers. One way to extend freeze-dried dinners is to add instant rice or noodles.

The empty aluminum foil pouches don't burn, so slip them into your litter bag and pack them out with the rest of your garbage.

FREEZE-DRIED BREAKFAST FOODS ▶ include scrambled eggs, omelets and pancakes.

FREEZE-DRIED LUNCH FOODS ▶ include tuna salad, chicken salad and cottage cheese.

FREEZE-DRIED SUPPER FOODS ▶ include rib eye steaks, beef stroganoff, chicken chop suey, beef amandine, chicken stew, beef stew, turkey tetrazzini, chicken with rice, cheese romanoff, turkey supreme, and spaghetti (with freeze-dried meatballs). There are also meatless dishes such as chili, lasagna, vegetable stew and couscous.

FREEZE-DRIED VEGETABLES ▶ are available separately and include green peas, green beans, carrots and corn.

FREEZE-DRIED DESSERTS ▶ include vanilla, chocolate and strawberry ice cream, blueberry and raspberry cobbler, banana cream pudding, and a no-bake pineapple cheesecake with a graham cracker crust.

Quick Energy Trail Snacks

Take a break about once an hour to rest, drink water and have something to eat. Foods high in carbohydrates are best for snacks during rest stops. *Gorp* (for Good Old Raisins and Peanuts) is the name given to a snacking mixture combining some of these quick energy foods: raisins, currants, dates, peanuts, chocolate chips, dried fruit, coconut, roasted soybeans, pumpkin seeds, sunflower seeds and nuts (cashews, almonds, walnuts and others). Mix the gorp in a plastic bag and keep it in a pocket that you can easily dig into on those short trips when you don't take off your pack.

Growing Sprouts on the Trail

To eat fresh vegetables on backpacking trips, grow sprouts in your pack. Sprouts are germinated seeds. They provide roughage—usually lacking in dried foods—and are high in protein, minerals and vitamins B, C and E. Alfalfa sprouts are easy to grow on a backpacking trip. Add them to sandwiches and soups, and as garnishes on macaroni, stews and casseroles.

TO GROW SPROUTS ▶ Soak two tablespoons of alfalfa seeds (available in health food stores) overnight in a wide-mouth plastic bottle. In the morning drain the water and stretch a piece of nylon or cheesecloth over the mouth of the bottle, securing it with a rubber band. Store the bottle in a part of your pack where it will be out of the light but not cut off from air. The seeds must be kept moist and should be rinsed through the strainer twice a day.

At the end of the second day little sprouts will appear. On the third or fourth day, expose the sprouts to sunlight by carrying them in a plastic bag on top of your pack. The sunlight produces chlorophyll, which rapidly turns the sprouts green. The sprouts are now at the peak of flavor and nutritional value—and ready to eat. Start some of your seeds before leaving, and the sprouts will be ready early in your trip. Mung beans, soybeans, mustard seeds and lentils are some of the many seeds that can be sprouted.

Water

When in Doubt, Purify It

In areas where the purity of the water is questionable—if there is even just the slightest doubt—play it safe and purify the water. Boil the water for at least 20 minutes to ensure killing bacteria, or treat the water with iodine, available in drugstores and hiking equipment shops. Don't use iodine for more than two to three weeks. Don't use it at all if you're pregnant, have a thyroid condition or are allergic to iodine. You can use a lightweight water filter and iodine, or a water purifier that combines a filter and iodine. Filters and purifiers are sold in hiking equipment shops.

SAFEGUARDING THE WATER SUPPLY ▶ Don't let anyone wash themselves or their dishes in any lake, river or stream.

Fish and Wild Food

Enjoy Fresh Fish

Lakes and streams along many of Canada's trails contain trout and other fish that hikers with angling equipment can catch and eat fresh. Telescoping and other fishing rods that attach to packs are available. Check into fishing rules and license requirements.

Edible Wild Plants

Edible wild plants gathered fresh from the wilderness are at their tastiest and most nutritious. Raspberries, blueberries and cranberries can be picked and eaten fresh. Try boiling a cupful of berries to spread on pancakes. A crisp backcountry salad can be made of wild leeks, fiddlehead ferns and other edible wild greens. Edible mushrooms can be sautéed to add a gourmet touch.

If you are not absolutely certain a berry, plant or mushroom is edible, leave it alone. Study a book on edible wild food and learn a few of the safe, easily recognizable varieties that grow where you're hiking.

Menu Planning and Organizing Your Food

Bringing the Right Amount

Beginning hikers sometimes worry about starving in the wilderness and overload their packs with too much food. Carefully plan your menu in advance to be sure you bring along the right amount.

Make a simple chart, with three menu columns—breakfast, lunch, supper. In the left margin, mark the days of your trip. Then fill in the foods and amounts required for each meal on each day. Then, referring to the menu, draw up a shopping list and buy the food. Don't forget trail snacks.

Organizing Food at Home

Preparing meals on the trail will be easier if you organize the food at home. It takes little time and saves fumbling around with a measuring cup as suppertime approaches. It also means you won't run out of food because you used too much for other meals.

TIPS *for packing food*

- Carry the amount you need of each food, not the whole box. This reduces the weight and bulk of your load.

- Put dry ingredients for each meal into individual plastic bags.

- Label with masking tape bags of food that may be confused, such as sugar, powdered milk and flour.

- Pack food in strong plastic bags and close them securely. There's nothing worse than opening your pack to find a rocklike clump of flour, salt, sugar and coffee.

Containers

Hiking equipment shops and grocery stores carry a variety of plastic food containers. Plastic bottles can be used to carry grains, beans and other dry food. Salt, pepper and other seasonings can be carried in small plastic bottles or in an old 35 mm film container. Egg carriers of durable plastic, in six- and twelve-egg sizes, are available if you like fresh eggs in the morning.

WATER BOTTLES ▶ The narrow-mouth poly bottles with attached screw-on caps are popular. Some hikers prefer the wide-mouth bottles that fill more quickly, an advantage when you submerge the bottle in an ice-cold mountain stream.

Groups can use a collapsible water carrier at camp. Available in 5-, 10- and 20-litre (about 1-, 2- and 4-gallon) sizes, these containers let you get all the water needed for a meal at one time.

Our Romance with Campfires

At the end of a day on the trail, we savor the warm glow of a fire. It draws us together. We sings songs. Out come harmonicas, recorders and spoons.

Given the dwindling amount of dead wood remaining at back-country campsites, many national and provincial parks discourage or prohibit the use of fires, encouraging hikers to carry backpacking stoves for their cooking needs. Some parks prohibit campfires during hot, dry weather because of the risk of forest fires

Building a Campfire

There are backcountry areas in Canada where hikers can safely build campfires.

BEGIN BY FINDING A SAFE SITE FOR A FIRE BOWL ▶ If there already is one at the campsite—and chances are there will be—use it rather than making your own. If there isn't, collect stones and arrange them in a small circle to confine the fire. Clear a one-metre (one-yard) circle of all loose burnable material around the fire bowl. The safest place for a campfire is on rock, or on sandy or clay soil. If you must build the fire on loam soil, line the bottom of the fire bowl with rocks. Roots and other organic materials that will burn are found in loam soil. The fire can smolder along roots and, when it eventually reaches the surface, can cause a forest fire.

COLLECT A GOOD SUPPLY OF DRY TINDER AND TWIGS ▶ White birch makes excellent tinder because it burns slowly and provides a lot of heat, even when damp. Use bark that has already fallen off the tree; don't strip live trees. Crumple the tinder into a ball and place it in the center of the fire bowl. Starting with the small twigs and adding sticks of gradually increasing thickness, build a teepee-shaped structure around the tinder. When this is completed, light the tinder. The flame should soon have the kindling and larger wood burning. If the fire requires air, blow gently at its base. Don't add more wood until the base of the fire is burning well, since you may suffocate the fire.

KEEP THE FIRE SMALL ▶ Use wood about 3 cm (1 inch) in diameter— about the thickness of the length of your thumb. You don't need to carry an axe, hatchet, saw or machete, which will only scar the forest. Use any wood you can break in your hands or against a rock. Dead wood snaps easily when broken. Green wood is still living, doesn't snap and won't burn. Rotting wood usually contains moisture and burns poorly. Gather only enough wood to use during your stay.

SOFTWOODS AND HARDWOODS ▶ Softwoods are easy to ignite, burn quickly and are best for starting a fire. Softwoods include balsam, poplar, pine, cedar and spruce. Hardwoods are more difficult to ignite but burn slower. They give off more heat and produce coals, which are best for cooking. Once the fire is burning well, add hardwoods like birch, maple, elm and ash.

DAMP CONDITIONS ▶ In wet weather, a fire gives warmth—often needed for drying out wet clothes. Starting a campfire under damp conditions may be more difficult, but it can be done. Begin by stripping the wet bark off dead wood. Shave slivers from the dry center for kindling.

PUTTING OUT A FIRE ▶ Know the rules. Drown the ashes with water and stir until they're cool to touch. Drench the fire-ring rocks. When breaking camp at a virgin campsite where you've made the fire bowl, remove every trace of the fire by returning the fire bowl rocks to their original locations and scattering the ashes and leftover wood.

Grates and Matches

USE A GRATE TO SUPPORT POTS OVER A FIRE ▶ Without a grate, cooking can be a tricky business. Anyone who has crunched on the remains of pea soup scooped from the sand will agree. If you don't have a grate, arrange logs or stones so pots can balance on them. Take care that the pots are steady. If they tip over, you may spill your supper and put out the fire. A backpacking grate makes cooking on a fire easier. One type has folding legs for better stability. Cake racks also can be used.

CARRY MATCHES IN A MOISTURE-PROOF CONTAINER ▶ If you expect to encounter wet and windy weather, carry waterproof and windproof matches. You can make matches waterproof. Dip the head of wooden matches in melted wax. Before using them, scrape the wax off the tips.

Safety matches have to be ignited on the striker panel on the matchbox. They won't light on any abrasive surface the way strike-any-where matches will. If you're bringing safety matches, be sure to take the box with the striker.

Wrap an emergency supply of matches in plastic and keep them in your pack. Some hikers bring a butane lighter in addition to matches.

Using a Stove—Saving Time and Trouble

With a stove, you don't have to spend half an hour gathering wood and building a fire while you're famished. On rainy days, a stove has obvious advantages. And during hot weather, cooking over a stove is more pleasant than dealing with an open fire. The regulating valve found on most models gives you heat control. It lets you boil water quickly, or simmer a freeze-dried dinner. Backpacking stoves can be divided between those that operate with a butane cartridge and those that burn white gas.

Butane Stoves

BUTANE STOVES ARE SIMPLEST TO OPERATE ▶ Butane burns quietly. The cartridges contain pressurized butane gas that vaporizes instantly when vented to atmospheric pressure. No priming, preheating or pumping required. Just open the valve and light. Unlike white gas stoves there is no fuel to spill and butane burns quietly.

Butane does have disadvantages. The cartridges weigh more for the same amount of heating energy. Butane is more expensive than white gas and has a lower maximum heat output, which means a longer overall cooking time. As the butane canister empties of fuel, the pressure and the stove's heat output decrease. The cartridge cannot be changed until it is empty. Because butane freezes at −9°C (15°F) and does not operate effectively at temperatures below freezing, butane stoves are impractical for winter use.

The Gaz S200-S Bleuet stove, the first model available, is widely sold. It weighs 400 grams (14 ounces) without a cartridge. A butane cartridge lasts about three hours and weighs 100 grams (4 ounces).

White Gas Stoves

WHITE GAS STOVES BURN HOTTER ▶ White gas stoves are better suited for longer trips. They burn hotter than butane stoves, and the fuel is cheaper. White gas backpacking stoves are manufactured by Svea, Optimus, Phoebus, Coleman, MSR and Primus. The traditional Svea 123, which weighs 510 grams (1 pound, 2 ounces), has a built-in windscreen; and the Optimus 8R, which weighs 700 grams (1 pound, 9 ounces), is carried in a sturdy steel box. Neither has a built-in pump, but an optional Optimus mini-pump attaches to the fuel tank cap, which increases efficiency of the stoves during cold weather.

The Coleman Peak 1 at 0.6 kg (1.3 pounds) and the MSR and Primus stoves have built-in pumps and use a fuel bottle as the stove's reservoir. MSR stoves have a high heat output and weigh only 0.5 kg (1.1 pounds). The Coleman and MSR stoves are available in multifuel models, which burn kerosene in addition to white gas.

The Optimus 111B, weighing 1.5 kg (3 pounds, 8 ounces), is better suited for winter camping and for large groups, given the extra heating capacity.

White gas stoves are noisier than butane stoves, and because they have more parts are likelier to break down. Spare parts can be purchased, and it's a good idea to carry a spare burner plate and burner head. Avoid problems with white gas stoves by using the proper fuel. Automobile gasoline burns dirty and gums up the nozzle.

White gas is a highly flammable liquid that should be carried in a leakproof metal container. The aluminum Sigg Fuel bottles, available in litre and half-litre sizes, fit easily into a side pocket of your pack, away from your food and clothing. A vented pouring cap, sold separately, makes pouring easier and eliminates the need for a funnel and eye dropper.

OPERATING A WHITE GAS STOVE ▶ Lighting a white gas stove is a little complicated. The process centers around priming, the purpose of which is to heat the vaporizing chamber so that the fuel burns as a gas rather than in its liquid form.

To start a Svea or an Optimus stove, first turn the throttle to the cleaning position. A needle will rise through the opening and remove soot and any other matter that can block the passage of the vaporized fuel. On older models, plunge the separate cleaning needle into the opening several times; then turn the valve to the off position, remove the tank cap and fill the reservoir with fuel. A funnel makes pouring easier and reduces waste.

The next step is to prime the stove. You do that by heating the vaporizing tube located between the tank and the burner. Using an eye dropper, withdraw gas from the tank and fill the priming cup at the bottom of the burner. Close the tank and place the fuel bottle away from the stove. Ignite the fuel in the cup and let it heat the vaporizing chamber. When the flame is nearly out, open the valve. A roaring blue flame should come out around the burner plate. If it doesn't, then probably the gas in the vaporizing tube has not been sufficiently heated. Try priming the stove again.

The manufacturer's instructions with some stoves say to warm the tank in your hands, which will force some gas out of the nozzle into the priming cup, and then ignite the fuel after closing the valve. This method does work, but most hikers find filling the priming cup directly much more efficient.

Before taking your stove on a trip, practice lighting it outside to learn its idiosyncrasies. Filling the tank, priming and lighting the stove should soon be routine.

Safety Guidelines

TREAT ALL STOVES AND FUEL WITH CAUTION ▶ Don't overheat the stove by insulating the tank. Don't obstruct air circulation by using the Svea 123 with windscreen inside a Sigg Cookset. Keeping the regulating valve open the whole way will also overheat the stove. When a white gas stove is overheated, the safety valve will blow—releasing gas vapor, which often immediately ignites.

TIPS *for safe practices*_____

- Don't use an excessive amount of gas to prime the stove.

- Fill the tank away from all open flames, and never when the stove is hot.

- If the stove runs out of fuel and you're in the middle of cooking a meal, let the stove cool before refilling it.

- If a small flame remains when you've turned the valve off, just blow it out.

- Don't open the fuel tank to release the pressure; it will allow gas vapor to escape and ignite in a ball of flames.

- Use the stove outside. Don't use it inside a tent as it can tip over and ignite your sleeping bag or the tent itself, or cause carbon monoxide poisoning and asphyxiation.

Cookware

The size of the hiking group usually determines the pots and pans you'll take on a trip. A solo hiker can often get by with one small pot for cooking and eating. Parties of four or more usually require two or more larger pots.

Cooksets sold in hiking gear shops are made of lightweight aluminum and are easy to clean. Many have tight-fitting covers that double as frying pans. If you need a pan for frying pancakes or freshly caught trout, and find the pans included in cooksets inadequate, get a lightweight aluminum frying pan. It will weigh about 360 grams (12 ounces).

You'll find a variety of cooksets for one or two people that come with a small pot, a frying pan, plates and a cup. A pot-gripper is handy for holding hot pots. The steel pot-gripper with a spring-loaded grip holds heavy pots best. This small item weighs 60 grams (2 ounces).

Utensils

Many hikers limit their eating ware to a cup and a spoon, but a fork sometimes comes in handy too. An insulated plastic cup can be used for eating and drinking. Some hikers, particularly those who hike in large groups and prepare meals in one big pot, may find just a cup insufficient, preferring to bring plastic bowls and plates as well.

A pocket knife, such as one of the Swiss Army knives, has many uses on a hiking trip, including cooking and eating. A knife equipped with two blades, can opener, reamer and corkscrew is sufficient for most backpackers. The fully equipped luxury models, which include magnifying glass, scissors and a miniature wood saw, tend to be too bulky and heavy for a shirt or pants pocket.

Cleanup

WASH DISHES AWAY FROM THE WATER SOURCE ▶ To wash dishes in the backcountry, use a nylon scouring pad to loosen the food, and a small amount of biodegradable detergent and hot water to cut grease. Heat water in the largest pot and use it as a wash basin.

Don't bother scrubbing the carbon off the bottom of pots used in a wood fire. It holds the heat and spreads it more efficiently. Carry the blackened pots in a stuff sack to keep the rest of your pack clean.

Dirty dishwater should be dumped on the ground, away from lakes and streams and preferably on soil that is deep enough to absorb and decompose the waste. Don't permit other hikers to pollute the water source with their dishwater.

4

Avoiding Insects
That Bite

- ► Wear loose clothing with a tight weave. Avoid dark colors.
- ► Use insect repellant with a high percentage of active ingredient diethyl toluamide.
- ► Don't use cologne or scented soap and shampoo.
- ► Camp in a dry, open, breezy area.
- ► Avoid stagnant water where mosquitoes breed.

Most hikers have a horror story to tell about camping during bug season. It's often something like: You hike from mountaintop to lake. You settle down for supper and to watch the sun shout its last hurrah for the day. But wait, what is that black cloud hovering yonder, emitting buzz-saw-like sounds? Within seconds the sound has become a not-so-dull roar and there are monsters chipping and mangling every available pore. The next sound is your scream as you dash for your tent, all thoughts of food forgotten.

Biting insects are found in many of Canada's natural areas. Using proper defenses against these pests can mean the difference between an enjoyable outdoor experience and a nightmare.

Mosquitoes, Blackflies and Other Pests

An Ojibwa legend says the Great Spirit Gitchi Manitou was angry when one day all the men married all the women. A mass honeymoon began, and no one harvested the rice and corn. Manitou created the mosquito and sent swarms of the bugs. Suddenly, all romance and intimacy disappeared. The honeymoon was over.

Mosquitoes and Blackflies

MOSQUITOES ▶ Mosquitoes, called flying piranhas by some, can be a problem during the spring and summer. They're most active at dusk, at night and during overcast days. Only the females bite—they require the blood to produce eggs. They inject anticoagulant to thin the blood, causing the irritation we feel.

Itching is usually minor and temporary. It's the buzzing sound and the swarming of mosquitoes around ears, eyes and nose that can drive us mad.

BLACKFLIES ▶ Although blackflies are widespread throughout Canada, the worst areas are northern Ontario, Quebec and the muskeg areas of the Canadian Shield. Ontario's Algonquin Park in June is filled with hungry bugs. It's not safe to yawn unless you want a mouthful of them. Unlike mosquitoes, blackflies attack only during the day and are most active at daybreak and at dusk. In warm and humid weather they feast all day.

Blackflies like to bite shaded areas of exposed skin around the collar and hairline and under hat rims and sunglasses. They're persistent and penetrate beneath clothing and into the nose, ears and eyes. A bite from a blackfly is painless, but irritation usually sets in, the result of a histamine reaction from the fly's digestive juices. The bites leave red bleeding spots and can be severe enough to cause painful swelling.

No-see-ums, Horseflies and Deerflies

NO-SEE-UMS ▶ These are flies so tiny that they can be mistaken for pieces of dust. Usually found in lowland areas, their bites give an itchy feeling all over. If you're snugly inside your bug-proof tent yet feel ravenous hordes attacking your body, don't panic. No-see-ums have probably snuck inside your haven. If you can, move to higher, windier ground.

HORSEFLIES AND DEERFLIES ▶ These are large insects found in open woodlands near water. They attack only during the day, and their bite is painful. Insect repellants are not effective against these flies. Use a strong slap to kill them.

Ticks

Ticks are wingless parasites about 5 mm ($\frac{1}{5}$ inch) long that are found in open areas such as trails, clearings and the edge of a forest. Of the 20 species in Canada, only the Rocky Mountain Wood Tick and the American Dog Tick bite humans. Encounters with them are most likely to occur in the southern interior of Alberta and British Columbia during spring and early summer. Rocky Mountain Wood Ticks are feared as carriers of Rocky Mountain Spotted Fever, but very few cases of tick-related diseases have been reported in Canada. The disease, which once was fatal, is now treated with antibiotics. Ticks are also associated with the spread of Lyme disease.

Ticks give a painless bite and begin to feed on your blood. When hiking in tick country, wear long pants treated with insect repellant. At the end of the day, inspect your body and scalp. If a tick has dug into your skin, touching it with a drop of repellant, kerosene or gas may induce it to withdraw. If that doesn't work, hold the front part of the tick and pull slowly. Should parts of the mouth remain in the skin, remove them like an ordinary splinter and treat with antiseptic.

Wasps, Hornets and Bees

These insects generally leave people alone except to investigate brightly colored clothing they mistake for flowers. Like mosquitoes and flies, they're attracted to perfumes and sweet scents. They bite humans only when threatened. Hornet nests are located on the ground—take care not to disturb them. Wasps and hornets can sting several times. Bees lose their stinger in the wound. If you are bitten by a bee, remove the stinger by scraping across the skin with a knife.

To treat a sting, apply a cold compress and a baking soda paste. If you're allergic to the venom from these insects, consult a physician and carry medication in case of bites.

Warding Them Off!

What to Wear—Loose Clothing and Light Colors

Dressing properly is an important defense against biting insects. Loose clothing with a tight weave will protect most of your body. Keep long-sleeved shirts closed at the collar and wrists. Tuck long pants into socks. Headnets will keep the bugs from biting your face.

Dark colors attract mosquitoes and blackflies, so avoid black, red, blue and dark-brown clothing. Both types of bugs are attracted to blue jeans. Wear light colors. White and yellow are best.

Insect Repellants

An effective insect repellant is vital to preserving your sanity during bug season. Repellants block the sensors on the insect's antennae and prevent the bugs from landing and biting. The pests remain only a few metres away, however, swarming about you—and they'll land on untreated areas of your body.

Most insect repellants contain M-diethyl-meta-toluamide (diethyl toluamide, or DEET for short), either as the sole or an active ingredient. The higher the percentage of active ingredients (as listed on the container), the stronger the repellant and the longer it lasts. For backcountry trips, use a repellant with the highest percentage of active ingredients.

Apply repellant evenly to all exposed skin and clothing, especially around the neck and waist. The repellant should keep bugs off you for several hours, unless it is washed off by water or perspiration.

TIPS *on a campsite*

CHOOSING A CAMPSITE ▶ Look for a dry and open area that has a breeze to keep insects from clustering. Tall grass and thick woods should be avoided, since they break the wind. Most important: stay away from areas with stagnant water, where mosquitoes breed.

BUILDING A SMUDGE FIRE ▶ A smudge fire can help keep mosquitoes away from your camp. Green grass or green pine needles on a bed of glowing coals will produce thick smoke. As the smoke drifts through the campsite the bugs will go elsewhere.

BUGPROOF TENTS ▶ Shop carefully for a bug-proof tent so you can retreat into an insect-free interior for a peaceful sleep.

Finally ...

WHAT YOU EAT ▶ The foods you eat can make you appealing to hungry insects. After you eat a banana, for example, your skin exudes an odor that mosquitoes just love. On the other hand, if you eat garlic the odor your skin exudes will keep biting insects away.

FLORAL SCENTS ▶ Floral scents attract bugs—so don't use colognes, scented soaps or shampoos while in the outdoors. Do wash, though. Mosquitoes like warmth and humidity, and are more attracted to people who perspire a lot.

YOU CAN STILL GET BITTEN! ▶ No matter how well prepared you are —dressed in light colors, bathed in repellant and smelling of garlic— some insects may get through, and you may get bitten. Calamine lotion helps reduce the swelling and relieve the itch. A paste of baking soda and water is also effective. If abnormal swelling develops, consult a physician.

5

Routefinding

When using a map and compass:

▶ Orient the map using landmarks and the compass.

▶ Determine where you are on the map.

▶ Take a bearing; then pick a landmark in that direction and hike there.

▶ Establish a baseline.

Finding Your Way

Most of the trails in this book are well marked. You walk along a cleared path and follow signs, blazes or cairns (piles of stones that mark routes above the treeline). There are times when you use a map—such as to determine the distance to a landmark, or where several trails meet and you're not sure which way to go.

If You Lose the Trail

If you lose the trail, stop and return to the last marker if it's visible. If you can't see one, first try to find the trail. If you can't find it, use a map and compass to determine your location on the map and a route back to the trail.

When hiking unmarked routes, you need a map and compass. Practice using a map and compass in different situations.

Carry Maps of the Area

Trail guides often include detailed maps. For some hikes you may need some of the 1:50,000 series topographical maps produced by the Centre for Topographic Information of Natural Resources Canada. These maps show dirt roads, trails, streams, rivers, lakes, cabins and other landmarks.

Get maps in advance to plan your route and choose campsites. You'll get an idea of landmarks along the route and know ahead of time where the difficult sections are.

Using a Map

When in the backcountry, carry maps in a clear plastic bag (such as a freezer bag with a zip-top seal) or a map case to keep them clean and dry. In windy or rainy weather, fold the map so it can be read without removing it from the case.

CONTOUR LINES SHOW THE TERRAIN ▶ Contour lines are light brown lines joining points of the same elevation on a topographical map.

How to read contour lines:
• Widely spaced contour lines represent a gentle slope, while lines that are close together indicate a steep hillside or cliff.
• Valleys and concave slopes appear as a series of V-shaped contours that point upstream.

- Ridges and convex slopes are a pattern of downhill-pointing Vs.
- A series of rough circles or closed loops represents a summit or hill-top.

As you use topographical maps, you'll be able to look at a map and have a picture of the land in your mind.

SCALE ▶ Scale is the relationship between a distance on the map and the actual distance on the ground. In the 1:50,000 series, 2 cm on the map equals 1 km on the ground. Use a small ruler—compasses usually have a ruler along the edge of the base—to measure map distances and pinpoint grid references. A map measurer is a mechanical device with a little wheel that you run over your course. It indicates the distance as though the trail were flat, so the measure can be deceiving in mountainous country.

More Information:
Topographical maps for the entire country can be purchased from:

Canada Map Office
130 Bentley Avenue
Nepean, ON K1A 0E9
Telephone: (toll-free): 1-800-465-6277
Fax: (899) 771-6277
Website: www.GeoCan.NRCan.gc.ca
E-mail: info@GeoCan.NRCan.gc.ca

Contact the Canada Map Office for a list of local dealers. National and provincial park offices often have maps, but check ahead of time that they are available.

Carry a Compass and Know How to Use It

Better compasses are liquid filled so the needle settles into position quickly and stays stable. Many have sighting devices for taking bearings. Along with the four cardinal points—north, south, east and west—compasses have an azimuth, a 360° marking system that allows for more accurate direction-finding. To keep your compass accessible, hang it around your neck with a string and slip the compass into your shirt pocket.

True North and Magnetic North

Most compasses have a pivoting needle that has one end marked with the letter N or colored red, black or blue to indicate north. The needle does not point to true north everywhere in Canada, but to magnetic north. The magnetic north pole is on Bathurst Island, about 1,560 km (970 miles) south of the true north pole. The compass needle points to true north only along the agonic line, which runs from Thunder Bay, Ontario, through Churchill, Manitoba, to the magnetic pole.

The difference in degrees between true north and magnetic north is known as declination. The local declination usually is indicated in the margin of a topographical map. East of the agonic line you add the number of degrees of declination to the bearing; and west of the line, you subtract. Some compasses can be adjusted to save correcting for declination each time you take a bearing.

Navigating with Map and Compass

Orienting the Map

The easiest way is to line up known landmarks with their symbols on the map. To orient the map using a compass, place the compass on the map with the direction-to-travel arrow parallel with map north and the meridian lines. Turn the map and compass together until the needle points to the number of degrees east or west of north, which is the local declination.

The map is now oriented. Be sure to keep the compass away from metallic objects such as belt buckles, knives, photo meters and lighters, which can affect the accuracy of the compass.

Place the compass edge on the map along the desired line of travel between your present location and your objective.

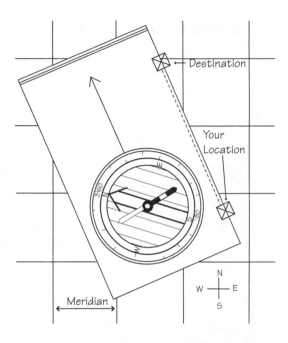

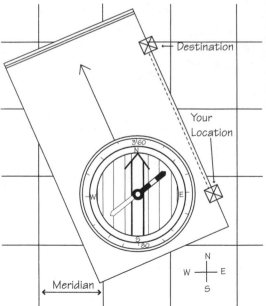

Turn the compass dial until the north-south lines on the base of the compass are parallel with the meridian lines on the map and the N on the compass points to north on the map.

Determining Your Location on the Map

If you know your position relative to a distinct landmark such as a trail junction, bridge or mountain, it should be no problem to determine your location. To make this easier, make a point of observing the terrain through which you are hiking, noting creeks, mountains and other landmarks you can identify on the map.

To take a bearing on a landmark:
- Face the object and point the compass's direction-of-travel arrow at the feature.
- Turn the dial on the compass until the needle is pointing to the N.
- The number of degrees indicated at the travel arrow is the bearing to the landmark.

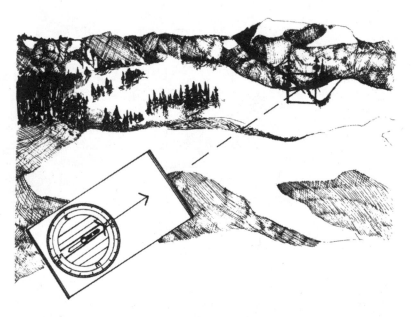

Without changing the dial setting and keeping the compass horizontal, turn the entire compass until the needle points to north on the dial. Your destination is in the direction of the compass's travel arrow.

TRIANGULATION ▶ If you don't know your position on the map, you can use triangulation to determine it. This involves taking a bearing on three natural features or landmarks that can be identified on the map:

- Make a line on the map, beginning at the first landmark. The line should be at the same angle of your compass reading to that point and should go from that landmark through the area you're located in.
- Repeat this step for two other features in other directions.
- The point where the three lines intersect on the map is your approximate location.

To take a map bearing:

- Place the compass edge on the map, along the desired line of travel between your present location and your objective.
- Turn the compass dial until the north-south lines on the base of the compass are parallel with the meridian lines on the map, and the N on the compass points to north on the map.
- Without changing the dial setting, keep the compass horizontal and turn the entire compass until the needle points to north on the dial.
- Your destination is in the direction of the compass's travel arrow.

To follow a compass bearing:

- Look along the bearing.
- Pick a landmark in this direction and hike there.
- When you reach this objective, sight with the compass to another landmark along the route and continue until you reach the destination.

Establish a Baseline

When navigating with map and compass, try to establish a baseline— an unmistakable feature that can be a boundary for your trip area. A road, railway line, river, power line, cliff, lakeshore, sea coast, canyon or mountain range is suitable.

When you're hiking to a destination that is on a baseline—a car on a road, for example, or a cabin on a lake—make an intentional deviation of several degrees in your compass bearing. It's safer to do that than to follow the bearing directly to your objective. This way, when you reach your baseline you'll know which way to turn to reach your objective. If you set your compass bearing directly on your objective—a car, for example—and you come out on the road around the bend and cannot see the vehicle, you won't know whether to turn left or right.

Navigating by Natural Signs

Finding the North Star

On a clear night, you can find true north by looking at the sky and finding Polaris—the North Star. In latitudes below 60° north, the bearing of Polaris is never more than 2¼° from true north.

To locate the North Star:
- Find the Big Dipper and identify the two pointer stars on the outer lip.
- These stars point to Polaris, which appears above the opening of the Big Dipper.

To tell direction using a watch and the sun:
- If daylight saving time is in effect, set the watch back to standard time.
- Hold the watch flat and point the hour hand in the direction of the sun.
- South will lie halfway between the hour hand and 12 on the dial. (Before 6 pm, use the smallest angle shown; after 6 pm, use the largest. At noon the sun will lie due south.)

Modern Technology

GPS Receivers

GPS stands for Global Positioning System. GPS receivers use radio signals from satellites to calculate the coordinates of where you are on a topographic map. They also help you navigate. Once you have the map coordinates of your location, you can enter the coordinates of your destination. The GPS receiver will tell the direction and distance.

Cellular Phones

Some cell phones may be useful to call for help if you're lost. They're also helpful in other emergency situations. When you carry one, however, you may lose the feeling of being away from it all. Keep in mind, too, that cell phones don't work everywhere, and that their batteries can run out. If you're going to carry one in case of emergencies, make sure it will work in the area in which you're going to be.

6

Discovering Nature with Children

► Have fun! Make that your first goal.

► Start with short outings, and hike from a base camp for overnights.

► Show children nature lore.

► When setting up camp, give each kid a job to do.

Make sure children enjoy their first hiking trips. They're likely to be more enthusiastic about wilderness activities than the walking itself. If you're leading hikes for kids, put the kids' needs first.

How Young?

What age to start hiking? Many parks have nature trails that are accessible to strollers. An infant can enjoy an outing in a carrier. You can begin exploring short nature walks soon after your child can walk. For overnight or longer hiking trips, five to eight is a good age to start. The child can carry a small pack with a sleeping bag and clothing. Kids between nine and twelve years are usually able to carry more.

Make Sure Kids Have Fun

Adult hiking goals are different from children's. Your goal may be to reach an objective—and to do that you make sure you keep to a schedule. A child's goal is to have fun. To make your children enthusiastic hikers, it's your job to be sure they have a good time.

Some parents think their kids can't endure the rigors of hiking. After all, if Mom and Dad are exhausted after a short climb, how will their child do? Though they have less stamina, children are stronger and can usually walk farther than you think. Teach them to keep a steady pace rather than tearing down the trail.

Start with Short Hikes

If you want to do an overnight trip, try to schedule it for warm, dry weather and when there are the fewest bugs. Mosquitoes and blackflies love children's tender skin. Since there are some bugs out during most of the summer, take proper precautions against bugs that bite. Insect repellant and proper clothing are musts. (See Chapter 4, Avoiding Insects That Bite.)

Plan to hike a shorter distance at a pace slower than on adult trips. Choose a trail you're familiar with. Until your children are older and more experienced hikers, avoid bushwhacking or scrambling over rocks.

Until children are old enough to carry their packs all day without complaining, set up a base camp and explore the surroundings on day-hikes. Base-camping gives you flexibility; should an illness or injury happen, you can quickly get back to the car.

Choosing a Route

Choose a route that kids will find exciting. Monotonous scenery will dampen a child's enthusiasm. Ocean beaches, lakeshores, riverbanks and meadows keep the mind occupied. They also make for easier walking.

Choose a trail that has frequent interesting natural and human-made features. Plan time to stop and look at wildflowers, plants, meadows, trees, birds, waterfalls, rockslides and mountain vistas. Study some nature lore so you can tell your children stories about the environment, wildlife and explorers of the area. Many parks have interpretive trails for exploring natural or historic themes.

Rest Stops

Stop often for snacks. To maintain the child's energy level, have a 15-minute rest/snack stop every hour. Stop at interesting places. Encourage kids to observe and listen to birds and other wildlife.

Bringing Friends Along

Most children enjoy the trip more if a friend comes along. Several families can go together. Take care, though, that the group is not too large.

Kids and Safety

Make your children aware of hazards, but don't scare them with horror stories. Tell young children to stay in your sight all the time. Teenagers want the independence to walk faster and discover the country by themselves. Let them get ahead of you on the trail, so long as they wait for you at junctions, road crossings and mountaintops. Give each child a whistle, telling everyone to blow three blasts on it if they get lost. (Three of anything is the universal distress signal.) Assure kids they'll be found if they stay in one place and don't wander around. Warn your children about poison ivy and poison oak. Tell them most berries and plants are not edible; they should check with you before picking any.

Drink Lots of Liquids

Encourage children to drink frequently. When you're hiking, the body loses a lot of water. Children often forget they're thirsty. Plan soup-in-a-cup as a first course. Keep a full water bottle in the tent for children who wake up thirsty in the middle of the night.

Help Kids Learn Skills

Delegating Jobs

"Are we there yet?" You're on an overnight hike and you finally arrive at the campsite. Take a few minutes with the children to celebrate, or just sit down and rest. Set up camp boundaries and tell your children to stay within them.

Give every child a job to do. Assign jobs before reaching camp so there won't be any squabbling over who does what. Involve children even though it may take longer to set up camp. Remember, they're learning and growing.

Chores children can do include setting up tents, going for water, helping cook dinner, gathering wood if you're having a fire, cleaning dishes after dinner, and looking for tree branches from which to hang the food.

These skills and experiences help children build self-confidence and learn to accept responsibility. Kids who avoid a task may fear they're not doing a good job. If a child is self-conscious about not being able to start a campfire, take the time to explain and demonstrate the job.

Teach children to use a map and compass. Let kids figure out the family's position on the map by identifying landmarks. Encourage kids to follow your route on the map.

Infants and Toddlers

Carrying Infants

If you wish to bring infants on a walking or hiking trip, use a child-carrier pack. A baby carrier for hiking should protect the child and have a pocket for carrying some of the baby's gear. It should be comfortable for both baby and parent. A carrier that stands on its own on the ground is handy.

In one type of carrier, the child faces forward—always seeing the parent. This design puts the child's weight close to the parent's back, which is a more comfortable position. Some parents prefer the child to face to the rear so as to keep fingers out of ears and hair, and to lessen the baby's chance of getting hit in the face by swinging branches. In this design the weight rides lower and tends to pull the parent backward. A padded hip belt on a carrier makes the load easier to carry.

Carriers that keep the baby on your front protect the child, but may strain your neck muscles. Carriers that hold the child on your back are more comfortable, but you need to watch that branches or twigs don't hit the child.

When carrying a child in a carrier, never bend forward from the waist—it can throw the child head-first out of the carrier. If you have to reach for something on the ground, bend from the knees. Watch for low-hanging branches that can brush against the baby's face. Have someone hold the branches while the parent and baby pass.

Plan Short Trips for Toddlers

Hiking with toddlers between two and four years old may be more difficult than taking babies. The child is too heavy to be carried for long distances and can't yet walk very far.

Because trips usually involve the child walking part of the way and being carried the rest, you find trips shorter and slower than with infants. Always keep an eye on toddlers. They haven't yet learned what is dangerous and are curious about everything in the new world around them. If you're camping, choose a site near a small stream, away from lakes and rivers into which the child can fall.

Exploring the Winter Wilderness

- ▶ Winter has fewer hours of daylight, so plan to reach your goal in time.
- ▶ Warm clothing, foods that provide heat energy, and ample rest all help to keep you warm.
- ▶ Dress in layers to keep warm.
- ▶ Avoid perspiring, which can chill you.
- ▶ Don't use a stove inside a tent.

The snow packs under your steps as you travel through forests and across frozen lakes. The winter wilderness is a quiet world of clean, sparkling white snow, crisp air, glistening snow-covered trees and frozen waterfalls. At the end of a day, you feel warmly accomplished.

Wandering in the winter landscape, relying on what you're carrying on your back, gives you a feeling of freedom and self-reliance.

Canadian Winters

Winters in Canada can be long. The first snow and frosty weather usually arrive in November. Winter conditions usually last until early April. At high elevations, snow cover remains until May.

Exploring the outdoors on cross-country skis or snowshoes is a welcome escape from the gray, slush-covered city. Fewer people are on backcountry trails. Blackflies and mosquitoes are gone.

Traveling over deep powder snow requires snowshoes or cross-country skis. Distributing your weight over the snow is all important. Otherwise, your steps may sink deeply into the snow, making it difficult to cover distance.

Snowshoes for Thick, Wooded Areas

Use snowshoes for traveling over unbroken snow in thick, wooded areas. A snowshoe's rough webbing gives you good traction to walk up a hill. Snowshoes provide more stability when you're carrying a heavy pack.

Walking naturally with snowshoes:
- Strap the snowshoes on and walk naturally with your feet the normal distance apart.
- Let the snowshoes glide over each other.
- To make a turn, take several short steps rather than changing direction in one step.
- When climbing or descending a steep hill, traverse the hill in a series of switchbacks.

Types of Snowshoes

WOODEN SNOWSHOES ▶ The Algonquin, Cree, beaver-tail and bearpaw are snowshoe designs that are widely available. Each is intended for a specific condition. The wider and shorter bearpaw is good in flat, open terrain, but its width makes it more difficult for climbing and descending hills in thickly wooded areas. Algonquin and Cree snowshoes are suited for most terrains—the tail keeps the snowshoe straight while you're walking. The lighter and easier-to-handle beaver-tail, also known as the modified bearpaw, combines the advantages of the bearpaw and Algonquin.

ALUMINUM SNOWSHOES ▶ The aluminum-framed snowshoes with neoprene webs are lighter and smaller than wooden ones, an advantage if you expect to carry your snowshoes for long distances. Most are long and narrow, with a rounded front and back.

Cross-country Skis for Open Terrain and Trails

Cross-country skis are ideal for trips over open terrain and trails. For day excursions, use touring or light-touring skis. For winter backpacking, touring skis are wider and heavier than light-touring skis, providing stability if you're skiing off prepared tracks. Mountaineering skis are used by skiers who climb peaks and ridges and ski down the open runs.

Cross-country skiing is similar to ice skating. The rhythm of striding should come naturally. If you can walk, you can ski.

Planning a Winter Trip

Start by going with an experienced winter backpacker. If you don't know anyone to help you, look for winter camping trips offered by outfitters and outing clubs.

Winter backpacking needs more planning than a summer trip. Worn paths and landmarks disappear under snow. Take extra care planning your food and shelter, keeping warm, getting enough rest, traveling over the snow, and watching for the signs of frostbite and hypothermia. And don't forget, of course, that you have fewer hours of daylight.

Before going on a winter trip, get experience backpacking in summer and autumn. Go on winter day trips to get an idea of snow conditions and to estimate how far you can travel in one day. Use the day trips to explore possible routes for a backpacking trip.

Clothing—Dress in Layers

Wearing several layers of light breathable clothing rather than a single heavy layer lets you shed layers while skiing or doing other vigorous activity, and helps you avoid perspiring.

Clothing damp from perspiration can chill the body. Get into the habit of brushing snow off all your clothes before it has a chance to melt.

Wool keeps you warm when it's wet or dirty outside. Cotton absorbs and retains moisture and, with the exception of fishnet underwear, is not good for winter trips.

INNER AND OUTER GARMENTS ▶ Wear woolen inner garments—pants, shirts and sweaters. For outer clothing, wear a down or synthetic-fill parka with a hood that extends in front of your face; a windproof nylon or waterproof breathable shell; mittens rather than gloves; and a wool hat or balaclava. While traveling during the day, you may be comfortable wearing just a sweater and pants. Soon after stopping, though, you'll reach for the parka and other warmer clothing.

BOOTS ▶ If you don't wear proper boots, your feet may soon feel like blocks of ice. Summer hiking boots with an extra pair of socks are not sufficient for Canadian winters. They don't provide enough insulation. As well, the tighter fit created by the extra socks constricts the blood flow, resulting in cold feet and frostbite.

For extreme dry cold conditions use mukluks. They have rubber soles, canvas or nylon uppers, and duffel or felt liners to keep your feet snug and toasty warm. Mukluks are not suitable for wet conditions because the uppers soak quickly. For traveling in wet snow, use insulated all-rubber boots. The trapper pack boots with rubber soles and leather uppers are suitable for general winter use, when you only occasionally meet up with wet conditions.

Nutritious Food and Lots of Liquids

To produce heat energy to keep warm, eat nutritious food high in protein, carbohydrates and fat.

Eating a piece of chocolate or other sweet food before going to bed helps keep you warm while you sleep. (For more information on nutrition and planning a proper menu, see Chapter 3, Eating Well on the Trail: Food and Cooking Gear.)

Though you may not feel as thirsty as on a hot summer day, it's important to drink as much as possible. That is because the body is dehydrated by dry cold air. Consume at least 1.5 litres (about 1½ quarts) per day. Snow has relatively little water, and eating a lot of it will chill your stomach. (If you do eat snow, let it first melt in your mouth.)

Start your trip with a full water bottle. When it's half empty, keep refilling it with wet, dense snow, which soon melts into water. Keep the container upside-down to prevent the cap from freezing.

When choosing a campsite, try to find a spot near an open stream or other running water. If the snow is deep and water difficult to reach, tie a pot or cup to the end of a ski pole or stick and scoop the water from a safe distance. Camping near open water saves fuel (you would need a stove to melt the snow) and time (it takes many pots of snow to make one pot of water). Another advantage is taste. Melted snow has a stale quality and needs to be flavored with coffee, tea or powdered juice.

Sleeping Bags

GET A WINTER SLEEPING BAG OR USE TWO BAGS ▶ A sleeping bag you can rely on to keep you warm is essential on a winter trip. Use a good quality sleeping bag rated to the lowest temperature you expect to encounter. If you don't want to buy a winter sleeping bag because of cost, or want more versatility than a single winter bag provides, use a lightweight sleeping bag inside a medium-weight bag. This arrangement keeps you warm, but tends to be heavier than a single winter bag. Check the loft—a winter bag rated to −30°C (−20°F) should have at least 18 cm (7 inches) of loft.

In winter, a sleeping pad is essential. Full-length closed-cell pads 1 or 1.3 cm (⅜ or ½ inch) thick provide the needed insulation. Self-inflating foam mattresses provide more insulation and comfort than closed-cell foam pads. But they're also heavier and more expensive.

Campsites and Tents

Choose a winter campsite sheltered from the wind. Trees are a good windbreak. Using your snowshoes or skis, pack down a platform for the tent.

A tent for winter backpacking, like a summer tent, should keep you dry, warm and comfortable. Also important in a winter tent is roominess. There should be sufficient space to allow you to sit up and stretch your arms and legs. During winter, you spend more hours per day inside the tent than you would in summer. Blizzards may keep you inside for days. You need a tent that will help keep you from going stir-crazy.

Tent poles should attach to the floor and top of the tent. Self-supporting tents are an advantage here. If poles go directly on the ground, put them on a piece of wood to keep them from sinking into the snow.

Winter expedition tents have special features. Snow flaps are edges of the tent floor extending 20 to 25 cm (8 to 10 inches). They can be banked with snow to prevent high winds from getting under the tent.

A frost liner is a canopy hung inside the tent to absorb the moisture that might otherwise condense and freeze on the tent walls. In the morning you detach the frost liner, shake off the frost outside and then rehang the liner inside the tent.

A vestibule is an extra sheltered space in front of the tent, useful for stowing gear and keeping out snow.

Not all these features are essential in winter camping. If you're camping in forested areas sheltered from high winds, a three-season tent may be adequate.

Packs—Internal Frame Pack for Winter

For ski-touring, an internal frame pack is preferred over an external frame pack. The internal frame pack's narrow cut doesn't protrude at the sides—so you don't knock into it when swinging your arms.

When traveling on skis, try to keep the pack's center of gravity low to prevent the pack from putting you off balance. External frame packs keep the weight high on the back. Though this is comfortable for summer hiking, for ski-touring it tends to overbalance skiers and cause them to fall. If you only have an external pack, put the heavier items near the bottom—the opposite of what you would do in the summer.

Stoves

For winter camping, use a white gas or kerosene stove equipped with a pump. Brand names include Optimus, Primus, MSR, Phoebus and Coleman. Butane and propane cartridge stoves don't work at below-freezing temperatures.

If you melt snow for water, make sure you bring extra fuel for this purpose. When using your stove on snow, place a closed-cell foam pad under the stove to prevent the snow from melting and sinking into it. *Don't use the stove inside a tent. It can cause carbon monoxide poisoning.* (See Chapter 3 for more information on stove types and safety.)

IF YOU COOK ON A WOOD FIRE ▶ Build your wood fire on a platform of green tree limbs to prevent it from sinking into the snow and being extinguished by melting snow.

Beware of Frostbite and Hypothermia

Two serious consequences of not being equipped for cold are frostbite and hypothermia.

Frostbite

Frostbite is the freezing of body tissue. If serious, it can permanently disable you. The cold causes reduced circulation in the body's extremities—hands, toes, feet, nose and ears. With superficial frostbite you feel a general numbness, and the flesh appears white and waxy. To restore circulation in a hand, toe or foot, warm it with body heat by placing it on a bare stomach, armpit or hand. If your nose, ears or cheeks are frostbitten, hold a warm hand on the frostbitten surface.

Deep frostbite is more serious and has a hard and woody feeling. Move a person who has deep frostbite inside, and get medical attention as soon as possible.

Several old ideas on treating frostbite can do more damage. Never rub it with snow or massage it. Don't try to rewarm a frozen part by exercising it. Don't soak the frozen part in cool water. Don't try to rewarm it near a fire, since the person may not feel the heat and get burned.

Hypothermia

Hypothermia is the lowering of body temperature, and it can be fatal. If the body loses heat faster than it produces it, the temperature of the body core will go down. If you're not wearing proper clothing, then cold, wet and windy conditions can chill the body.

PROTECTING THE HEAD AND THE BACK OF THE NECK IS IMPORTANT ▶ You lose a lot of heat if your head is uncovered. According to one outdoors maxim, "When your feet are cold, put a hat on." Keep your clothes dry. Your body gets colder much faster in wet clothing than in dry clothing. Wear woolen clothing—it keeps you warm when you're wet.

ALWAYS BE ALERT FOR SIGNS OF HYPOTHERMIA ▶ Early symptoms include shivering and a general numb feeling. As the condition worsens, the shivering is more intense, speech becomes slurred, judgment becomes impaired and the person loses coordination.

IF SOMEONE SHOWS SIGNS OF HYPOTHERMIA, GET THEM OUT OF THE COLD ▶ Remove all wet clothing, and put the victim in a sleeping bag with another person, who has also removed his or her clothes. If you have a double sleeping bag, huddle the victim between two people to transfer their body heat. Putting someone with hypothermia in a cold sleeping bag alone is not sufficient because the body may not be able to produce enough heat. Warm the person with warm drinks and with candy and other sweetened foods. These are high in carbohydrates and quickly provide heat energy.

DON'T GIVE ALCOHOL OR TOBACCO TO A HYPOTHERMIA VICTIM ▶ In fact, avoid these products on winter outings. Alcohol can lower the body's resistance to cold since it may cause a sudden release of cold blood from the surface blood vessels to the core. This can reduce the body's core temperature. Nicotine constricts the flow of blood, which can cause the extremities to become cold and get frostbitten.

Preserving Our Natural Environment

- ► Camp at designated campsites.
- ► If you use a campfire at all, keep it small.
- ► Don't cook or eat in your tent.
- ► Carry garbage out with you—don't bury it.
- ► Wash yourself and your dishes away from the water source.
- ► Where there's an outhouse, use it; if there isn't one, go at least 60 metres (200 feet) from water, scoop a small hole and bury everything.

Canada is fortunate to have a great diversity of natural environments within its natural areas for people to explore and enjoy. To preserve our outdoors, we must minimize our impact on the environment.

Guidelines for Hikers

Stay on the Path and Minimize Your Impact

Steep sections of trails are often built with switchbacks to make hiking easier and reduce erosion. Cutting across switchbacks encourages run-off.

Modern equipment has eliminated the need for a campsite to provide wood and shelter, making it easier to carry a lightweight stove and tent than to build shelters and cook on a fire. It also lets you camp in bare spots—near a glacier, for example, or on treeless barrens.

On trails where campsites are designated, camp only at these sites. This confines impact on the environment to particular spots and leaves surrounding areas intact. Where there are no restrictions, camp at previously used campsites. When forced to use a virgin site, set up camp at least 30 metres (100 feet) away from the shores of lakes and streams.

QUOTAS ▶ Several parks have quotas on the number of hikers permitted on a trail at one time. Some also restrict the size of hiking groups allowed to camp at one site at the same time. Large groups occupy more space and have more impact on the environment than do the same number of campers using the same site over an extended period. If a large number of hikers happen to be camping at the same site, be extra courteous, especially after dark when people want to listen to the night sounds of the forest. Nothing is more obnoxious than loud, rowdy people at a campsite.

Clearing vegetation to make a site for your tent and digging ditches around the tent contribute to erosion. When setting up your tent, choose a site from which rain will drain away. If it rains and ditches are needed, dig them only as deep as necessary to carry away the water. Fill them in before you leave.

Are Campfires Needed?

Campfires exude a cozy warmth that brings people together. Unfortunately, in many areas the depletion of deadwood is a serious problem. In some areas people have cut green trees, which don't burn.

Backpacking stoves are more efficient than fires, and they leave no trace. If there is an adequate supply of wood and you want to have a fire, keep it small. (Building a campfire is described in Chapter 3, Eating Well on the Trail: Food and Cooking Gear.)

Keeping Animals Out of Your Food

At backcountry campsites, animals lurk—waiting to feast on your food. These scavengers range from cute little mice to large bears, masked raccoons and unlovable porcupines. They've learned that hikers bring food. With the increase in the number of people visiting their habitat, they're no longer afraid of humans. Even noise doesn't bother them. In the good old days when a bear came into your camp, you banged two pots together and the beast would be scared away. Now, many bears will let you smash your cookware till it's crumpled tin—oblivious to the noise as they fill their stomachs.

HANG FOOD BETWEEN TWO TREES ▸ All food that is not canned should be placed in a sack and suspended between two trees. The sack should be at least 3 metres (10 feet) above the ground, 1.2 metres (4 feet) down from a branch and 3 metres (10 feet) out from the trunk. It's important the sack be between two trees. Hanging it over one branch is virtually useless because black bears can climb trees and get at the sack of food.

DON'T COOK OR EAT IN YOUR TENT ▸ The lingering odors attract bears. Cook away from the tent. When preparing a meal, take the required food out of the sack and immediately put the remainder back up between two trees. If you leave the food unattended on the ground, even for a few minutes, you may end without food—and will have to cut your trip short and walk out hungry.

PORCUPINES LOVE SALT ▶ Hanging the food will take care of problems with bears, raccoons and mice. Porcupines are another matter. These unsociable creatures love salt and will eat anything that has absorbed perspiration—like boots, hip belts and jackets (the armpit areas). Keep any such items inside the tent or hang them between two trees. Lean-tos and cabins are favorite places for porcupines; you should always hang your pack, boots and food from the ceiling, away from the walls.

DON'T FEED THE BEARS ▶ Don't encourage problems with bears and other animals by leaving litter or burying trash around camp. Don't feed bears for any reason, even to take that special picture to show the folks back home. Take photographs with a telephoto lens. Forget the Yogi Bear and Winnie the Pooh storybook images. Feeding bears is dangerous and unlawful. It encourages them to come around people, which increases the chances of a bear attacking a person. Remember, you're a visitor in the bear's country.

Carry Garbage Out with You

Don't bury garbage. Cans take up to 40 years to decompose, plastics take two centuries, aluminum takes half a millennium, and glass will still be around in one million years. Often the garbage does not remain buried. Animals smell the traces of food, dig things up and strew them around, making a mess and possibly injuring themselves.

"If you pack it in, pack it out," is the rule in the backcountry. Empty food containers are much lighter than the full ones you carried in. There's no excuse for not packing them out.

When buying food for your trip, avoid cans and bottles. Repackage food in plastic bags. On a trip, rinse empty cans, crush them with your foot or a rock, and pack them out in a plastic garbage bag. We can preserve the wilderness environment if we all conscientiously pack out all our garbage, right down to the last chocolate bar wrapper.

Safeguard Water Sources on the Trail

Camp at least 30 metres (100 feet) from lakes, rivers and streams. Washing near the water source can contaminate it, so carry water to wash yourself and your dishes at least 60 metres (200 feet) away. Use a biodegradable soap, if you use any soap at all. Dump the soapy water where the ground can absorb it.

Dispose of Human Waste Properly

To preserve a healthy environment around campsites, use privies—outhouses—when available.

WHERE THERE ARE NO PRIVIES ▶ Take care not to pollute water sources. Choose a spot that is at least 60 metres (200 feet) from any water source and is not a potential campsite. An isolated spot in the woods high on a hill is a good place. Scoop a small hole about 10 to 15 cm (4 to 6 inches) deep. The bacteria at this depth will decompose the waste. After use, bury everything by covering it with loose dirt, stones and dead leaves.

Be Responsible with Your Dog

Many parks prohibit dogs in the backcountry. Dogs may be a nuisance to other hikers and can disturb the wildlife. If you would like to hike with a dog, check the rules in advance with the park superintendent.

On trails where dogs are permitted, dog owners should use common sense and courtesy and respect the rights of other hikers. Don't let the dog chase wildlife, and restrain it when there are hikers, horses or other dogs that appear nervous because of its presence. Make sure the dog stays away from other hikers' food and out of the water source. Bury dog droppings. Loud yapping dogs are annoying to hikers. If you can't keep your dog quiet, leave it at home. Responsible behavior by dog owners will ensure that man's best friend is not banned from backcountry trails.

Now You're Ready

The next part of the book describes walking, day-hiking and back-packing opportunities in Canada. Whether you want an easy walk for the family or a wilderness trek, the next chapters will help you choose where to go.

Enjoy the trip!

Appendix A

Health and Safety

Here are some safety considerations to review before heading out. This list isn't exhaustive. For more comprehensive information, check a good book on first-aid and outdoor survival.

Blisters:
- Make sure your hiking boots or shoes are well broken in before you head out on the trail. If you feel a hot spot on a foot, stop immediately and cover the chafed area with moleskin or molefoam.
- If a blister develops, treat it right away. Cover a small blister with moleskin.

Hip Belts:
- When fording a stream or walking on logs and stretches of terrain with slippery footing, unbuckle the hip belt of your backpack so you can quickly jettison the pack in case you fall. If you fall while fording a swift flowing stream—and if the pack belt is secured

around your hips—the weight of the floating pack can hold your face down in the water.

Sleeping Bags:

- Make sure your sleeping bag is rated to the coldest temperatures you're likely to encounter.

Head Protection:

- Always have a sun hat and a regular hat or cap to protect your head from cold, wind, sun and rain.

Cooking Safety:

- Avoid eating food in your tent. The lingering odors may attract bears or other animals.
- When priming a white gas stove, don't use an excessive amount of gas. Fill the tank away from all open flames, and never fill it when the stove is hot. If the stove runs out of gas in the middle of cooking a meal, let the stove cool before refilling it. If a small flame remains after you've turned the valve off, just blow it out. Don't open the fuel tank to release the pressure; it will allow gas vapor to escape, which can ignite explosively.
- Use a backpacking stove outside. Don't use it inside a tent. It can cause carbon monoxide poisoning and asphyxiation.

Insects:

- If you're hiking during bug season, bring light-colored clothing with long sleeves and full-length pants.
- Use insect repellant with a high percentage of the active ingredient. (Most repellants contain diethyl toluamide, abbreviated DEET.)

Cold Weather:

- When hiking in winter, make sure your head and the back of the neck are protected.
- If hands, toes or feet have superficial frostbite, warm them by placing on a bare stomach, armpit or hand. If nose, ears or cheeks are frostbitten, hold a warm hand over the affected area.

- Never rub a frozen part of the body with snow.
- Never massage a frozen part of the body before, during or after rewarming.
- Don't try to rewarm a frozen part of the body by exercising it. Exercising will most likely increase injury to the tissue.
- Deep frostbite is serious. Move the person inside as soon as possible, and get prompt medical attention.
- Don't use a gradual rewarming process by soaking the frozen part of the body in cool water.
- Never try to rewarm a frozen part of the body near a fire. The person may not be able to feel the heat and may burn the limb.
- Be alert for the signs of hypothermia. The early symptoms are shivering and a general numb feeling. As the condition worsens, the shivering becomes more intense, speech is slurred, judgment is impaired and there is a loss of coordination.
- If someone in your group shows signs of hypothermia, prevent further heat loss by immediately getting the victim out of the cold. Remove all wet clothing and put the person in a sleeping bag with another individual who has also removed his or her clothing. If you have a double sleeping bag or can put two bags together, huddle the victim between two people to transfer their body heat. Putting someone with hypothermia in a cold sleeping bag alone may not be enough because the body may not be able to produce heat by itself. Warm the person with warm drinks, candies and other sweetened foods, which are high in carbohydrates and quickly transform into heat energy.
- Avoid alcohol and tobacco on winter outings. Alcohol has the effect of lowering the body's resistance to the cold because it can cause a sudden release of cold blood from the surface blood vessels to the core of the body, reducing the core temperature. Nicotine constricts the flow of blood through the blood vessels, causing extremities to become more susceptible to frostbite.

Appendix B

Checklist: What to Take

Prepare your own checklist, and revise it after each trip.

Begin by looking at each piece of equipment and deciding if you really need it. Avoid filling your pack with unnecessary gadgets. When you're lugging them up a steep climb, they feel pretty heavy.

Below is a sample checklist. Go through the list and select items you think you'll need. After the trip, note the items you lacked and those you didn't use. Then decide what you'll take on the next trip.

Items that should be carried on all trips in the back country:

Extra clothing

Extra food

Fire starter (candle)

First-aid kit

Flashlight

Map and compass

Plastic tarp

Pocketknife

Sunscreen lotion and sunglasses

Waterproof matches

Whistle

Transportation:
Frame pack
Hiking boots or shoes

Shelter:
Groundsheet
Sleeping bag
Sleeping pad
Tent or tarp

Cooking gear:
Can opener
Cooking pots and utensils
Cup
Food containers
Pot gripper
Salt and pepper shaker
Scouring pad
Spoon and fork
Stove and fuel
Sugar container
Water bottle
Water purification tablets, filter or purifier

Clothing:
Bandana
Belt or suspenders
Down booties
Gaiters
Gloves
Insulated vest
Long pants
Long underwear
Long-sleeved shirt(s)
Nylon windbreaker or breathable waterproof parka
Raingear
Short pants
Sneakers or moccasins
Socks
Sun hat
Swim suit
T-shirts
Underwear
Wool sweater
Wool toque

Toiletries:

Biodegradable soap
Comb
Foot powder
Handkerchief
Insect repellant
Lip salve
Moleskin

Personal items
Scissors
Suntan cream
Toilet paper
Toothbrush and toothpaste
Towel
Washcloth

Miscellaneous items:

Binoculars
Camera and film
Candles
Fishing gear
Money for emergency phone calls
Nature guides
Notebook and pen or pencils
Nylon cord

Plastic bags
Reading material
Safety pins
Sewing kit
Signal flare
Spare flashlight batteries and bulb
Thermometer
Watch

part two

Where to Walk, Hike and Backpack in Canada

British Columbia

British Columbia's snowcapped mountain ranges were once a major obstacle to reaching the Pacific coast from the east. In 1793 Alexander Mackenzie was the first European to journey overland across North America, 14 years before a comparable expedition was made in the United States. In that year Mackenzie reached Bella Coola near present-day Tweedsmuir Provincial Park. In the park, part of the trail he followed has been restored for hikers. When British Columbia joined Canada in 1871, the construction of a railway from central Canada to the coast was promised. Over the next decade, surveyors explored mountain passes for possible routes. These ranges now provide hikers with many exhilarating opportunities to hike through colorful alpine meadows, through forests of towering Douglas fir and over rugged mountain passes.

British Columbia covers 1,048,234 square km (366,255 square miles) almost wholly in the Western Cordillera. In the west are the

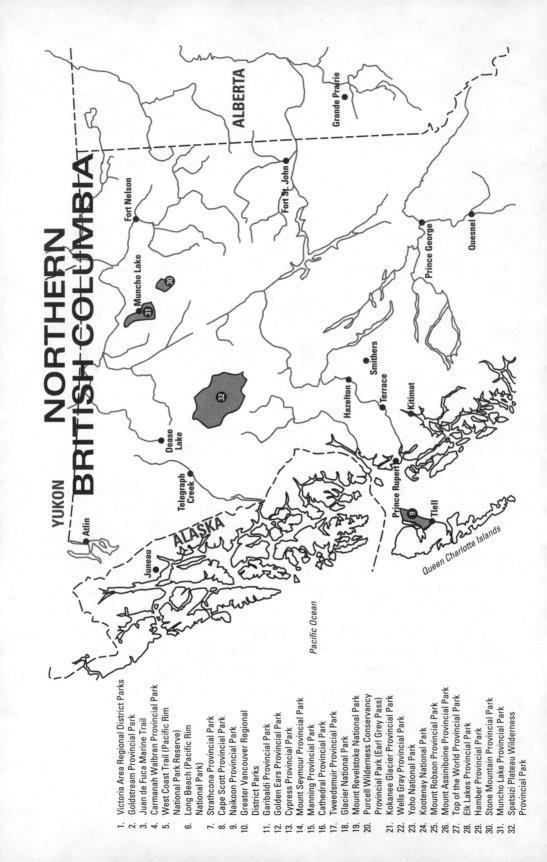

NORTHERN
BRITISH COLUMBIA

YUKON

ALASKA

ALBERTA

Grande Prairie

Fort Nelson

Fort St. John

Muncho Lake

Prince George

Quesnel

Dease Lake

Smithers

Hazelton

Terrace

Kitimat

Telegraph Creek

Atlin

Juneau

Prince Rupert

Tlell

Queen Charlotte Islands

Pacific Ocean

30

31

32

9

1. Victoria Area Regional District Parks
2. Goldstream Provincial Park
3. Juan de Fuca Marine Trail
4. Carmanah Walbran Provincial Park
5. West Coast Trail (Pacific Rim National Park Reserve)
6. Long Beach (Pacific Rim National Park)
7. Strathcona Provincial Park
8. Cape Scott Provincial Park
9. Naikoon Provincial Park
10. Greater Vancouver Regional District Parks
11. Garibaldi Provincial Park
12. Golden Ears Provincial Park
13. Cypress Provincial Park
14. Mount Seymour Provincial Park
15. Manning Provincial Park
16. Cathedral Provincial Park
17. Tweedsmuir Provincial Park
18. Glacier National Park
19. Mount Revelstoke National Park
20. Purcell Wilderness Conservancy Provincial Park (Earl Grey Pass)
21. Kokanee Glacier Provincial Park
22. Wells Gray Provincial Park
23. Yoho National Park
24. Kootenay National Park
25. Mount Robson Provincial Park
26. Mount Assinboine Provincial Park
27. Top of the World Provincial Park
28. Elk Lakes Provincial Park
29. Hamber Provincial Park
30. Stone Mountain Provincial Park
31. Muncho Lake Provincial Park
32. Spatsizi Plateau Wilderness Provincial Park

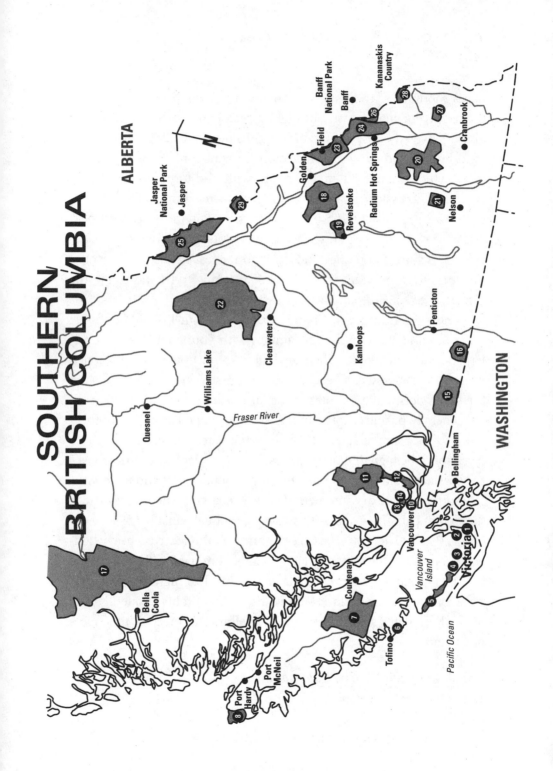

SOUTHERN BRITISH COLUMBIA

ALBERTA

WASHINGTON

N

Jasper National Park

• Jasper

Banff National Park

• Banff

Kananaskis Country

28

27

• Cranbrook

26

24

Field

23

Golden

29

25

20

18

Revelstoke

Radium Hot Springs

21

• Nelson

19

22

Penticton

• Clearwater

• Williams Lake

• Kamloops

16

• Quesnel

Fraser River

15

• Bellingham

11

12

13 14

10

Vancouver

Courtenay

Vancouver Island

• Victoria

2

1

3

4

5

17

• Bella Coola

7

6

• Tofino

Pacific Ocean

• Port McNeil

• Port Hardy

8

Coast Mountains, averaging 130 km (80 miles) wide and extending to the deeply indented coast. The highest peak in the lush rain forest and glacier-covered Coast Mountains is 3,978 metre (13,260 foot) Mount Waddington. On the eastern side of the province are the Rocky Mountains, which average 80 km (50 miles) wide and form an almost continuous succession of ridges and peaks—reaching 3,892 metres (12,972 feet) at Mount Robson, the highest peak in the Canadian Rockies. West of the Rockies are the Columbia Mountains, consisting of the Purcell, Selkirk, Monashee and Cariboo ranges. In the south-central portion of the province is the Interior Plateau. To the north are the Hazelton, Skeena, Omineca and Cassiar mountains.

The large number of hiking opportunities in British Columbia range from gentle rambles for families with young children to challenging wilderness treks. There are highly scenic trails along unspoiled beaches, where you can beachcomb for mussels and other shellfish in the tidal pools. Hiking routes in the far northern part of the province are generally primitive routes not as well developed as in the south.

British Columbia has many different climates, thanks to the Pacific Ocean and the high mountain ranges. The warm Japanese current gives the coastal region a very moderate climate of mild, wet and foggy winters and moderate dry summers. The west coast of Vancouver Island is the wettest part of Canada, with an average annual rainfall of 305 to 483 cm (120 to 190 inches). The Coast Mountains also receive a heavy rainfall as a result of the moisture-laden winds from the Pacific. East of the Coast Mountains, the Interior Plateau is dry. The higher air currents travel on to the lofty Selkirk Mountains, where it rains frequently. The Rocky Mountains are protected by the Selkirks and receive much less precipitation.

British Columbia Tourist Information
Tourism British Columbia
Box 9830
Station Provincial Government
1803 Douglas St.

Victoria, BC V8W 9W5
Toll-free telephone, within North America: 1-800-663-6000
Telephone, from overseas: (250) 387-1642
Website: www.snbc-res.com

Hostels
Hostelling International
British Columbia Region
Suite 402, 134 Abbott St.
Vancouver, BC V6B 2K4
Telephone: (604) 684-7111
Fax: (604) 684-7181
E-mail: info@hihostels.bc.ca
Reservations: www.hihostels.bc.ca

Vancouver Island

1. Victoria Area Regional District Parks
Trails near British Columbia's capital city

WALKS/DAY-HIKES. A variety of environments are preserved in 17
Capital Regional District Parks. Among them:

- **East Sooke Regional Park.** Covers 14 square km (5 square miles)
  of the rugged coast of the Strait of Juan de Fuca; noted for rocky
  hills, rain forest, and Coast Salish Indian rock carvings. Its 60 km (37
  miles) of trails include the 10 km (6 mile) Coast trail along the shore
  with views of the Olympic Mountains. Other trails wind through
  the park's interior, which offers a variety of animal and plant life.
- **Galloping Goose Regional Park.** Part of the Trans Canada Trail, a
  46 km (28.5 mile) long park corridor along a former railway right-
  of-way. Links View Royal, Colwood, Langford, Metchosin and
  Sooke. Part of it is along the coast. Hiking, cycling and horseback
  riding are permitted on the trail.

- **Mount Work Regional Park.** Encompasses 4 square km (1.5 square miles) on the Saanich Peninsula, about 20 km (12 miles) northwest of Victoria. The park's 426 metre (1,400 foot) Mount Work is the peninsula's highest point. Trails lead to its summit and to the McKenzie Bight.

Guidebooks ▶ *Hiking Trails I: Victoria and Vicinity* and *Nature Walks Around Victoria.* (See end of chapter.)

More Information:
Capital Regional District Parks
400 Atkins Ave.
Victoria, BC V9B 2Z8
Telephone: (604) 478-3344;
or (604) 474-PARK (recorded information)

2. Goldstream Provincial Park
Variety of large trees, northwest of Victoria

Situated 19 km (11.8 miles) northwest of Victoria, Goldstream Provincial Park covers 3 square km (1.1 square miles) of south Vancouver Island forest land. The park is traversed by the Trans-Canada Highway and the Goldstream River. The discovery of gold in the area in 1885 spurred a brief gold rush. Though little gold was retrieved, old shafts and tunnels dug by the early miners may be seen along some of the park's trails.

Forest Cover ▶ Because the area was not logged, a variety of large trees —including red alder, big leaf maple, western hemlock and black cottonwood—still stand. Also found here are Douglas fir, western red cedar—some up to 600 years old—and the arbutus, Canada's only broad-leafed evergreen. Salt marsh plants may be seen at the marsh where the Goldstream River empties into the sea at Finlayson Arm.

WALKS. The park's short nature trails, ranging from 5 to 25 minutes, are:

* The Arbutus Trail, through forested upland.
* The Upper Goldstream Trail, along the Goldstream River.
* The Lower Falls Trail, along Niagara Creek to the base of the falls.
* The Lower Goldstream Trail, to the nature center.

DAY-HIKES. The park's hiking opportunities include:

* The Gold Mine Trail, which leads past gold rush remains to 47.5 metre (150 foot) high Niagara Falls; about 60 minutes one-way.
* The Prospector's Trail, which leads past giant Douglas fir trees beside the Goldstream River; about 90 minutes one-way.

More Information:
BC Parks
2930 Trans Canada Highway
Victoria, BC V9E 1K3
Telephone: (250) 391-2300
Fax: (250) 478-9211
Website: http://www.elp.gov.bc.ca/bcparks/

3. Juan de Fuca Marine Trail

Roaring surf along rugged Pacific coast wilderness. China Beach, at the park's southern end, is just west of the community of Jordan River—which is 60 km (36 miles) from Victoria. The park's northern end at Botanical Beach, near Port Renfrew, is 134 km (80 miles) from Victoria. The park can be reached by Highway 14 from Victoria.

Winding along the west coast of southern Vancouver Island, this 47 km (29 mile) wilderness trail is in Juan de Fuca Provincial Park. There is camping at beach and forest campsites.

Wildlife ▶ Black bear and cougar inhabit the region.

WALKS/DAY-HIKES/BACKPACKING. You can walk to the beach, do a longer day-hike or start a backpacking trip from the four trailheads:

*   China Beach: At the southern end of the Juan de Fuca Marine Trail, the fine-sand China Beach is popular for family outings and is suitable for young children and seniors. A 20-minute walk (each way) along a wide, gravel trail—some steep sections—leads through a Sitka spruce, Douglas fir and western red cedar forest. A waterfall is at the western end of the beach. Grey whales migrate along the beach during spring and fall.
*   Sombrio Beach: A 10-minute walk (each way) leads to this beach. From China Beach, it's a 29 km (18 mile) hike along the Juan de Fuca Marine Trail to Sombrio Beach. From here, you can hike 9 km (5 miles) to Parkinson Creek.
*   Parkinson Creek: From here, it's 10 km (6 miles) to Botanical Beach or 9 km (5 miles) to Sombrio Beach.
*   Botanical Beach: At the northern end of the Juan de Fuca Marine Trail are tide pools. Marine life includes coralline algae, periwinkles, sea urchins, giant anemones, chitons and sea stars. Trails in this area, about 20 minutes each way, are popular with children and seniors.

Guidebook ▶ Hiking Trails I: Victoria and Vicinity. (See end of chapter.)

More Information:
BC Parks
2930 Trans Canada Highway
Victoria, BC V9E 1K3
Telephone: (250) 391-2300
Fax: (250) 478-9211
Website: http://www.elp.gov.bc.ca/bcparks/

Tide Tables:
For information on tide pools, refer to volume 6 of *Canadian Tide and Current Tables*; "Tofino" section. (See Guidebook Sources at end of chapter.)

4. Carmanah Walbran Provincial Park
World's largest spruce trees. The park is 20 km (12 miles) northwest of Port Renfrew, which is 134 km (83 miles) north of Victoria. You can reach the Carmanah Valley by road: from Port Alberni to the Caycuse River Bridge and then into the park; from Highway 14 and Port Renfrew to the Caycuse River Bridge and then into the park.

The Carmanah Valley and Walbran Valley preserve an old-growth forest of large Sitka spruce, including the 800-year-old Carmanah giant —95 metres (311 feet)—thought to be the world's tallest Sitka spruce. On the hillsides are thousand-year-old gnarled cedars.

The 165 square km (64 square mile) park is a wilderness area. The trails in the Carmanah are primitive and muddy; the Walbran has no trails, and because of potentially unsafe conditions the park discourages hiking there.

Wildlife, Birds and Fish ▶ Black-tailed deer, wolves, cougars, black bears, squirrels, mice, voles, marten and raccoons inhabit the park. Hairy woodpecker, pileated woodpecker, northern flicker, red-breasted sapsucker, winter wren, varied thrush, pygmy owl and the marbled murrelet may be seen. The lower sections of Carmanah Creek are populated with Coho and Chinook salmon, steelhead trout, cutthroat trout and sculpins.

WALKS/DAY-HIKES/BACKPACKING. From the parking area it is a 1.3 km (0.8 mile) hike to the Carmanah Valley Trail. From the trail junction, you can hike 7.5 km (4.6 miles) up the valley to August Creek, or 2.6 km (1.6 miles) down the valley to Heaven Grove. There are four tent camping sites along the trail.

Supplies ▶ Be completely self-sufficient. There are no nearby services —gas, food, lodging, telephone or medical. The nearest telephone is 33 km (20 miles) away at the Didtidaht Reserve.

Guidebooks ▶ *Hiking Trails II: Southeastern Vancouver Island* and *Hiking the Ancient Forests of British Columbia and Washington*. (See end of chapter.)

More Information:
BC Parks
2930 Trans Canada Highway
Victoria, BC V9E 1K3
Telephone: (250) 391-2300
Fax: (250) 478-9211
Website: http://www.elp.gov.bc.ca/bcparks/

5. Pacific Rim National Park Reserve—West Coast Trail
Historic lifesaving trail. Access to Port Renfrew is by highway from Victoria, or by logging road from Shawinigan Lake and Lake Cowichan. Bamfield can be reached by logging road from Port Alberni, or on the foot passenger boat MV Lady Rose, *which sails from Port Alberni (see below).*

In January 1906, the S.S. *Valencia*, a 77 metre (253 foot) passenger vessel ran aground on the notorious "Graveyard of the Pacific" on Vancouver Island's west coast, and 126 lives were lost. Following that tragedy, a lifesaving trail for shipwrecked mariners was built between the villages of Bamfield and Port Renfrew. The 75 km (47 mile) West Coast Trail follows the route of the historic lifesaving trail along the unspoiled coast of Vancouver Island. You'll see sandstone cliffs, waterfalls, caves, sea arches and beaches. It's a wilderness trail not suited for inexperienced hikers or children under 12.

Be prepared for rainy weather. Average annual rainfall in Bamfield is 269 cm (106 inches), with moderate summer temperatures between 10° and 24°C (50° and 75°F).

Forest Cover ▶ Heavy rain, prolonged cloudiness and moderate temperatures have produced a dense forest of western red cedar, western hemlock and amabalis fir, with Sitka spruce on the coastal fringe. The forest floor is hidden by a thick growth of salal, salmonberry and huckleberry.

Wildlife, Birds and Marine Life ▶ Living in the park are a small number of red squirrels, mink, marten, raccoons, black-tailed deer, black bears and cougars.

Because the park is on the Pacific Flyway, thousands of migrating ducks and geese stop to feed and rest on the shore during the spring and fall. Birds that inhabit the park include forest species such as woodpeckers, Steller's jays, brown creepers, red crossbills and chickadees. Shoreline birds that may be seen include red-throated loons, great blue herons, bald eagles and oystercatchers.

During the summer grey whales and sea lions may be seen offshore. Harbor seals inhabit the sheltered coves. At low tide mussels, barnacles, hermit crabs, starfish, limpets, sponges and sea anemones may appear in the tidal pools. Razor clams, beach hoppers and sea worms may be found on the beaches. Trout swim in many of the streams crossed by the West Coast Trail.

DAY-HIKES/BACKPACKING. The 47 km (29 mile) section, from the trail's northern terminus at Pachena Bay near Bamfield to Carmanah Point, was part of the historic lifesaving trail and is easier hiking than the more difficult southern section. A large part of the northern section can be covered on the scenic sandy beaches and sandstone shelves. A highlight is Tsusiat Falls, which cascade 15 metres (50 feet) down to the beach.

The 29 km (18 mile) section, from Carmanah to Port Renfrew, requires hikers to cross gullies on fallen trees, wade through fast-moving streams, climb numerous vertical ladders and walk on logs laid end to end. This section should be attempted by experienced backpackers only.

There are two river crossings along the trail that require the ferry services operated by local First Nations people: the Gordon River at the southern end of the trail, and the Nitinat Narrows near the midpoint. They cannot be forded.

Hiking the entire West Coast Trail takes between six and ten days. To avoid the difficult southern section, you can start from Bamfield and hike as far as Tsusiat Falls; then turn back or leave the trail at Nitinat Narrows.

Supplies ▶ Supplies cannot be acquired near the trail. Register for a free permit before beginning the hike.

Guidebooks ▶ *The West Coast Trail and Other Great Hikes*; and *Blisters and Bliss*. (See end of chapter.)

More Information:
Pacific Rim National Park Reserve
Box 280
Ucluelet, BC V0R 3A0
Telephone: (250) 726-7721
Fax: (250) 726-4720
Website: http://www.parkscanada.gc.ca/
E-mail: pacriminfo@pch.gc.ca

Ferry Service:
Alberni Marine Transportation Ltd.
PO Box 188
Port Alberni, BC V9Y 7M7
Telephone: (250) 723-8313

Reservations:
The number of hikers permitted to begin the trail each day is limited between May 1 and September 30. You may reserve quota spaces up to 90 days in advance by calling Super Natural British Columbia **Reservation Service**: (604) 663-6000 in the Greater Vancouver area; 1-800-663-6000 from Canada and the United States; and (250) 387-1642 from overseas. A limited number of wait-list spaces are available each day on a first-come/first-served basis at the Gordon River and Pachena Bay Park information centers. (*The West Coast Trail Hiker Preparation Guide* and *West Coast Trail Map* are sent to hikers making a reservation.)

Tide Tables:
Carry the Tofino tide tables found in *Canadian Tide and Current Tables* (vol. 6). (See Guidebook Sources at end of chapter.)

6. Pacific Rim National Park—Long Beach

Stretching along the Pacific coast of Vancouver Island. It is 108 km (65 miles) by steep and winding Highway 4 from Port Alberni; or on the foot passenger boat MV Lady Rose, which sails from Port Alberni to Ucluelet (see below).

Long Beach is 11 km (7 miles) of surf-swept sandy beaches and rocky headlands between the tiny fishing villages of Tofino and Ucluelet on Vancouver Island's west coast. It's backed by almost impenetrable rain forests and snowcapped 1,200 metre (4,000 feet) mountains. Long Beach offers easy walking, less rigorous than the West Coast Trail.

WALKS. Walk some of the 20 km (12 miles) of sandy beaches, absorb the ocean scenery, and explore tidal pools and rocky shoreline. Then explore some of the nine nature trails:

- The wheelchair- and stroller-accessible Bog Trail is a 0.8 km (0.5 mile) self-guiding nature trail along a boardwalk crossing the park's wettest forest.
- The wheelchair- and stroller-accessible Shorepine Bog Trail boardwalk is 1 km (0.6 mile).
- The wheelchair- and stroller-accessible Lismer Beach Trail is 300 metres (100 feet).
- The 5 km (3 mile) Wickaninnish Trail is part of the overland path from Ucluelet to Tofino.
- The Rain Forest Trail, with two loops, each 1 km (0.6 mile), leads to trunks of fallen trees that were saplings before the first European set foot in North America.
- The 2.8 km (1.7 mile) Willowbrae Trail leads to the seacoast at the south end of Florencia Bay.

Guidebook ▶ *Hiking Trails II: Southeastern Vancouver Island.* (See end of chapter.)

More Information:
Pacific Rim National Park Reserve
Box 280
Ucluelet, BC V0R 3A0
Telephone: (250) 726-7721
Voice/TTY (press space bar): (250) 726-7721
Fax: (250) 726-4720
Reservations: 1-800-689-9025
Website: http://www.parkscanada.gc.ca/
E-mail: pacriminfo@pch.gc.ca

Ferry Service:
Alberni Marine Transportation Ltd.
Box 188
Port Alberni, BC V9Y 7M7
Telephone: (250) 723-8313

7. Strathcona Provincial Park

Highest waterfall in Canada; on central Vancouver Island, west of Courtney and Comox, and southwest of Campbell River

Dominated by rugged snow-covered mountain peaks, lakes, alpine tarns and rivers, Strathcona Provincial Park is a 2,505 square km (974 square mile) mountain wilderness almost at the center of Vancouver Island. The park includes 2,200 metre (7,216 foot) Golden Hinde Mountain, the highest point on Vancouver Island. Strathcona also contains the highest waterfall in Canada, Della Falls, which drops 440 metres (1,443 feet) in three cascades.

British Columbia's oldest provincial park, Strathcona Park was created in 1911. The area's history dates to 1778, when Captain James Cook of the Royal Navy landed at Nootka Sound on Vancouver Island's west coast, a few kilometres from the park's western boundary.

Forest Cover ► In the valley and lower mountain slopes, the forest cover comprises western red cedar, Douglas fir, grand fir, amabialis fir and western hemlock of the Coast Forest. In the subalpine areas are alpine fir, mountain hemlock, lodgepole pine and creeping juniper. Wildflowers, giving some areas of the park a spectacular display of flora, grow at elevations between 1,200 and 1,800 metres (4,000 and 5,900 feet).

Wildlife and Birds ▶ The park is a wildlife sanctuary that contains some of the last remaining Roosevelt elk on Vancouver Island, as well as deer, black bear, cougar, wolves and wolverines. Birds are not numerous, but grouse, jays and the occasional eagle may be sighted. The park's lakes and rivers provide good fishing for cutthroat trout, rainbow trout and Dolly Varden.

WALKS. For walkers:

- The five-minute Auger Point loop shows how nature is reclaiming an area burned in a forest fire.
- The 2 km (1.2 mile) Karst Creek Trail explores limestone features, including sinkholes, disappearing streams, and waterfalls.
- The 1 km (0.6 mile) Paradise Meadows-Battleship Lake Trail provides access to the Forbidden Plateau area.

DAY-HIKES. The park offers more than 100 km (60 miles) of marked hiking trails in the Buttle Lake and Forbidden Plateau areas:

- Hikes from Buttle Lake include the 10 km (6 mile) Elk River Trail to Landslide Lake; the 5 km (3 mile) Crest Mountain Trail (views of the surrounding valleys); and the 6 km (3.7 mile) Flower Ridge Trail (through an alpine area).
- In the Forbidden Plateau area, trails include the 4.5 km (2.7 mile) Mount Belcher Trail offering panoramic views of the Coast Mountains on the British Columbia mainland; and the 15 km (9.3 mile) trail to Kwai Lake, from where short trails lead to surrounding lakes.

BACKPACKING. With the exception of the areas around Buttle Lake and Forbidden Plateau, Strathcona Park is largely undeveloped, so its primary appeal is to backpackers. Unique to the park are the interconnecting alpine ridges that form spectacular hiking circuits. Many of the park's trails are access routes to these high-ridge routes, which are not marked and should be attempted only by experienced, well-equipped hikers:

- From Buttle Lake there are four routes, each taking about a week to hike. The easiest and most popular begins and ends at Phillips Creek. The route follows the entire Phillips Creek watershed along the high divide and crosses Marble Meadows. Reaching the access trail to this route involves crossing Buttle Lake by boat.
- The other high-ridge routes follow the Ralph River watershed; the Shepherd Creek watershed; and the Henshaw Creek watershed, which includes the Flower Ridge Trail.
- A three-week-long trip on the Buttle Lake watershed is almost entirely in alpine parkland or high alpine terrain; it includes the highest sections of the four routes described above. From Mount Becher near the Forbidden Plateau the route follows the ridges south to Comox Glacier, west to Septimus and Big Interior, and then north to Mount Thelwood and Burman Lake, skirting south of Golden Hinde Mountain and going north down to the Elk River Valley.

Guidebook ▶ The routes and access trails are described in *Hiking Trails III: Central & Northern Vancouver Island & Quadra Island*. (See end of chapter.)

More Information:
BC Parks
1812 Miracle Beach Drive
Black Creek, BC V9J 1K1
Telephone: (250) 337-2400
Website: http://www.elp.gov.bc.ca/bcparks/

8. Cape Scott Provincial Park
Wide sandy beaches at Vancouver Island's isolated northwestern tip; 448 km (278 miles) from Victoria and 65 km (39 miles) from Port Hardy. Access is by logging roads from Port Hardy, 64 km (40 miles) east of the park. Port Hardy can be reached from Prince Rupert by BC Ferry.

Cape Scott Park is a rugged coastal wilderness of 149 square km (57 square miles). The 64 km (40 miles) of scenic ocean frontage include 23 km (14 miles) of shoreline spread over nine beaches. The wide sandy beaches from Nissen Bight in the north to San Josef Bay in the south are divided by rocky headlands and promontories. Nels Bight, a fine white-sand beach 2.4 km (1.5 miles) long and 210 metres (689 feet) wide, is the most impressive. The park's highest point is Mount St. Patrick at 415 metres (1,361 feet) above sea level.

In 1897 and again in 1910, Danish pioneers attempted to settle the area but were unsuccessful, given the weather conditions, the distance from markets, and the lack of suitable access routes. A few frame buildings and rusting farm implements remain.

Be prepared for adverse weather conditions. Annual precipitation in the area, almost all in the form of rain, is between 375 and 500 cm (146 and 195 inches). Prolonged sunny periods are rare, even during the summer. Trails can be very muddy, so bring high rubber boots in addition to hiking boots. Exploring all of Cape Scott Park takes about one week.

Forest Cover ▶ Within the park are red cedar, yellow cedar, lodgepole pine, hemlock and true fir in the upland areas. Undergrowth is mainly salal, salmonberry, evergreen huckleberry and fern.

Wildlife, Birds and Marine Life ▶ Deer, elk, bear, otter, cougar and wolves inhabit the forests and open upland areas. Seals and sea lions can be observed on the offshore islands. Canada geese and other water-fowl traveling the Pacific Flyway stop at Hansen Lagoon. Sea birds may be seen on the shoreline.

DAY-HIKES/BACKPACKING. Cape Scott Park, which can be entered only by foot, has 50 km (30 miles) of hiking trails:

- The 24 km (15 mile) Cape Scott Trail begins at the parking area near the southeastern park boundary and follows the old telephone line from Holberg Inlet northwest to Cape Scott Lighthouse, Fisherman Bay and Hansen Lagoon. The trail also provides access to the beaches at Nissen Bight, Nels Bight, Experiment Bight and Guise Bay.
- From the wildlife marshes and wide sandy beaches at San Josef Bay, a 10 km (6 mile) trail leads to the summit of Mount St. Patrick and then to the beach at Sea Otter Cove. From there a 2 km (1.2 mile) trail goes to another beach at Lowrie Bay.
- Hiking on the coastline off designated trails should not be attempted, since many of the headlands are impassable. Any other coastal travel should be attempted at low tide.

If you hike on the beaches, carry a tide table (see below).

Supplies ▶ Cape Scott is a wilderness area. Bring complete supplies with you.

Guidebook ▶ *Hiking Trails III: Central & Northern Vancouver Island & Quadra Island*. (See end of chapter.)

More Information:
Cape Scott Area Supervisor
BC Parks, Bag 11000
8785 Gray St.
Port Hardy, BC VON 2P0
Telephone: (250) 949-6346.
Website: http://www.elp.gov.bc.ca/bcparks/

Tide Tables:
Tide listings for Cape Scott are found in *Canadian Tide and Current Tables*. (See Guidebook Sources at end of chapter.)

Queen Charlotte Islands

9. Naikoon Provincial Park

Fine sandy beaches stretching endlessly; may be reached by air from Vancouver and Prince Rupert, and by ferry from Prince Rupert to Skidegate.

The Queen Charlotte Islands lie in the Pacific Ocean about 100 km (62 miles) west of Prince Rupert on the British Columbia coast. Naikoon Park covers 718 square km (277 square miles) of the northeastern tip of Graham Island, the largest of the islands.

A fine sandy beach stretches 32 km (20 miles) from the park's northwest boundary at the mouth of the Sangan River to Rose Point, where the 5 km long (3 mile) Rose Spit separates the waters of Dixon Entrance and Hecate Strait. Naikoon, a Haida word meaning "long nose," is the Indian name for Rose Point.

South of Rose Point to the park boundary at the Tlell River is 80 km (50 miles) of beaches backed by sand bluffs ranging from 5 to 60 metres (16 to 20 feet) above the surf. The northern inland section of the park consists of the Argonaut Plain, a wild land of muskeg, stunted pine, meandering streams, meadows and low flat-topped hills that reach 120 to 150 metres (400 to 500 feet).

Weather changes rapidly: Cool, rainy or foggy conditions with high winds can happen at any time. Storms up to three or four days long occur. Precipitation, mostly rain, averages 140 cm (55 inches) annually. Be prepared for cold, wet conditions.

Wildlife, Birds, Fish and Marine Life ▶ Black bear, marten and blacktail deer inhabit the northern area. Bald eagles, sea birds and migrating waterfowl traveling the Pacific Flyway may be seen. Trout may be found in Mayer Lake in the southern section of the park and in some of the other lakes and streams. Fur seals and whales may be sighted from the beach. Beachcombers can find numerous types of shellfish in the tidal pools.

WALKS. For walkers:

- The 5 km (3.1 mile) Tlell River Trail winds along the river shore to the beach.
- The half-hour Tow Hill Trail leads to a Blow Hole on the beach and the summit of Tow Hill.

DAY-HIKES. For hikers:

- The Cape Fife Trail leads 10 km (6 miles) one-way to Fife Point.

BACKPACKING. For backpackers:

- Naikoon's main backpacking resource is the scenic 95 km (59 mile) hike along the sandy beaches from the park headquarters at Tlell to Tow Hill. The route can be covered in six or seven days, but some hikers take ten days walking at a leisurely pace. The route has three major river crossings—the Oeanda, Cape Ball and Mayer rivers.
- The 21 km (13 mile) return Cape Fife loop is a two-day trip through coastal forest and bogs, and along sandy beaches and the 5 km long (3 mile) Rose Spit.

Supplies ▶ Food can be purchased at most towns on the islands but it's recommended you bring complete supplies with you.

More Information:
BC Parks
3790 Alfred Ave.
Bag 5000
Smithers, BC V0J 2N0
Telephone: (250) 847-7320
Fax: (250) 847-7659
Website: http://www.elp.gov.bc.ca/bcparks/

Tide Tables:
All rivers in Naikoon are tidal. Hikers should carry tide tables and plan their crossings for low tide. The Queen Charlotte Islands are listed in *Canadian Tide and Current Tables* (vol. 6). (See Guidebook Sources at end of chapter.)

Southwestern British Columbia

10. Greater Vancouver Regional District Parks

Hikes close to the city

Regional Parks offer diverse walking and hiking trails close to the city.
Among the district parks offering hiking opportunities are:

*   **Lynn Headwaters Regional Park** in North Vancouver, a 47 square
    km (18 square mile) wilderness mountain park. During the 1880s
    giant fir, hemlock and cedar trees from Lynn Valley were used for
    beams and spars. The park's 20 km (12 miles) of trails include: (1)
    the 5.4 km (3.3 mile) Lynn Loop Trail, an interpretive path that
    leads to an abandoned cabin with a view of the Lynn Valley; (2) the
    15 km (9 mile) round-trip Headwaters Trail, which starts at the top
    of the switchback of the Lynn Loop Trail and leads to Norvan Falls.
    A 4.5 km (2.7 mile) hike from the top of Grouse Mountain Skyride
    leads to Goat Ridge, a point for panoramic views.
*   **Seymour Demonstration Forest**, covering 56 square km (22
    square miles) between Lynn Headwaters Park and Mount Seymour
    Provincial Park, offers over 40 km (25 miles) of trails – including
    the 1.5 km (0.9 mile) Integrated Forest Resource Management Loop
    Trail and the 0.4 km (0.2 mile) Forest Ecology Loop Interpretive
    Trail. Among the park's other routes are the 2.2 km (1.3 mile) Twin
    Bridges Trail, the 5.5 km (3.4 mile) Fisherman's Trail and the 1 km
    (0.6 mile) Homestead Trail.
*   **Pacific Spirit Regional Park** encompasses upland forest of trem-
    bling aspen, old-growth fir and cedar; ocean beaches of rock and
    sand; and river frontage beside the University of British Columbia,
    near downtown Vancouver. The park's more than 50 km (31 miles)
    of trails follow the ocean shore (and include a clothing-optional
    beach) and traverse the interior. Most of the trails are multi-
    purpose routes used for hiking, cycling and horseback riding. Sev-
    eral trails are wheelchair and stroller accessible.

- **Belcarra Regional Park** covers 6 square km (2.5 square miles) at Burrard Inlet's entrance to Indian Arm, a 19 km (11 mile) fiord. The 9 km (5.5 miles) of marine shoreline is accessible by trail. Sun stars, moon jellyfish and beds of eelgrass may be seen. The park's Sasmat Lake offers swimming plus a trail along the shore.

Guidebook ▶ *Best Hikes and Walks of Southwestern British Columbia.* (See end of chapter.)

More Information:
Greater Vancouver Regional District Parks
4330 Kingsway
Burnaby, BC V5H 4G8
Telephone: (604) 432-6350
Fax: (604) 432-6296
Website: http://www.gvrd.bc.ca/

Phone Numbers of Parks:
Lynn Headwaters Regional Park: (604) 985-1690
Seymour Demonstration Forest: (604) 432-6286
Pacific Spirit Regional Park: (604) 224-5739

11. Garibaldi Provincial Park

Coast Range alpine wilderness, north of Vancouver

Garibaldi Provincial Park is a 1,920 square km (741 square mile) alpine wilderness in the Coast Range, 97 km (60 miles) north of Vancouver. The park is named for and encompasses 2,678 metre (8,784 foot) Mount Garibaldi. Many of the peaks in the park, particularly those in the area around Garibaldi Lake—including Price Mountain, the Table, Mount Garibaldi, the Cinder Cone and the Glacier Pikes—are the result of recent volcanic action. The Black Tusk has been intensely eroded and is the most interesting of the peaks formed by volcanoes.

Forest Cover ▶ At lower levels of the park, the growth of Douglas fir, western red cedar and western hemlock is dense. Birch and alder grow along the waterways. Mountain hemlock, yellow cedar, alpine fir and white bark pine are at higher elevations. The alpine areas are carpeted with many varieties of colorful wildflowers, including western anemone, lupine, arnica, Indian paintbrush and snow lily.

Wildlife and Birds ▶ Deer, mountain goat, grizzly bear and black bear inhabit the park but are seldom seen. Birds that can be observed include the Canada jay, bald eagle and ptarmigan.

DAY-HIKES/BACKPACKING. The park's main hiking areas are Diamond Head in the southwest section, and Black Tusk/Garibaldi Lake in the central area.

In the Diamond Head area:

- An 11.2 km (7 mile) trail begins at the parking lot 16 km (10 miles) off Highway 99 and goes along Paul Ridge to the Elfin Shelter and primitive campsites near Elfin Lakes and Red Heather Meadows. An A-frame shelter providing accommodation for up to 30 people is also located near Elfin Lakes. Hikers can establish a base camp and explore the area on day-hikes.
- From Elfin Lakes, an 11 km (7 mile) trail to Mamquam Lake passes Diamond Head, the Gargoyles (strange visages formed in eroding lava), and the Opal Cone (a disintegrating volcanic mound).

In the Black Tusk area:

- A 9 km (5.6 mile) trail leads to a campsite on the shore of Garibaldi Lake, where a base camp can be set up. Some of the scenic features in this area are Panorama Ridge, Mimulus Lake, Black Tusk Lake and Helm Lake. Hikers may also pass near Helm Glacier and the volcanic Cinder Cone.

- From Black Tusk Meadows a 14.4 km (9 mile) trail leads to Cheaka-mus Lake, a glacier-fed lake at 914 metres (2,998 feet) elevation surrounded by towering mountains rising up to 1,500 metres (5,000 feet) from the shore. This lake, which offers fishing for rain-bow trout and Dolly Varden, can also be reached by a 3.2 km (2 mile) trail. The trailhead is 8 km (5 miles), along a logging road from Highway 99.

Supplies ▶ Garibaldi Park is a wilderness area; and hikers should arrive with complete supplies, which can be acquired in Vancouver, Squamish and Whistler. The park is closed to fires and domestic animals.

Guidebook ▶ *Best Hikes and Walks of Southwestern British Columbia.* (See end of chapter.)

More Information:
BC Parks
Box 220
Brackendale, BC V0N 1H0
Telephone: (604) 898-3678
Fax: (604) 898-4171
Website: http://www.elp.gov.bc.ca/bcparks/

12. Golden Ears Provincial Park
Twin peaks of Mount Blanshard in rugged Coast Mountains north of the Fraser River

One of British Columbia's largest provincial parks, Golden Ears Park is situated 48 km (30 miles) east of Vancouver. The 550 square km (212 square mile) park is named for the prominent twin-peaked Mount Blan-shard. Garibaldi Park is on the northern park boundary, but an almost impenetrable mountain barrier in the region of Mount Glendinning makes travel between the two parks almost impossible.

Forest Cover ▶ Vegetation in the area is typical of the Coast Mountains. Douglas fir, western hemlock, western red cedar and balsam grow at lower elevations. Cottonwood and alder are found along creek and river banks.

Fish ▶ The park's lakes and rivers contain coastal cutthroat, kokanee and Dolly Varden.

WALKS. Walking opportunities include:

- The wheelchair- and stroller-accessible Spirea Bog interpretive trail, a 45-minute walk that explores a bog from a series of boardwalks.
- The 1.5 km (0.9 mile) Viewpoint Trail, which provides good views —including a waterfall during the wet season.
- The 2.7 km (1.6 mile) Lower Falls Trail, a popular walk along Gold Creek to the 10 metre high (33 foot) falls.

DAY-HIKES. The park has more than 50 km (30 miles) of hiking trails, including:

- The 4.2 km (2.6 mile) Mike Lake Trail, which links with the 1.2 km (0.7 mile) Incline Trail. The Incline in turn joins with the 10 km (6 mile) Alouette Mountain hiking trail, offering panoramic views of Alouette Mountain.

BACKPACKING. For backpackers:

- The Golden Ears Trail is a strenuous 12 km (7.5 mile) hike (each way) through second-growth, first-growth and subalpine forest to alpine terrain on Panorama Ridge—with magnificent views in all directions. A mountain shelter is located near the ridge.

More Information:
BC Parks
1610 Mt. Seymour Rd.
North Vancouver, BC V7G 1L3
Telephone: (604) 924-2200
Fax: (604) 924-2244
Website: http://www.elp.gov.bc.ca/bcparks/

13. Cypress Provincial Park
In the North Shore Mountains, which form a backdrop to Vancouver

Situated north of West Vancouver, 30 square km (11 square mile) Cypress Provincial Park is just 12 km (8 miles) from downtown Vancouver via the Lions Gate Bridge.

Cypress Park is bounded on the west by Howe Sound. On the northeast it's bounded by 1,454 metre (4,770 foot) Mount Strachan and 1,325 metre (4,347 foot) Hollyburn Mountain; these, along with 1,217 metre (3,992 foot) Black Mountain, are the park's highest peaks.

Forest Cover ▶ A Coastal Douglas fir forest is found at lower elevations, while near ridge tops are mountain hemlock, 40 metre (130 foot) high amabalis fir, and yellow cypress.

Wildlife and Birds ▶ Animal life includes deer, black bears, coyotes, squirrels, hares and weasels. A variety of birds may be seen, among them ravens, gray jays, chickadees, warblers and woodpeckers.

WALK. For walkers:

- The Yew Lake interpretive trail, a 1.4 km (0.8 mile) loop skirting Yew Lake. Focuses on the role of water, snow and ice in the development of plants and animals.

DAY-HIKES/BACKPACKING. For hikers and backpackers:

- The 6 km (3.7 mile) Hollyburn Mountain Trail leads from the Hollyburn Ridge parking area to the mountain's peak.
- The Howe Sound Crest Trail offers good views of Howe Sound and the Coastal Mountain Range. It's a 29 km (18 mile) route along mountain ridges from Cypress Bowl in Cypress Park to Highway 99 just south of Porteau Cove Provincial Park on Howe Sound.
- The Baden Powell Centennial Trail extends for 42 km (26 miles) from Eagle Ridge near Horseshoe Bay to Deep Cove along the North

Shore Mountains. Two sections traverse Cypress Park: an 8.5 km (5.2 mile) section from Horseshoe Bay, up Eagle Ridge and over Black Mountain to Cypress Bowl ski area; and a 9.5 km (5.9 mile) section from the Cypress Bowl ski area to Hollyburn Lodge, along Blue Gentian Lake and Lawson Creek to the British Properties.

Guidebook ▶ *Best Hikes and Walks of Southwestern British Columbia.* (See end of chapter.)

More Information:
BC Parks
1610 Mt. Seymour Rd.
North Vancouver, BC V7G 2R9
Telephone: (604) 924-2200
Fax: (604) 924-2244
Website: http://www.elp.gov.bc.ca/bcparks/

14. Mount Seymour Provincial Park

30 minutes from downtown Vancouver

Located just 15 km (9 miles) from downtown Vancouver, this 35 square km (15 square mile) park encompasses most of 1,453 metre (4,766 foot) Mount Seymour and is bounded on the north by the Coast Mountain Range.

The park is mainly a day-use area for the Vancouver and Lower Mainland area, but overnight trips are permitted.

Forest Cover ▶ The forest, typical of the Coastal Range, is made up of Douglas fir and western red cedar at lower elevations, and alpine fir and pine at higher elevations. Some areas above the treeline are carpeted with alpine flowers.

Wildlife and Birds ▶ Park animals include black bear, deer, coyote and a large variety of birds.

WALKS. For walkers:

- The Goldie Lake Trail is a 2 km (1.2 mile) loop through a mountain hemlock forest.
- The Dinky Peak Trail leads almost 1 km (0.6 mile) to a view of the Vancouver area.

DAY-HIKES. For hikers:

- The 4 km (2.4 mile) Mount Seymour Trail climbs to the summit. Several trails lead off from this trail.

BACKPACKING. For backpackers:

- The 42 km (26 mile) Baden Powell Trail, which connects Deep Cove with Eagle Ridge near Horseshoe Bay, passes through the park.

Guidebook ▶ *Best Hikes and Walks of Southwestern British Columbia.* (See end of chapter.)

More Information:
BC Parks
1610 Mt. Seymour Rd.
North Vancouver, BC V7G 2R9
Telephone: (604) 924-2200
Fax: (604) 924-2244
Website: http://www.elp.gov.bc.ca/bcparks/

15. Manning Provincial Park
Cascade Mountains—with deep valleys, alpine meadows, lakes and rivers

Situated in the Cascade Mountains, 224 km (139 miles) east of Vancouver, Manning Park is 850 square km (325 square miles) of mountains, deep valleys, alpine meadows, lakes and rivers. Within the park are the sources of two major rivers: the Skagit, which flows west and south to the Pacific Ocean; and the Similkameen, a major tributary of the Columbia River flowing east into the Okanagan.

Forest Cover ▶ Mountain slopes are covered with conifers including Douglas fir, western red cedar, hemlock, Engelmann spruce and lodgepole pine. Wildflowers carpet the alpine meadows, including the spectacular meadows that cover an area of 24 km (15 miles) in length and up to 4.8 km (3 miles) in width stretching from Blackwall Mountain to Nicomen Ridge. The Heather Trail traverses this subalpine meadow.

Wildlife and Birds ▶ Mule deer, coyote, moose and black bear inhabit the park. Over 190 bird species have been observed.

WALKS. Trails include:

- The 0.5 km (0.3 mile) Beaver Pond Trail, which offers excellent bird watching in May and June.
- The 1 km (0.6 mile) Paintbrush Trail, which leads through subalpine meadows.
- The 0.5 km (0.3 mile) Rein Orchid walk, with orchids and other bog flora.

DAY-HIKES. For hikers:

- The Three Falls Trail, a 9 km (5.5 mile) hike leads to Shadow, Nepopekum and Derek Falls.
- The 14 km (8.6 mile) return Windy Joe Mountain Trail presents scenic views and features a fire-lookout interpretive display.
- The 17 km (10.5 mile) Whatcom Trail leads through forest and meadows to Whatcom Pass.

BACKPACKING. Manning Park is laced with 270 km (167 miles) of trails that can be linked to create a number of trips:

- The 21 km (13 mile) Heather Trail through alpine meadows to Three Brothers Mountain connects with the 22 km (14 mile)

Bonnevier Trail at Big Buck Mountain and continues to Nicomen Ridge, where the trail links with the 17 km (11 mile) Granger Creek Trail.

- The Pacific Crest Trail's northern terminus is in the park. The 3,864 km (2,400 mile) Pacific Crest Trail is a high mountain wilderness route along the crests of the Cascade Range (Washington and Oregon) and the Sierra Nevada and other California mountains. Manning Park contains 12.5 km (7.5 miles) of the trail, from the park headquarters to Monument 78 on the United States border. Hikers crossing the border must comply with all customs regulations.

Supplies ▶ There are no large stores near the park, so hikers should bring supplies with them.

More Information:
Manning Provincial Park
Box 3
69 Hope-Princeton Highway
Manning Park, BC V0X 1R0
Telephone: (250) 840-8836
Fax: (250) 840-8700
Website: http://www.elp.gov.bc.ca/bcparks/

16. Cathedral Provincial Park

Azure lakes, alpine meadows and jagged Okanagan Mountain peaks; 30 km (19 miles) southwest of the town of Keremeos

The Cathedral Lakes and peaks of the Okanagan Mountains are found in this 332 square km (130 square mile) wilderness area that is bounded on the south by the United States border, on the east by Ewart Creek, and on the west and north by the Ashnola River, a tributary of the Similkameen.

The park is known for the five turquoise-colored Cathedral Lakes, for the Haystack Lakes, and for Stone City—a wind-eroded quartzite formation looking like a city of a future age. The highest peak in the park is 2,628 metre (8,620 foot) Lakeview Mountain.

Plant life and wildlife are typical of the transition zone between the rain forests of the Cascade Mountains and the drier Okanagan Valley.

Forest Cover ► The forest is made up mainly of Douglas fir at lower levels, with cottonwood and aspen along creeks and rivers. At higher elevations are lodgepole pine and Engelmann spruce, which give way to subalpine fir and alpine fir near the timberline.

Wildlife and Fish ► Inhabiting the park are mule deer, mountain goat and California bighorn sheep. Most of the lakes contain Kamloops trout and cutthroat trout.

DAY-HIKES/BACKPACKING. Cathedral Park has about 90 km (56 miles) of trails:

- The Centennial Trail goes for 24 km (15 miles) along Wall Creek, the Ashnola River and Easygoing Creek to the Paysayten River.
- From Quiniscoe Lake, a network of 46 km (29 miles) of trails radiates to the other scenic lakes, Lakeview Mountain, Bomford Mountain, Pyramid Mountain and Stone City.
- Visitors are not allowed to drive their cars in the Cathedral Lakes area, but a commercial jeep service is available to it from the park entrance. Otherwise, access is either by a 20 km (12 mile) trail that follows Wall Creek from the Ashnola River; or via a secondary road and the Ashnola Forest Development Road, 22 km (14 miles) from Highway 3—and a hike of about 16 km (10 miles) from the park entrance to the Cathedral Lakes area.

Supplies ► Arrive self-sufficient. Cathedral Park is a wilderness area; supplies are not available at the park.

More Information:
BC Parks
Box 399
Summerland, BC V0H 1Z0
Telephone: (250) 494-6500
Fax: (250) 494-9737
Website: http://www.elp.gov.bc.ca/bcparks/

West-Central British Columbia

17. Tweedsmuir Provincial Park

Vast unspoiled wilderness; approximately 480 km (290 miles) north of Vancouver

Tweedsmuir Park is divided by the Dean River into the northern region covering 4,675 square km (1,820 square miles), and the southern region covering 5,064 square km (1,970 square miles). It's bounded on the west and southwest by the Coast Mountains, which average 2,100 metres (6,900 feet); on the east by the Interior Plateau; and on the north and northwest by the Ootsa-Whitesail Lakes reservoir. Monarch Mountain in the Coast Range, at 3,533 metres (11,588 feet), is the park's highest peak. Glaciers cling to many of the mountain slopes. The Rainbow Mountains, a range of brightly colored peaks of glistening reds, yellows, grays, lavenders and violets, are in the east central area of the park.

Forest Cover ▶ Douglas fir, cedar, hemlock and balsam cover the lower slopes of the Coast Mountains. Pine and spruce grow in the northern and central areas. Along the eastern boundary are the rolling grasslands of the Cariboo Plateau.

Wildlife, Birds and Fish ▶ Found in the park are moose, mule deer, mountain caribou, black bear and grizzly bear. Bald eagles, golden eagles, ospreys, hummingbirds, horned owls, grouse, ptarmigan, Canada jays, ravens, trumpeter swans and loons may be seen. The lakes contain steelhead, kokanee, rainbow trout, cutthroat trout, Dolly Varden, Rocky Mountain whitefish, and salmon.

WALKS. For walkers:

- The two-hour Kettle Ponds Trail loop leads to a kettle pond and a bog.
- The two-hour Burnt Bridge Trail loops to a viewpoint overlooking the Bella Coola Valley.

DAY-HIKES. For hikers:

- The Rainbow Trail leads 8 km (4.9 miles) to an alpine lake, from where hikers can explore surrounding terrain.
- The Octopus Trail leads 18 km (11 miles) through the Rainbow Mountains, where it connects with a trail in the Capoose Valley.
- The 20 km (12 mile) Capoose Trail follows a network of lakes and waterfalls through the Capoose Valley.

BACKPACKING. For backpackers:

- Tweedsmuir Park's most popular trail is the 32 km (20 mile) route. It travels along the Atnarko River from Highway 20 to the 260 metre (853 foot) Hunlen Falls and then onto Turner and Lonesome lakes.
- The Alexander Mackenzie Heritage Trail stretches 300 km (186 miles) from Blackwater River near Quesnel to Bella Coola. The 80 km (50 mile) section within Tweedsmuir Park, considered the most scenic part of the route, takes about five days to a week to hike. This trail was originally used by Indians for packing oolichan oil (a food rendered from the oolichan fish and highly valued for its tonic qualities) to the interior for trade. In 1793, fur trader Alexander

Mackenzie traveled the route on his journey to the Pacific coast, the first overland crossing of North America.

Supplies ▶ Arrive self-sufficient. Supplies are not available locally.

More Information:
Tweedsmuir North Provincial Park
BC Parks
3790 Alfred Ave.
Bag 5000
Smithers, BC V0J 2N0
Telephone: (250) 847-7320
Fax: (250) 847-7659
Website: http://www.elp.gov.bc.ca/bcparks/

Tweedsmuir South Provincial Park
BC Parks
281-1st Ave. North
Williams Lake, BC V2G 1Y7
Telephone: (250) 398-4414
Fax: (250) 398-4686
Website: http://www.elp.gov.bc.ca/bcparks/

Columbia Mountains

18. Glacier National Park

More than 400 glaciers clinging to mountain slopes; straddles the Trans Canada Highway, 55 km (35 miles) west of Golden

In the heart of the Columbia Mountain system, Glacier Park covers 1,350 square km (521 square miles) of the jagged Purcell and Selkirk ranges that rise to 3,000 metres (10,000 feet). The narrow valleys and massive bedrock contrast with the broad valleys and sedimentary bedrock of the Rocky Mountains to the east. Half of Glacier Park is above 1,800 metres (6,000 feet), and about 12 percent of the park is covered with snow and ice the year round.

Expect some rain about every second day: The moist air from the Pacific rises and condenses when it hits the Selkirk Mountains, resulting in heavy rainfall.

Forest Cover ▶ The park's wet valley bottoms are covered with a thick rain forest of huge cedar and hemlock. Spruce and fir are found on the mountain slopes below the timberline.

Wildlife and Birds ▶ Grizzly and black bear inhabit the park, along with other large animals such as deer and moose. A small number of birds such as ravens, Steller's jays, gray jays and Clark's nutcrackers may be seen year-round in the park.

WALKS. Walks include:

- The 1.2 km (0.7 mile) one-way Abandoned Rails Trail, which travels along an abandoned railway grade, explores the history of Rogers Pass. Wheelchair- and stroller-accessible for most of its route.
- The 1.6 km (1 mile) round-trip Loop Brook Trail highlights railway history.
- The 0.4 km (0.25 mile) Hemlock Grove Boardwalk—barrier free, for people with mobility or visual impairments—explores old-growth western hemlock trees.

DAY-HIKES. Among the variety of day-hikes in Glacier Park:

- The 2.8 km (1.7 mile) Hermit Trail, a climber's access route into the Hermit Range, takes hikers from 1,287 metres to 2,057 metres (4,222 to 6,748 feet), with views of Rogers Pass and the Selkirk and Purcell ranges of the Columbia Mountains.
- The Bostock Creek Trail leads 9 km (5.5 miles) to views of the Selkirk Ranges.
- The 4.2 km (2.6 mile) one-way Avalanche Crest Trail leads to views of Rogers Pass, the Hermit Range and the Illecillewaet River Valley.

BACKPACKING. Glacier Park has more than 160 km (100 miles) of hiking trails:

- The best overnight trip in the park is the 16 km (10 mile) Copper-stain Trail. It traverses the extensive alpine meadows on Bald Mountain and provides a view of the eastern side of the Sir Donald Range.
- The 42 km (26 mile) route up the Beaver River—which divides the Purcell and Selkirk Mountain ranges—leads to the southern park boundary. It takes about three days to hike each way, linking with the Copperstain Trail to provide a multi-day hike.

Supplies ▶ Revelstoke and Golden are the closest communities.

More Information:
Glacier National Park
Box 350
Revelstoke, BC V0E 2S0
Telephone: (250) 837-7500
Fax: (250) 837-7536
Website: http://www.harbour.com/parkscan/glacier/
E-mail: revglacier_reception@pch.gc.ca

19. Mount Revelstoke National Park

*Massive, steep-walled mountains and narrow valleys; straddles
the Trans Canada Highway, 21 km (14 miles) east of Revelstoke*

The Columbia Mountains contrast with the broad valleys and sedimentary bedrock of the Rocky Mountains to the east. Mount Revelstoke Park occupies 260 square km (100 square miles) between the Columbia and Illecillewaet rivers and includes the Clachnacudainn Range of the Columbia Mountain system.

This is one of Canada's wettest areas. Precipitation produced by moist Pacific air hits the mountains and is forced to rise. As it rises, the air cools and the moisture condenses and falls as rain.

Forest Cover ▶ Valleys are covered by a thick rainforest of huge western red cedar, western hemlock, western white pine and devil's club. The subalpine forest between 1,300 and 2,000 metres (4,000 and 6,500 feet) is made up of subalpine fir and Engelmann spruce. Above the treeline, the alpine meadows are ablaze in late July and August with scarlet Indian paintbrush, blue lupine, yellow arnica and white valerian.

Wildlife and Birds ▶ Black bears, mountain goats and deer inhabit the park. Bird species include Steller's jays, gray jays and blue grouse.

WALKS. For walkers:

- The Giant Cedars Trail is a 0.5 km (0.3 mile) walk along a boardwalk through a stand of 800-year-old red cedars.
- The 1.2 km (0.7 mile) Skunk Cabbage Trail leads through a swamp with muskrats, beaver, skunk cabbages and many birds.
- Meadows in the Sky Trail is a 1 km (0.6 mile) paved trail through a subalpine meadow.

DAY-HIKES. For hikers:

- The Summit Trail leads 10 km (6 miles) one-way to the summit of 1,938 metre (6,350 foot) Mount Revelstoke.
- The 3 km (1.8 mile) Inspiration Woods Trail is a hike through a typical Columbia forest.
- The 8 km (4.9 mile) Lindmark Trail leads to meadows just below the summit of Mount Revelstoke.

BACKPACKING. For backpackers:

- The 6 km (3.7 mile) Eva Lake Trail crosses gently rolling country and subalpine meadows to a small cabin.
- The 9 km (5.5 mile) Jade Lakes Trail leads hikers to the jade-green waters of the Upper and Lower Jade lakes.

Supplies ▶ Supplies may be purchased in the city of Revelstoke, which borders the park.

More Information:
Mount Revelstoke National Park
Box 350
Revelstoke, BC V0E 2S0
Telephone: (250) 837-7500
Fax: (250) 837-7536
Website: http://www.harbour.com/parkscan/mtrev/
E-mail: revglacier_reception@pch.gc.ca

20. Purcell Wilderness Conservancy Provincial Park— Earl Grey Pass

High mountains, alpine lakes, grasslands. Toby Creek can be reached by 32 km (20 miles) of logging roads from the town of Invermere. Argenta is accessible by a secondary road from Highway 31, north of the town of Lardeau.

The Purcell Wilderness Conservancy preserves 1,996 square km (776 square miles) of the Purcell Mountains, the most easterly of the three southern ranges of the Columbia Mountain system. Mount Toby at 3,212 metres (10,537 feet) is the highest peak in the area.

The Earl Grey Pass Trail is a rigorous hike and should be attempted only by experienced, well-equipped backpackers.

Forest Cover ▶ The forest changes as the trail gains elevation. At lower levels are young alder, hemlock and Douglas fir. Above this zone is an area of hemlock and cedar, where some of the trees are almost a thousand years old. Just below the timberline are Engelmann spruce and subalpine fir, and above it are alpine meadows and tarns.

Wildlife ▶ Elk, grizzly bear, mountain goats, mule deer, black bear, and moose inhabit the park. Pileated woodpeckers may be seen here as well.

BACKPACKING. The wilderness conservancy is known for the Earl Grey Pass Trail, named for the Canadian governor-general who traveled the pass in 1911–12:

• The 61 km (38 mile) Earl Grey Pass Trail straddles the summit of Kootenay Divide. It extends from the town of Argenta on the east side of Kootenay Lake (in the West Kootenay) to Invermere (in the East Kootenay). From the old mining community of Argenta, the trail follows Hamill Creek and climbs 1,341 metres (4,398 feet) over a distance of 45 km (28 miles), reaching an elevation of 2,256 metres (7,400 feet) at Earl Grey Pass. Suggested hiking time from Argenta to the pass is five days. The eastern side of the trail from Invermere follows Toby Creek for 16 km (10 miles), with an elevation gain of 1,070 metres (3,510 feet) to the pass, and takes about three days to hike.

More Information:
BC Parks
Box 118
Wasa, BC V0B 2K0
Telephone: (250) 422-4200
Fax: (250) 422-3326
Website: http://www.elp.gov.bc.ca/bcparks/

21. Kokanee Glacier Provincial Park
More than 30 gem-colored alpine lakes; 34 km (21 miles) north-east of Nelson. Reached by Kokanee Creek via Highway 3A, Woodbury Creek via Highway 31, Keen Creek via Highway 31A, Enterprise Creek via Highway 6, or Lemon Creek via Highway 6.

Glaciers, glacial and freshwater lakes, alpine meadows and steep rocky canyons make up this 320 square km (123 square mile) mountain wilderness in the rugged Slocan Range of the Selkirk Mountains in the West Kootenay region. The park is named for the glacier that clings to the easterly slopes of 2,774 metre (9,099 foot) Kokanee Peak. Most of the park is at an elevation of over 1,800 metres (5,900 feet), and half of it is above 2,100 metres (6,900 feet). The alpine lakes are nestled at elevations ranging from 1,700 to 2,100 metres (5,575 to 6,900 feet).

Forest Cover ▶ The deep valleys are covered with hemlock, western red cedar, lodgepole pine, larch and Engelmann spruce. Dwarf huckleberry, white rhododendron and alpine flowers carpet the alpine meadows.

Wildlife, Birds and Fish ▶ Wildlife is not abundant, but includes mountain goat, deer, black bear, grizzly bear, hoary marmot, pika and rockrabbit. Blue grouse, Franklin grouse and golden eagles may be seen. The streams contain cutthroat trout, as do several lakes, which are stocked with them.

WALK. For walkers:

- A 2 km (1.2 mile) self-guiding nature trail loops around Gibson Lake.

DAY-HIKES/BACKPACKING. Most of the more than 80 km (50 miles) of trails follow creeks to scenic lakes and provide the only access to the park's main area:

- From the park access road at Gibson Lake in the south is a 10 km (6 mile) trail, which parallels Kokanee Creek past Kokanee Lake and Kaslo Lake. From there, a trail leads to Slocan Chief Cabin, which accommodates 12 people.
- A 10 km (6 mile) trail from the access road on the western park boundary follows Enterprise Creek to Enterprise Pass.
- From the southwestern boundary there is a 10 km (6 mile) trail that parallels Lemon Creek to the Sapphire Lakes.

- There is a 9 km (5.5 mile) trail along Silver Spray Creek from Woodbury Creek at the eastern park boundary. It leads to Silver Spray Cabin, which provides accommodation for eight.
- Another trail starting at Woodbury Creek leads 9 km (5.5 miles) to Woodbury Cabin, which accommodates six.

Supplies ▶ Supplies are available in Nelson, Kaslo, Balfour, New Denver and Slocan City.

More Information:
BC Parks
Box 118
Wasa, BC V0B 2K0
Telephone: (250) 422-4200
Fax: (250) 422-3326
Website: http://www.elp.gov.bc.ca/bcparks/

22. Wells Gray Provincial Park

Waterfalls, extinct volcanoes, mineral springs, glaciers and alpine meadows; 384 km (230 miles) northeast of Vancouver. To reach the park's main entrance at Hemp Creek, take the Clearwater Valley Road—40 km (24 miles) north of Highway 5.

A vast primitive area in the Cariboo Mountains, Wells Gray Park takes in a wide variety of scenery, including glaciers, alpine meadows carpeted with colorful flowers, numerous waterfalls, extinct volcanoes, lava beds and mineral springs. Helmcken Falls, at 135 metres (450 feet), is the highest waterfall. The 5,400 square km (2,100 square-mile) wilderness area—bordered by mountains on the east and north, and the upland plateau on the west—encompasses the Clearwater River watershed.

Forest Cover ▶ On lower mountain slopes grows a dense forest of Douglas fir, western red cedar and hemlock. Above 1,200 metres (3,900 feet) are alpine fir and white spruce, and above the timberline is alpine tundra.

Wildlife and Fish ▶ Wildlife is plentiful and includes mule deer, caribou, moose, mountain goat, black bear, grizzly bear, weasel, fisher, marten, mink, wolverine, beaver, squirrel, coyote, timber wolf, pika and marmot. Lakes, rivers and streams contain rainbow trout, lake trout, Dolly Varden and Coho and Chinook salmon.

WALKS. Walks ranging from half an hour to four hours explore a variety of sites, including a pioneer farm and the rim of Helmcken Falls. In addition:

• The 1.5 km (0.9 mile) Trophy Mountain Trail allows walkers to experience an alpine meadow within 45 minutes of the trailhead.

DAY-HIKES/BACKPACKING. The park's varied scenery may be seen through the network of over 240 km (150 miles) of trails. Many trails can be reached from Clearwater Valley Road:

• The 25 km (15 mile) trail to Battle Mountain traverses alpine meadows and links with a 16 km (10 mile) route to Stevens Lake; a 5 km (3 km) route to Mount Philip; and an 8 km (5 mile) hike to Table Mountain. These routes may be hard to follow and require routefinding skills.
• Murtle Lake, reserved for canoeing only, offers an opportunity to combine backpacking and canoeing.
• Six trails, ranging from 1 to 12 km (0.6 to 7.2 miles), lead from the lakeshore to alpine meadows, productive fishing spots, or points for enjoying panoramic views.

Supplies ▶ Limited camping supplies are available in the town of Clearwater, 40 km (25 miles) south of the park.

Guidebook ▶ *Exploring Wells Gray Park* and *Nature Wells Gray: Volcanoes, Waterfalls, Wildlife, Trails & More*. (See end of chapter.)

More Information:
BC Parks
1210 McGill Rd.
Kamloops, BC V2C 6N6
Telephone: (250) 851-3000
Fax: (250) 828-4633
Website: http://www.elp.gov.bc.ca/bcparks/

Rocky Mountains

23. Yoho National Park

Steep hollow cirques, glacial lakes, waterfalls, and hoodoo pillars. The park straddles the Trans Canada Highway just west of the British Columbia-Alberta boundary.

Glaciers, wind and water have produced the alpine scenery in 1,313 square km (507 square mile) Yoho National Park. Lying on the western slopes of the Rocky Mountains, Yoho includes 28 peaks over 3,000 metres high (10,000 feet). The Kicking Horse River begins at the Continental Divide and crosses the park from east to west. Banff and Kootenay national parks are on the eastern and southern borders.

Yoho's 400 km (250 miles) of trails reach nearly every part of the park. The extensive trail networks in the Yoho Valley and at Lake O'Hara are popular for day-hiking and overnight trips.

Forest Cover ▶ The grassy meadows and forests of Douglas fir, white spruce, trembling aspen and lodgepole pine are typical of the montane zone.

Wildlife, Birds and Fish ▶ Moose, deer, elk, black bear, cougar and mountain goat live at lower elevations, while marmot, pika, and grizzly bear inhabit the alpine areas above 2,100 metres (6,900 feet). The varied bird life includes Canada geese, ducks, pine siskin, red-breasted nuthatch and golden-crowned kinglet. The golden eagle, white-tailed ptarmigan and gray-crowned rosy finch are seen at higher elevations. The park's lakes and streams are populated by Dolly Varden, cutthroat trout, brook trout, lake trout and splake trout.

WALKS. For walkers:

- The wheelchair- and stroller-accessible Takakkaw Falls Trail is a 1 km (0.6 mile) return interpretive path beside the falls.
- The wheelchair- and stroller-accessible 4.6 km (2.8 mile) return Emerald Lake Trail is a self-guided nature path that winds around the blue-green lake and offers views of Mount Burgess.
- The 4 km (2.4 mile) return Walk in the Past is a self-guiding trail leading to the wreck of an old steam locomotive.
- The 4.4 km (2.7 mile) return Point Lace Falls and Angel Staircase Trail travels along the Yoho Valley Trail from the Takakkaw Falls campground.

DAY-HIKES. For hikers:

- The 3.2 km (2 mile) return Hoodoos Trail is a steep trail to Hoodoos.
- The Emerald Basin, an 8.6 km (5.3 mile) trail, travels through a yew and hemlock forest to a natural amphitheater of hanging glaciers and avalanche paths.
- The 7 km (4.3 mile) Paget Lookout Trail climbs across open slopes with good views of the Kickinghorse Valley and Cataract Valley.

BACKPACKING. In the Yoho Valley, four backcountry campsites let backpackers hike circuit routes or establish base camps from which to explore the surrounding area:

- The 16.6 km (10.3 mile) Iceline Trail over glacial moraines offers excellent views.
- The Lake O'Hara area can be reached only by hiking the 12.8 km (7.9 mile) Cataract Brook Trail or by reserving a seat on the bus. Trails in the Lake O'Hara area include the 5 km (3 mile) Opabin Pass loop, which crosses the Opabin Plateau; the 3 km (1.8 mile) trail past Seven Sisters Falls to Lake Oesa in a high alpine region; and the 3.5 km (2.1 mile) McArthur Lake Trail. (For bus service, telephone Lake O'Hara reservation line: (250) 343-6433.)
- Longer backpacking trips can be undertaken on the less-used trails in other areas of Yoho Park. Some of these are: the 40 km (24 mile) Arniskwi Trail; the 23 km (14 mile) Ice River Trail; and the 14 km (9 mile) Ottertail River Trail, which links with the trail system in Kootenay National Park to the south. There are two backcountry campsites in the Ottertail Valley.

Because of the popularity of the Lake O'Hara and Yoho Valley back-country camping areas, reservations are necessary.

Equipment and Supplies ▶ Hikers should be equipped with a back-packing stove, since fires are not permitted in the backcountry. Limited supplies are available in Field; a full selection is found in the larger centers of Banff or Golden.

Guidebooks ▶ *The Canadian Rockies Trail Guide, The Wonder of Yoho,* and *Lake O'Hara Trails.* (See end of chapter.)

More Information:
Yoho National Park
Box 99
Field, BC V0A 1G0
Telephone: (250) 343-6324
Fax: (250) 343-6330
Website: http://www.parkscanada.gc.ca/
E-mail: yoho_info@pch.gc.ca

24. Kootenay National Park

Radium Hot Springs mineral waters. The park is along Highway 93 and west of the British Columbia-Alberta boundary.

Kootenay National Park spans the Vermilion, Mitchell and Brisco ranges of the western Rocky Mountains. It's bounded on the north by Yoho National Park and on the east by Banff National Park and Mount Assiniboine Provincial Park. The 1,406 square km (547 square mile) park extends for about 8 km (5 miles) on both sides of the Banff-Radium Highway, and is cut by the Vermilion River Valley and sections of the Sinclair and Kootenay river valleys.

Kootenay has more than 200 km (125 miles) of trails in the park.

Forest Cover ▶ Douglas fir and spruce are found in the Columbia and Kootenay valleys, which have hot and dry summers. The Vermilion Valley to the north, which has moderate summers, is characterized by Engelmann spruce at lower elevations and alpine fir higher up. Above the timberline at 2,100 metres (6,900 feet), the alpine meadows are covered with red and white mountain heather, dwarf willow and bog laurel.

The park is known for the mineral waters at the Radium Hot Springs. Hikers and backpackers with trail-tired muscles may wish to relax in them.

Wildlife, Birds and Fish ▶ Elk, mule deer, bighorn sheep, mountain goats, black bears and grizzly bears inhabit the park. Among the 160 bird species seen in Kootenay Park are the western tanager, pine siskin, Audubon warbler, olive-sided flycatcher, northern three-toed woodpecker, Canada jay and nuthatch. Dolly Varden, brook trout, cutthroat trout, rainbow trout and whitefish populate the park's rivers.

WALKS. For walkers in Kootenay Park:

- The 0.8 km (0.5 mile) Paint Pots Nature Trail explores ochre beds where Indians obtained vermilion paint used to decorate their skin and tipis.
- The Marble Canyon self-guiding trail leads 0.8 km (0.5 mile) along the rim of this narrow chasm to waterfalls.
- The 0.8 km (0.5 mile) Fireweed Trail explores the renewal of a forest burned in a fire in 1968.

DAY-HIKES. Kootenay Park's hikes include:

- The 2.7 km (1.6 mile) Dog Lake Trail.
- The 2.7 km (1.6 mile) Cobb Lake Trail.
- The 4.2 km (2.6 mile) Stanley Glacier Trail, which leads up the Vermilion Valley to the Stanley Glacier basin.
- The 7.2 km Sinclair Creek Trail, which leads through alpine meadows and links with the 9.3 km (5.7 mile) Kindersley Pass Trail to form a circuit.

BACKPACKING. For extended trips, several trails from the Banff-Radium Highway to the spectacular Rockwall region in the northwest corner of the park may be linked or combined with trails in Yoho Park. The Rockwall, the eastern escarpment of the Vermilion Range, has a sheer vertical rise of 700 metres (2,300 feet). The main routes to this area are:

- The 17 km (11 mile) trail along Helmet Creek
- The 15 km (9 mile) route along Tumbling Creek.
- The 55 km (34 mile) Rockwall Highline route.
- In the eastern section of the park is the 32 km (20 mile) route in to Mount Assiniboine via the Simpson River, Surprise Creek and Ferro Pass.

Supplies ▶ A limited selection of hiking supplies is available in the town of Radium, but it's best to do your shopping in Banff.

Guidebook ▶ *The Canadian Rockies Trail Guide,* and *Invermere & the Columbia River Valley.* (See end of chapter.)

More Information:
Kootenay National Park
Box 220
Radium Hot Springs, BC V0A 1M0
Telephone: (250) 347-9615
Fax: (250) 347-9980
Website: http://www.parkscanada.gc.ca/
E-mail: kootenay_info@pch.gc.ca

25. Mount Robson Provincial Park
Lofty and usually cloud-topped; along Highway 16, west of the British Columbia-Alberta boundary and Jasper National Park

The highest peak in the Canadian Rockies, Mount Robson reaches 3,954 metres (12,972 feet). Bounded on the east by the Continental Divide and Jasper National Park, Mount Robson Park is 2,172 square km (839 square miles) of rugged snowcapped mountains, broad valleys, steep canyons and glacier-fed lakes, rivers and streams.

Forest Cover ▶ Spruce, fir, cedar, balsam, alder, lodgepole pine and birch make up the forest.

Wildlife ▶ Mule and white-tail deer, moose, elk and black bear are found at lower elevations. Grizzly bears, caribou, mountain goat and mountain sheep live at higher elevations.

WALKS. Walks include:

• The 2 km (1.2 mile) Fraser River nature walk, which explores plant life, wildlife and the Fraser River.
• The 1 km (0.6 mile) Robson River walk, which follows gravel flats along the river.

- The 0.5 km (0.3 mile) Portal Lake Walk, which goes along the shore of Portal Lake.

DAY-HIKES. Hikes include:

- The popular 7 km (4.3 mile) each-way Kinney Lake Trail.
- The 5 km (3.1 mile) Overlander Falls Trail.
- The Mount Fitzwilliam Trail, which climbs 7.2 km (4.4 miles) and affords good views.

BACKPACKING. Of the park's 100 km (60 miles) of backpacking trails, the most popular is:

- The 22 km (14 mile) trail to Berg Lake. Mount Robson rises 2,400 metres (7,872 feet) above the lake. Hikers can see icebergs calving (rolling off) Berg Glacier and falling into Berg Lake. Elevation gain on the trail is 725 metres (2,380 feet) and includes a rigorous 450 metre (1,475 foot) climb over a distance of 3.5 km (2 miles) in the Valley of the Thousand Falls. From Berg Lake the trail continues 2 km (1.2 miles) to Robson Pass, where it links with the North Boundary Trail in Jasper Park.

Supplies ▶ Supplies may be purchased in the Jasper townsite.

Guidebooks ▶ *The Canadian Rockies Trail Guide*, and *Jasper-Robson: A Taste of Heaven*. (See end of chapter.)

More Information:
BC Parks
Box 579
Valemount, BC M0E 2Z0
Telephone: (250) 566-4325
Fax: (250) 566-9777
Website: http://www.elp.gov.bc.ca/bcparks/

26. Mount Assiniboine Provincial Park

Resembling Switzerland's Matterhorn; bounded by two national parks—on the east by Banff, and on the west by Kootenay

At 3,561 metres (11,680 feet), Mount Assiniboine is the highest peak in the Rocky Mountains between the United States border and the Trans Canada Highway. Mount Assiniboine Park, which occupies 390 square km (150 square miles), is bounded on the east by Banff National Park and on the west by Kootenay National Park.

Access is only by hiking from Banff and Kootenay parks, and from the Spray Reservoir Road from Canmore.

Forest Cover ▶ The entire park lies at an elevation of more than 1,500 metres (5,000 feet). The lower areas of the park have a boreal forest of spruce, alpine fir and lodgepole pine. At higher levels are alpine larch and Engelmann spruce. Above the timberline, the colorful alpine meadows are carpeted with western anemone, alpine arnica, columbine, Indian paintbrush, spring beauty, alpine fleabane and mountain daisies.

Wildlife and Birds ▶ Rocky Mountain elk, mule deer, mountain goats and bighorn sheep inhabit the area. Among the 93 species of birds observed in the park are Canada jay, Clark's nutcracker, white-tailed ptarmigan, golden eagle, broad-winged hawk, sparrow, nuthatch, robin, sapsucker and chickadee.

DAY-HIKES/BACKPACKING. Lake Magog at the base of Mount Assiniboine is the goal of most hikers in the park. Here are the four Naiset cabins, open to hikers at a fee, and camping sites. There are four main routes to Lake Magog:

- The 27 km (17 mile) route from Sunshine Ski Village travels over Citadel Pass and through Golden Valley and Valley of the Rocks.

- From the Spray Reservoir south of the town of Canmore there are two routes: a 24 km (15 mile) route along Bryant Creek and over Assiniboine Pass; and a 25 km (15 mile) route via Wonder Pass.
- Beginning in Kootenay National Park is the 32 km (20 mile) route along the Simpson River and Surprise Creek, and over Ferro Pass.
- From the park's core area there are various trails that let you explore the surrounding area on day-hikes. Among them are the 5.6 km (3.4 mile) Og Lake Trail; the 4.8 km (2.9 mile) Mount Cautley Trail; the 5.6 km (3.4 mile) Wonder Pass Viewpoint Trail; and the 5.7 km (3.5 mile) Windy Ridge Trail.

Guidebooks ▶ *The Canadian Rockies Trail Guide, Banff-Assiniboine: A Beautiful World,* and *Invermere & the Columbia River Valley.* (See end of chapter.)

More Information:
BC Parks
Box 118
Wasa, BC V0B 2K0
Telephone: (250) 422-4200
Fax: (250) 422-3326
Website: http://www.elp.gov.bc.ca/bcparks/

27. Top of the World Provincial Park
Magnificent alpine plateau; 64 km (40 miles) east of Kimberley, and reached by logging roads from Highway 93/95

Most of 80 square km (31 square mile) Top of the World Park is an alpine plateau—at an elevation of more than 1,800 metres (6,000 feet) —enclosed by 2,700 metre (9,000 foot) peaks in the Kootenay Range of the Rocky Mountains of southeastern British Columbia. West of the plateau are the jagged peaks of the Hughes Range and to the east is the Van Nostrand Range dominated by 2,912 metre (9,551 foot) Mount Morro, the park's highest peak.

Forest Cover ▶ The forest consists of alpine fir and Engelmann spruce in the subalpine area. The plateau is carpeted with colorful alpine flowers, including mountain meadow cinquefoil and mountain forget-me-nots.

Wildlife, Birds and Fish ▶ The park has a small number of moose, elk, white-tailed deer, wolverine, porcupine, Rocky Mountain bighorn sheep and mountain goats. The abundant bird life includes Clark's nutcrackers, Steller's jays, Canada jays, spotted sandpipers and white-winged crossbills. There is fishing for cutthroat trout and Dolly Varden in Fish and Blue lakes.

DAY-HIKES/BACKPACKING. Top of the World Park has about 40 km (25 miles) of hiking trails. At the end of most trails are wilderness routes that can be explored by hikers experienced in routefinding. Trails include:

• The 6 km (3.7 mile) Fish Lake Trail, an easy hike through dense forest and past rock slides to open meadows, which features 28 primitive campsites, plus a cabin at Fish Lake (accommodates 24). From Fish Lake there are several scenic hiking trails, including the 7 km (4.3 mile) trail to the Sugarloaf; the 4 km (2.4 mile) route to Summer Pass; the 3.2 km (2 mile) hike to Wildhorse Ridge; and the 2.8 km (1.7 mile) trail to Sparkle Lake.

Guidebook. ▶ *Mountain Footsteps: Hiking Southeastern British Columbia.* (See end of chapter.)

More Information:
BC Parks
Box 118
Wasa, BC V0B 2K0
Telephone: (250) 422-4200
Fax: (250) 422-3326
Website: http://www.elp.gov.bc.ca/bcparks/

28. Elk Lakes Provincial Park

Bounded by towering glaciated peaks; 104 km (65 miles) north of Sparwood and 55 km (34 miles) north of Elkford. From Sparwood, north on Highway 3 to Elkford and then a secondary road to the park.

Lying in an isolated area of the Front Ranges of the Rocky Mountains on the Alberta boundary, much of this 172 square km (67 square mile) wilderness is above the treeline.

Among the park's scenic highlights are Upper and Lower Elk lakes. Upper Elk Lake, at an elevation of 1,800 metres (5,900 feet) is fed by the Petain, Elk and Castelneau glaciers. Lower Elk Lake is 100 metres (328 feet) lower and about 800 metres (2,600 feet) southwest of Upper Elk Lake.

Forest Cover ▶ Engelmann spruce, lodgepole pine and alpine fir grow below the timberline. Scrub birch, cinquefoil, saskatoon, gooseberry and a variety of colorful alpine flowers carpet the alpine meadows.

Wildlife, Birds and Fish ▶ Small numbers of elk, moose, mountain goats, Rocky Mountain bighorn sheep, grizzly bears and black bears are indigenous to the park. Spruce grouse, several members of the jay family and a variety of waterfowl may be seen. The park's lakes contain Rocky Mountain whitefish, cutthroat trout and Dolly Varden.

DAY-HIKES/BACKPACKING. Elk Lakes Park shares a common boundary along the Continental Divide with Alberta's Kananaskis Country. Among Elk Lakes Park's 20 km (12.4 miles) of trails are:

- A 4 km (2.4 mile) trail from the park entrance to Kananaskis Country via West Elk Pass.
- Another route from Kananaskis Country leads 7 km (4.3 miles) to Upper Elk Lake.

- A 1.6 km (1 mile) trail from Lower Elk Lake to Upper Elk Lake, a 2.4 km (1.5 mile) trail along Upper Elk Lake, and a 4 km (2.4 mile) route from Upper Elk Lake to Petain Creek Waterfall.

Supplies ▶ Complete supplies should be carried.

Guidebook ▶ *Mountain Footsteps: Hiking Southeastern British Columbia.* (See end of chapter.)

More Information:
BC Parks
Box 118
Wasa, BC VOB 2K0
Telephone: (250) 422-4200
Fax: (250) 422-3326
Website: http://www.elp.gov.bc.ca/bcparks/

29. Hamber Provincial Park
One of the least accessible of the Rocky Mountain parks; reached by a 24 km (15 mile) trail that starts at Sunwapta Canyon in Jasper, then goes along the Athabasca and the Chaba rivers to Fortress Lake.

This 240 square km (93 square mile) wilderness area of spectacular beauty can only be reached by hiking a difficult trail. The park adjoins Jasper National Park on three sides and encompasses several peaks over 3,000 metres (10,000 feet) including 3,058 metre (10,032 foot) Chisel Peak. The park features 26 square km (10 square mile) subalpine Fortress Lake, the South Alnus and Serenity glaciers on the western part of the park and part of the Chaba Icefield in the southeast corner. Fortress Lake has good fishing for brook trout.

The route is relatively level but has one river ford. Although murky, the Chaba River is usually shallow and has a sandy bottom. It can be treacherous depending on seasonal run-off. The best time to wade across the river is early September prior to fall freeze-up when the glacier-fed Chaba River is at its lowest level. The trek should be attempted by experienced backpackers only.

Wildlife ▶ Grizzly bears and black bears inhabit the park.

Supplies ▶ Backpackers should be self-sufficient.

Guidebook ▶ The Fortress Lake Trail is described in *The Canadian Rockies Trail Guide*. (See end of chapter.)

More Information:
BC Parks
Box 579
Valemount, BC MOE 2Z0
Telephone: (250) 566-4325
Fax: (250) 566-9777
Website: http://www.elp.gov.bc.ca/bcparks/

Northern British Columbia

30. Stone Mountain Provincial Park
Barren imposing peaks in northern Rocky Mountains. The Alaska Highway traverses the park for 13 km (8 miles), from the eastern entrance at Km 619 (Mile 385)—which is 159 km (99 miles) northwest of Fort Nelson—to the western boundary at Km 634 (Mile 394). Summit Pass, situated in the park, is the highest point on the Alaska Highway.

Named after the 2,041 metre (6,695 foot) mountain situated north of the park, Stone Mountain Park covers 256 square km (99 square miles) of the northern Rocky Mountains characterized by many barren and imposing peaks. Mount St. George at 2,261 metres (7,419 feet) in the southern section is the park's highest. The northern section of the park is dominated by Mount St. Paul which reaches 2,127 metres (6,979 feet). Glacial green Summit Lake, 2,000 metres (6,560 feet) long and 400 metres (1,312 feet) across at its widest point, is the park's largest lake.

Wildlife ▶ There are small populations of moose, mountain goats, stone sheep and Osborne caribou. Grizzly bears are occasionally sighted.

WALK. For walkers:

- The Erosion Pillars are a 0.5 km (0.3 mile) walk across from Rocky Crest highway pullout.

DAY-HIKES. For hikers:

- Summit Peak is a 5 km (3 mile) round trip offering an alpine view.
- The Flower Springs Trail is a 5.7 km (3.5 mile) hike to alpine lakes and waterfalls.

BACKPACKING. For backpackers:

- MacDonald Creek Valley offers a one- to three-day trip where caribou, sheep and moose may be seen.
- A two-day hike up the Churchill Mine Road leads to the Wokkpash Valley where there are hoodoos.
- The Wokkpash and MacDonald Creek hikes can be combined for a 70 km (43 mile) trip.

Supplies ▶ Hikers should bring complete supplies with them. The few stores on the Alaska Highway have limited selections and high prices.

More Information:
BC Parks
150-10003 110th Ave.
Fort St. John, BC V1J 6M7
Telephone: (250) 787-3407
Fax: (250) 787-3490
Website: http://www.elp.gov.bc.ca/bcparks/

31. Muncho Lake Provincial Park

"Big water" glacial jade lake. The Alaska Highway bisects the park, with the eastern boundary at Km 683 (Mile 424)—which is 223 km (139 miles) northwest of Fort Nelson—and the western boundary at Km 771 (Mile 479).

Muncho Lake Park covers 885 square km (342 square miles) of rugged wilderness in the Terminal and Sentinel Ranges of the northern Rocky Mountains, which rise to 2,134 metres (7,000 feet) surrounding Muncho Lake.

Muncho—a native word for "big water"—is a glacial jade lake. The area is considered the most scenic on the British Columbia section of the Alaska Highway.

Forest Cover ▶ The valley bottoms in the park are covered with white spruce and lodgepole pine. The heavy growth at low elevations thins to scrubby alpine spruce, then ends abruptly at the treeline. Dwarf alpine plants are scattered on the higher slopes.

Wildlife, Birds and Fish ▶ The park is inhabited by moose, mountain goat, stone sheep, Osborne caribou, elk, coyote, fox, marten, grizzly bear and black bear. Golden eagles, hawks, spruce grouse, willow ptarmigan and Canada jays are among the birds that have been observed. Anglers fish for Dolly Varden, Arctic grayling and Rocky Mountain whitefish in Muncho Lake and the Todd and Trout rivers.

WALK. For walkers:

- A 45-minute loop trail explores natural mineral lick formations near the banks of the Trout River.

DAY-HIKES/BACKPACKING. For hikers and backpackers:

• Trails parallel to the Trout River provide access to a variety of remote areas suitable for wilderness backpacking. Hiking cross-country is possible as well. Because of problems with grizzly and black bears, hikers should not travel alone. Package all food in sealed containers, and be sure your clothing is free of food odors.

Supplies ▶ Complete supplies should be acquired before traveling to the park.

More Information:
BC Parks
150-10003 110th Ave.
Fort St. John, BC V1J 6M7
Telephone: (250) 787-3407
Fax: (250) 787-3490
Website: http://www.elp.gov.bc.ca/bcparks/

32. Spatsizi Plateau Wilderness Provincial Park

Preserves spectacular alpine plateau scenery and top-quality wildlife habitat. Access into the park by trail is along McEwan Creek or Eaglenest Creek from the BC Rail grade south of the Ealue Lake Road. Can also be reached by float plane, chartered at Dease Lake, Eddontenajon Lake, Terrace and Smithers.

This 6,567 square km (2,553 square mile) wilderness park is situated east of the British Columbia Railway and 320 km (200 miles) north of Smithers. The diverse terrain ranges from bogs to alpine and glacial areas.

Wildlife ▶ The park is inhabited by woodland caribou, Stone sheep, Osborne caribou, mountain goat, moose, wolf and grizzly bear.

BACKPACKING. A variety of trails in Spatsizi Park lead to alpine areas, many with extensive plateaus that provide good hiking terrain. Most of the park's trails—originally game trails and later horse trails—are blazed and usually cleared. Many have water crossing them, and should be attempted on foot only in late summer, when water levels are lower.

- The McEwan Creek Trail leads through the Stikine River Provincial Recreation Area to Cullivan Creek, which it follows to Cold Fish Lake.
- The Eaglenest Creek Trail traverses the Gladys Lake Ecological Reserve—populated by Stone sheep and mountain goats—to Cold Fish Lake.
- From Cold Fish Lake, trails lead to Black Fox Creek, Caribou Mountain, Ice Box Canyon and Bates Mountain.

Supplies ▶ Backpackers should carry complete supplies. Individuals or groups may wish to use the services of a licensed outfitter.

More Information:
BC Parks
3790 Alfred Ave.
Bag 5000
Smithers, BC V0J 2N0
Telephone: (250) 847-7320
Fax: (250) 847-7659
Website: http://www.elp.gov.bc.ca/bcparks/

Trans Canada Trail—British Columbia
From the Pacific Ocean to Alberta boundary

The Trans Canada Trail's western terminus in Victoria will overlook the Strait of Juan de Fuca, which opens into the Pacific Ocean. On mainland

British Columbia, the trail will use the old Kettle Valley Railway right of way from Brookmere near Hope to Grand Forks in the West Kootenays. The trail will lead across southern British Columbia to Invermere. From here, it will cross the Kootenay River and the Kiko River before heading up to the headwaters of Cross Creek to Alberta.

More Information:
Trails BC
PO Box 2965
Creston, BC V9B 1G0
Telephone: (250) 428-5925
Fax: (250) 428-8447
Website: www.luco.gov.bc.ca/trancan/home2.htm

National Office:
Trans Canada Trail
43 Westminster Ave. North
Montreal West, QC H4X 1Y8
Telephone: 1-800-465-3636
Fax: (514) 485-4541
Website: www.tctrail.ca
E-mail: info@tctrail.ca

Guidebook Sources

Some of these books have been published by:

Gordon Soules Publishers
1359 Ambleside Lane
West Vancouver, BC V7T 2Y9
Telephone: (604) 922-6588
Fax: (604) 688-5442
Website: http://www.gordonsoules.com
E-mail: books@gordonsoules.com

Greystone Books
Douglas and McIntyre Publishing Group
201-2323 Quebec St.
Vancouver, BC V5T 3A3
Telephone: (604) 254-7191
Fax: (604) 254-9099
E-mail: dm@douglas-mcintyre.com

Lone Pine Publishing
Suite 206
10426-81 Ave.
Edmonton, AB T6E 1X5
Telephone: (780) 433-9333
Fax: (780) 433-9646
Website: http://www.lonepinepublishing.com

Rocky Mountain Books
#4 Spruce Center SW
Calgary, AB T3C 3B3
Telephone: (403) 249-9490
Toll-free: 1-800-566-3336
Website: http://www.rmbooks.com
E-mail: tonyd@rmbooks.com

Banff-Assiniboine: A Beautiful World. Don Beers. A guide to trails in the Palliser Pass to Castle Junction area of Banff National Park and the core area of Mount Assiniboine Provincial Park. Rocky Mountain Books.

Best Hikes and Walks of Southwestern British Columbia. Dawn Hanna. Describes 77 hikes. Lone Pine Publishing.

Blisters and Bliss: A Trekker's Guide to Vancouver Island's West Coast Trail. David Foster and Wayne Aitken. Rocky Mountain Books.

The Canadian Rockies Trail Guide. Brian Patton and Bart Robinson. A guide to many of the trails in the Rocky Mountains of British Columbia and Alberta. (Available from Book and Art Den, PO Box 1420, Banff, AB T0L 0C0, Telephone: (403) 762-4126).

The Canadian Rockies Access Guide. John Dodd and Gail Helgason. Includes hikes in Banff, Jasper, Waterton Lakes, Kootenay and Yoho national parks and Kananaskis Country. Lone Pine Publishing.

Canadian Tide and Current Tables. (Available from Canadian Hydrographic Service, Box 6000, 9860 West Saanich Rd., Sidney, BC V8L 4B2, Telephone: (250) 363-6358, Fax: (250) 363-6841).

Easy Hiking Around Vancouver. Jean Cousins and Heather Robinson. Vancouver, BC: Greystone Books.

Exploring Wells Gray Park. Roland Neave. A guide to the park's trails. (The Friends of Wells Gray Park, Box 1386, Kamloops, BC V2C 6L7, Telephone: (250) 674-4010, Fax: (250) 376-8928, E-mail: friends@wellsgraypark.com).

A Guide to Climbing and Hiking in Southwestern British Columbia. Bruce Fairley. Gordon Soules Publishers.

Hiking the Ancient Forests of British Columbia and Washington. Randy Stoltmann. Vancouver, BC: Greystone Books.

Hiking Trails I: Victoria and Vicinity. Ranges from neighborhood walks to week-long backpacking trips. (Compiled by Vancouver Island Trails Information Society, Website: http://www.vanisle.net/bctrails/, available from Orca Book Publishers, PO Box 5626, Station B, Victoria, BC V8R 6S4, Telephone: 1-800-210-5277, Website: http://www.pinc.com/home/orca, E-mail: orca@pinc.com).

Hiking Trails II: Southeastern Vancouver Island. Covers the area from the Koksilah River Park to Mount Arrowsmith. Victoria, BC: Orca Book Publishers (see above).

Hiking Trails III: Central & Northern Vancouver Island & Quadra Island. Includes trails and high ridge routes in Strathcona Park, and trails in Cape Scott Park. Victoria, BC: Orca Book Publishers (see above).

Hiking the Gulf Islands. Charles Kahn. Victoria, BC: Orca Book Publishers (see above).

Invermere & the Columbia River Valley. Aaron Cameron and Matt Gunn. Includes Kootenay National Park and the western side of Mount Assiniboine. Rocky Mountain Books.

Jasper-Robson: A Taste of Heaven. **Don Beers**. A guide to trails in Jasper National Park and Mount Robson Provincial Park. Rocky Mountain Books.

Lake O'Hara Trails. **Don Beers**. A guide to trails around Lake O'Hara in Yoho National Park. Rocky Mountain Books.

Mountain Footsteps: Hiking Southeastern British Columbia. Janice Strong. Includes Top of the World and Elk Lakes provincial parks. Rocky Mountain Books.

Nature Walks Around Vancouver. Jean Cousins. Vancouver, BC: Greystone Books.

Nature Walks Around Victoria. Helen Lansdowne. Vancouver, BC: Greystone Books.

Nature Wells Gray: Volcanoes, Waterfalls, Wildlife, Trails & More. Trevor Goward and Cathie Hickson. Lone Pine Publishing.

Okanagan Trips & Trails. Judie Steeves and Murphy Shewchuk. Merritt, BC: Sonotek Publishing (PO Box 1752, Merritt, BC V1K 1B8, Telephone/Fax: (250) 378-5930, Website: http://www.sonotek.com).

One-Day Getaways from Vancouver. Jack Christie. Vancouver, BC: Greystone Books.

103 Hikes in Southwestern British Columbia. David Acaree. Details hiking trails on the North Shore, Vancouver Island, the islands on the Strait of Georgia, the Garibaldi area, the Fraser Valley and the Manning Park area. Vancouver, BC: Greystone Books.

109 Walks in BC's Lower Mainland. David and Mary Macaree. Includes hikes in the Vancouver, North Shore, Fraser Valley, Chilliwack River, Hope Canyon, Fraser Canyon and Howe Sound areas. Vancouver, BC: Greystone Books.

Regional Parks in the Lower Mainland. Ed Rychkun. Vancouver, BC: Gordon Soules Publishers.

Scrambles in the Canadian Rockies. Alan Kane. Rocky Mountain Books.

The Similkameen Hiking Guide. Macdonald Burbidge, ed. Merritt, BC: Sonotek Publishing (PO Box 1752, Merritt, BC V1K 1B8, Telephone/Fax: (250) 378-5930, Website: http://www.sonotek.com).

The Southern Cariboo. Colin Campbell. Rocky Mountain Books.

Sunshine and Salt Air: *The Sunshine Coast Visitor's Guide*. Peter A. Robson. Madeira Park, BC: Harbour Publishing (PO Box 219, Madeira Park, BC V0N 2H0, Telephone: (604) 883-2730 or 1-800-667-2988, Fax: (604) 883-9451, E-mail: harbour@sunshine.net).

Tofino Tide Tables (see *Canadian Tide and Current Tables*).

Trails to Timberline in West Central British Columbia. Einar Blix. A guide to trails in the Kitimat, Smithers and Terrace areas. Vancouver, BC: Gordon Soules Publishers.

The West Coast Trail and Other Great Hikes. Tim Leadem. Vancouver, BC: Greystone Books.

Where to Walk Your Dog in Greater Vancouver. Ross W. Powell and Hero. Vancouver, BC: Gordon Soules Publishers.

Wilderness Trails in the Lower Mainland. Ed Rychkun. Vancouver, BC: Gordon Soules Publishers.

The Wonder of Yoho. Don Beers. Describes trails in Yoho National Park. Rocky Mountain Books.

10

Yukon Territory

The three men stared in awe at the flecks of yellow in the cold waters of Rabbit Creek. The year was 1896, and George Carmack and his two Indian companions had found gold in this lonely tributary of the Klondike River. Soon it was lonely no more, as thousands of excited "sourdoughs" tore up the streams and valleys in the great Klondike Gold Rush of 1898. They came by sea and then packed hundreds of pounds of food and gear, climbing in an endless file up the towering Chilkoot Pass. Their trail, still marked, is an exhilarating adventure for hikers.

The Yukon Territory is 536,326 square km (207,087 square miles) of high mountains and hills, fast-flowing streams and broad valleys cut by great rivers. The Yukon Plateau is a basinlike area 600 to 900 metres (2,000 to 3,000 feet) high of rolling hills, deep valleys and isolated mountain ranges, drained by the Yukon River and its tributaries. West of the plateau are the St. Elias and Coast Mountain Ranges, to the north is the Ogilvie Range, and the Mackenzie Mountains are to the east.

Southern Yukon is at a higher elevation and averages 45 days without frost. The Dawson City area averages 75 frost-free days. The interior is generally dry. Average annual precipitation in the Yukon ranges from 23 to 33 cm (9 to 13 inches), with about half of it falling during the four summer months.

The best time of year for hiking is from the middle of June to the end of August. Conditions for hiking during September and October depend on weather conditions; snow storms may occur at high elevations in September. During the summer, the Yukon has long hours of daylight.

Supplies ▶ Whitehorse is the Yukon's capital and largest city. Hiking supplies may be acquired there. Prices in the Yukon are higher than in southern Canada. If traveling north, you may wish to stock up on supplies beforehand.

Yukon Tourist Information
Yukon Tourism
Box 2703
Whitehorse, YK Y1A 2C6
Telephone: (867) 667-5340
Website: http://www.touryukon.com
E-mail: info@touryukon.com

Hostels
Hostelling International (Canada)
Suite 402, 134 Abbott St.
Vancouver, BC V6B 2K4
Telephone: (604) 684-7111
Fax: (604) 684-7181
E-mail: info@hihostels.bc.ca
Reservations: www.hihostels.bc.ca

1. Chilkoot Pass Trail
Symbol of the Gold Rush stampede. Skagway may be reached by ferry; Bennett, by car from Whitehorse or via the White Pass & Yukon Route. For information call 1-800-343-7373 or (907) 983-2217.

Between the summers of 1897 and 1898 about 40,000 men and women challenged the Chilkoot Pass through the Coast Mountains on their way to the Klondike gold fields. The North-West Mounted Police required that anyone traveling to the Yukon have one year's provisions, which weighed about 900 kg (2,000 pounds). The grueling trek relaying supplies over the Chilkoot Pass has remained a symbol of the Gold Rush stampede.

The 53 km (33 mile) trail runs between Dyea, 14 km (9 miles) from Skagway, Alaska, to Bennett, British Columbia. It's maintained for hikers and has several shelters and campsites. Hikers can see many Gold Rush artifacts remaining along the trail. Wildlife that may be observed include bald eagles, hummingbirds, bears and an occasional lynx. Blueberries, salmonberries, currants, high-bush and low-bush cranberries and gooseberries grow along many parts of the trail.

The route has an elevation gain of over 600 metres (2,000 feet) and is considered difficult. It usually takes three to five days to hike. For a day-hike you can hike in part way and return.

Weather is variable, and hikers should be prepared for cool temperatures with rain, fog, snow and high winds.

More Information:
Parks Canada
Suite 200 - 300 Main St.
Whitehorse, YK Y1A 2B5
Telephone: (867) 667-3910
Toll-free telephone (North America) 1-800-661-0486
Fax: (867) 393-6701
Website: http://www.parkscan.harbour.com/ct/
E-mail: whitehorse_info@pch.gc.ca

2. Kluane National Park Reserve

Encompassing Canada's highest peak; in the southwest corner of the Yukon

Embraced in 22,104 square km (8,500 square mile) Kluane Park are the lofty peaks of the St. Elias Mountains, including 5,950 metre (19,520 foot) Mount Logan, Canada's highest peak, and some of the world's largest nonpolar icefields. Covering the southwest corner of the Yukon, Kluane is characterized by rugged mountains, wide valleys, mountain lakes, valley glaciers, alpine meadows and tundra.

There are two major mountain ranges in the park. The Kluane Range is a chain of 2,200 metre (7,500 foot) summits interrupted by several large valleys and cut by rivers, three of them glacier-fed. The Icefield Range includes Mount Logan and a number of other high peaks with elevations of 4,500 to 5,400 metres (15,000 to 18,000 feet). Separating the Kluane and Icefield ranges is a narrow trough known as the Duke Depression. Several large plateaus make up this depression, along with a series of valleys in which the "tongues" of glaciers protrude.

Forest Cover ▶ Below the timberline at 1,050 to 1,200 metres above sea level (3,500 to 4,000 feet) is a mountain forest of white spruce, trembling aspen and poplar. Willow, shrub birch, alder and many small plants and flowers are found above the timberline.

Wildlife, Birds and Fish ▶ Inhabiting the Kluane are moose, Dall sheep, mountain goats and caribou. Grizzly bears are found throughout the park, and black bears in the forested areas. Over 170 species of birds have been observed, including the upland sandpiper, Arctic tern, peregrine falcon, bald eagle, golden eagle, mountain bluebird and sharp-tailed grouse. Large lake trout, pike, grayling and kokanee may be found in the park's lakes and streams.

WALKS. Opportunities for walking:

- The wheelchair- and stroller-accessible Kokanee Trail extends 0.5 km (0.3 mile) on a boardwalk along Kathleen Lake.
- The 6.5 km (4 mile) Dezadeash River Wetland Trail goes along the Dezadeash River, offering views of wildflowers, waterfowl, and the Auriol Range.
- The Rock Glacier Trail, a self-guiding route, leads 0.5 km (0.3 mile) to the toe of a rock glacier and a view of Dezadeash Lake.
- The 0.5 km (0.3 mile) Soldiers' Summit Trail leads to the site of the official opening in 1942 of the Alaska Highway.
- The St. Elias Lake Trail leads 3.8 km (2.4 miles) to an alpine lake.

DAY-HIKES. For hikers:

- The 9 km (5.5 mile) one-way Mt. Decoeli route travels along a rocky stream bed and a steep ridge to the mountain's summit, with views of Mt. Logan.
- The 12 km (7.4 mile) one-way Bullion Plateau Trail follows an old mining road to an alpine plateau.
- The 15 km (9 mile) loop Auriol Trail climbs to subalpine terrain, with access to the Auriol Range.

BACKPACKING. For backpackers:

- The 26 km (16 mile) Alsek Trail is a one- to three-day hike along an old mining road. It extends into the only major river valley flowing from the Yukon to the Pacific Ocean.
- The 83 km (51.5 mile) Cottonwood Trail is a four- to six-day trip through two alpine passes and alpine scenery.
- The 30 km (19 mile) Slims West Trail leads along the Slims River west to Canada Creek, with access to an alpine plateau and the summit of Observation Mountain.

Guidebook ► *The Kluane National Park Hiking Guide.* (See end of chapter.)

More Information:
Kluane National Park
Box 5495
Haines Junction, YK YOB 1LO
Telephone: (867) 634-2251
TDD: (867) 634-7289
Fax : (867) 634-7265
Website: http://www.parkscanada.gc.ca/
E-mail: kluane_info@pch.gc.ca

3. Canol Heritage Trail

Hikers can access the Canol Heritage Trail from Ross River in the Yukon, then travel through the Mackenzie Mountains to Norman Wells in the Northwest Territories. (See Chapter 12, Northwest Territories.)

Trans Canada Trail—Yukon

In the Yukon, the Trans Canada Trail follows the route of the Dawson Overland Trail—a historic stage coach route north from Whitehorse to Braeburn. From Dawson City, the Trans Canada Trail follows the Dempster Highway, a 735 km (456 mile) gravel highway that winds across the Continental Divide three times and crosses tundra and the Arctic Circle to Inuvik in the Northwest Territories.

More Information:
Klondike Snowmobile Association
Box 9034
24 Wann Rd.
Whitehorse, YK Y1A 4A4
Telephone: (867) 667-7680
Fax: (867) 667-7684
Website: www.tctrail.ca/yukon/htm

Guidebook Sources

The Kluane National Park Hiking Guide. Vivien Lougheed. Vancouver, BC: New Star Books (2504 York Ave., Vancouver, BC V6K 1E3).

Whitehorse & Area Hikes & Bikes. Yukon Conservation Society. Whitehorse, YK: Lost Moose Publishing (58 Kluane Cres., Whitehorse, YK Y1A 3G7, Telephone: (867) 668-5076, Fax: (867) 668-6223, Website: www.yukonweb.com/business/lost_moose, E-mail: lmoose@yknet.yk.ca).

Alberta

The majestic Rocky Mountains are Alberta's widely known outdoor resource. The province's three Rocky Mountain national parks—Jasper, Banff and Waterton Lakes—have over two thousand kilometres of trails through spectacular alpine scenery. These lend themselves to walks of several hours; day-hikes; and backpacking trips from overnight to several weeks. Less well known and also offering good hiking are Kananaskis Country and the wilderness areas bordering the national parks.

The Rocky Mountains make up only a part of Alberta's 660,933 square km (255,200 square miles). To the east are the Foothills as well as the Alberta Plateau—the third prairie level, characterized by rolling prairie in the south and forest, lake and river country in the north.

Alberta receives the most sunshine in Canada; in Banff, the July average is 255 hours. Summers are hot and winters are cold, since the Rocky Mountains block the moderating influence of the Pacific Ocean.

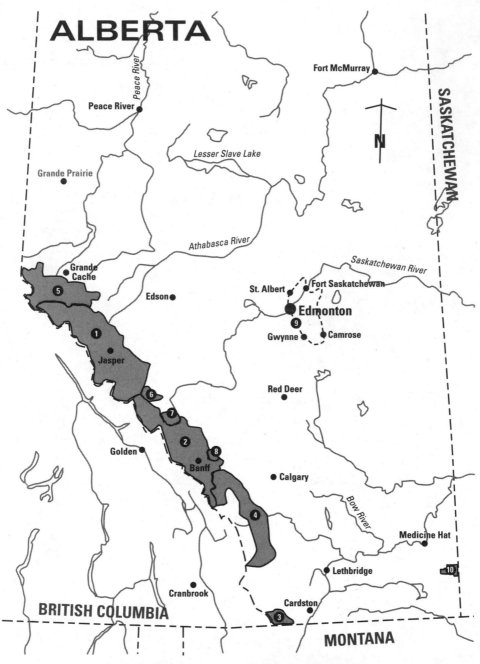

ALBERTA

Peace River

Lesser Slave Lake

N

SASKATCHEWAN

Fort McMurray

Peace River

Grande Prairie

Athabasca River

Saskatchewan River

Grande Cache

Edson

St. Albert

Fort Saskatchewan

Edmonton

Gwynne

Camrose

Jasper

Red Deer

Golden

Banff

Calgary

Bow River

Medicine Hat

Lethbridge

Cranbrook

Cardston

BRITISH COLUMBIA

MONTANA

1. Jasper National Park
2. Banff National Park
3. Waterton Lakes National Park
4. Kananaskis Country
5. Willmore Wilderness Park

6. White Goat Wilderness Area
7. Siffleur Wilderness Area
8. Ghost River Wilderness Area
9. Waskahegan Trail
10. Cypress Hills Interprovincial Park

By the beginning of May, the snow is usually gone from trails in valleys below 1,500 metres (5,000 feet). Trails at elevations between 1,500 and 2,100 metres (5,000 to 6,900 feet) are free of snow by June. Routes above 2,100 metres (6,900 feet) are clear by late June or early July.

Alberta Tourist Information
Alberta Tourism
City Centre
10155 - 102 St.
Edmonton, AB T5J 4L6
Toll-free telephone: from Canada and the United States, 1-800-661-8888; from other countries, (780) 427-4321
Fax: (780) 427-0867
Website: www.discoveralberta.com

Hostels
Hostelling International (Southern Alberta)
#203, 1414 Kensington Rd. NW
Calgary, AB T2N 3P9
Telephone: (403) 283-5551
Fax: (403) 283-6503
Website: http://www.hostellingintl.ca/alberta
E-mail: sab@hostellingintl.ca

Hostelling International (Northern Alberta)
10926 - 88th Ave.
Edmonton, AB T6G 0Z1
Telephone: (780) 432-7798
Fax: (780) 433-7781
Website: http://www.hostellingintl.ca/alberta
E-mail: nab@hostellingintl.ca

Rocky Mountains

1. Jasper National Park

Spectacular alpine scenery, remnant of last Ice Age; on the eastern side of the Continental Divide

Jasper Park covers 10,878 square km (4,200 square miles) and is the largest of the national parks in the Canadian Rocky Mountains. To the west is British Columbia's Mount Robson Provincial Park; Banff National Park is on the southern boundary. Jasper's peaks and broad flat valleys were carved by glaciers of the last Ice Age. The Columbia Icefield, a remnant of the glacial age, straddles the Continental Divide at the south end of the park. Waters from its glaciers feed rivers that flow west to the Pacific Ocean, north to the Arctic Ocean and northeast to Hudson Bay. The Athabasca River flows north through the park's mountain ranges and then on to the Arctic Ocean.

Jasper is known for its well-developed trail system. More than 960 km (595 miles) of hiking trails wind through the mountains. Some go through areas that were important to the fur trade of the early 1800s.

Forest Cover ▶ Lodgepole pine, poplar, aspen, white spruce and grassy meadows are found on lower mountain slopes. Just below the timberline at 2,100 metres (6,900 feet) are continuous bands of Engelmann spruce and alpine fir. Stunted alpine vegetation produced by a subarctic climate is found above the treeline.

Wildlife and Birds ▶ Mule deer, elk, moose, coyote, marten and black bear inhabit the lower elevations; and grizzly bear, mountain goats, bighorn sheep, marmot and pika are in the remote upper regions. The bird population, which is smaller than on the wetter western side of the Rockies, includes eagles, pipits and ptarmigans at higher elevations, and gray jays, ravens and black and white magpies at lower elevations.

WALKS. Jasper Park offers a large variety of walks:

- **Near Jasper townsite**, paths include the 3.5 km (2.1 mile) return Old Fort Point Trail, which offers views of the Athabasca Valley; and the 4.8 km (2.9 mile) Patricia Lake Circle, where you can see loons, ducks, beavers and moose. The wheelchair- and stroller-accessible 2.4 km (1.5 mile) Lake Annette loop is known as the Clifford E. Lee Wheelchair Trail.
- **Maligne Canyon's** walks include the 2.1 km (1.3 mile) one-way Maligne Canyon Trail, with good views of this limestone gorge; and the 2.6 km (1.6 mile) Moose Lake loop through hills and hollows and landslide debris. The first section of the 3.2 km (1.9 mile) Mary Schaffer Trail along Maligne Lake is wheelchair- and stroller-accessible.
- From the **Icefield Parkway** in Jasper Park, walks include the 2 km (1.2 mile) Athabasca Glacier Forefield Trail through boulders and moraine exposed by the melting glacier; the 1 km (0.6 mile) Toe of the Athabasca Glacier Trail across limestone that was under the glacier; and the 6.4 km (3.9 mile) Beauty Creek and Stanley Falls Trail, which passes seven waterfalls on its way to Stanley Falls.

DAY-HIKES. For hikers, Jasper Park offers:

- The 8 km (4.9 mile) return Wilcox Pass route, which provides a good view of several mountains.
- The 8 km (5 mile) Cavell Meadows loop, which offers views of Angel Glacier.
- The 9.5 km (5.9 mile) one-way Old Fort Point to Maligne Canyon route.
- The 10.4 km (6.4 mile) return Bald Hills hike, which travels through alpine meadows and leads to a panoramic view of Maligne Lake.

BACKPACKING. Backpacking ventures range from overnight to extended trips:

- Overnight trips include the 27.4 km (17 mile) Saturday Night Lake loop on a plateau; the 12 km (7.4 mile) Jacques Lake hike, which has little climbing; the 6 km (3.7 mile) one-way Second Geraldine Lake Trail with waterfall, boulder field and small glacial lake; and the 9.8 km (6 mile) Watchtower Basin route, which climbs to an alpine meadow.
- Three-day hikes include the 44 km (27 mile) Skyline Trail, which is mostly above the treeline; the 42 km (26 mile) Tonquin Valley Trail through a scenic alpine region; and the 20 km (12.4 mile) Fryatt Valley hike.
- For trips of four to five days, there are the 24.2 km (15 mile) Fortress Lake Trail, which fords the Chaba River; the 48 km (29.8 mile) Maligne Pass Trail in an alpine meadow; the 25 km (15.5 mile) Fiddle River Trail; and the 80 km (49.7 mile) Brazeau loop through alpine meadows and over two passes.
- Extended backpacking trips include the seven-day 100 km (60 mile) Athabasca Pass Trail along the Whirlpool River valley, which was a fur trading route; the eight- to ten-day 192 km (119 mile) North Boundary Trail, which leads to Mount Robson; and the 176 km (109 mile) South Boundary Trail.

Guidebooks ▶ *The Canadian Rockies Access Guide; The Canadian Rockies Trail Guide;* and *Jasper-Robson: A Taste of Heaven.* (See end of chapter.)

More Information:
Jasper National Park
PO Box 10
Jasper, AB T0E lE0
Telephone: (780) 852-6176
Fax: (780) 852-5601
Website: http://www.parkscanada.gc.ca/
E-mail: NatlParks-AB@och.gc.ca

2. Banff National Park
U-shaped valleys, glaciers, steep peaks and hot springs; on the Trans Canada Highway, an hour's drive west of Calgary

Established in 1885 as a 26 square km (10 square mile) reserve around hot sulphur springs, Banff National Park is Canada's oldest national park. It now occupies 6,641 square km (2,564 square miles) of spectacular glaciated scenery in the Rocky Mountains. The park stretches for 240 km (150 miles) along the eastern slope of the Continental Divide. To the west are Yoho and Kootenay national parks. The Columbia Icefields are at the northern boundary with Jasper Park.

The U-shaped valleys and steep peaks, characteristic of the Rocky Mountains, were carved by glaciers during the last Ice Age.

Banff National Park has more than 1,500 km (900 miles) of hiking trails reaching into all parts of the park.

Forest Cover ▶ Dense stands of lodgepole pine, white spruce and Douglas fir grow on lower slopes, and subalpine fir and Engelmann spruce at higher elevations. Above the treeline at 2,100 metres (6,900 feet) a semi-arctic climate has produced stunted, windswept vegetation. Alpine meadows are carpeted with colorful alpine flowers for a few weeks during the summer.

Wildlife and Birds ▶ Moose, elk, deer and black bear can be seen at lower elevations. The grizzly bear, mountain goat and bighorn sheep inhabit the high alpine areas, though grizzlies are found at low elevations as well. The park's evergreen forests do not support a large number of bird species. Chickadees, nutcrackers, gray jays and magpies can be seen the year round. During the summer, golden eagles, warblers and many types of waterfowl can be observed.

WALKS. Banff area self-guiding interpretive trails:

• The 2.2 km (1.3 mile) Fenland Trail traverses an area of marsh and forest.

- The 0.3 km (0.18 mile) Hoodoos Interpretive Trail leads to the Hoodoo formations (pillars of silt, gravel and rocks) and views of the Bow Valley and Mount Rundle.
- The 1.1 km (0.6 mile) Bankhead Trail explores the ruins of a coal mine from 1911.
- The wheelchair- and stroller-accessible Discovery Trail, 0.4 km (0.2 miles) leads to the Cave and Basin hot springs (geological and historical information).
- The wheelchair- and stroller-accessible Marsh Trail, 0.5 km (0.3 miles) travels through the lush vegetation that thrives on the hot mineral waters flowing out of the hillside.
- Short walking trails near the town of Banff include the 2.3 km (1.4 mile) trail to the summit of Tunnel Mountain; and the wheelchair- and stroller-accessible 3.7 km (2.3 mile) Sundance Trail, past swamps made by beavers and wetlands that are home to a variety of birds and animals.
- **Lake Louise area**. The most popular walking trails are the 3 km (1.8 mile) Lake Louise Shoreline Trail, leading along the level northwest shore of Lake Louise, which links with the 5.5 km (3.3 mile) Plain of Six Glaciers Trail; the 1.5 km (0.9 mile) Moraine Lake Shoreline Trail along Moraine Lake's northwest shore; and the 0.8 km (0.5 mile) Rockpile Trail, with views of the Valley of the Ten Peaks.
- **Icefields Parkway**. Self-guiding interpretive trails include the 2 km (1.2 mile) round-trip Bow Summit Trail overlooking Peyto Lake, Peyto Glacier and Mistaya Valley; the 0.3 km (0.2 mile) Mistaya Canyon path; and the 2.4 km (1.4 mile) Parker Ridge Trail through a tundralike environment.

DAY-HIKES. For hikers:

- **Near the town of Banff**. Day-hikes include the 5.3 km (3.2 mile) each-way Spray River loop; the 7.7 km (4.7 mile) Cascade

Amphitheater Trail through an alpine meadow to a cirque—the depression gouged by glacier in the mountainside on Cascade Mountain; and the 7.8 km (4.6 mile) each-way C-Level Cirque Trail past ventilation shafts of the old Bankhead mine and with views of Lake Minnewanka.

- **In the Lake Louise area**. The 5.5 km (3.3 mile) each-way Plain of Six Glaciers Trail. Begins at the end of the Louise Lakeshore Trail and continues up the valley to the Victoria Glacier and to views of Abbot Pass and the Death Trap. At Victoria Glacier is a teahouse for light lunches. Death Trap is the glacier-filled gorge between Mount Victoria and Mount Lefroy.
- **From Moraine Lake**. The Larch Valley Trail climbs 3 km (1.8 miles) and provides panoramic views. It joins with a 2.8 km (1.7 mile) trail to Sentinel Pass, one of the highest passes in Banff.
- **From the Icefields Parkway**. Hikes include the 4.3 km (2.6 mile) Bow Glacier Falls Trail, along Bow Lake to a huge waterfall; and the 3.5 km (2.2 mile) and 4.2 km (2.6 mile) Chephren and Cirque Lake trails to a subalpine lake.

BACKPACKING. Trips of overnight to a week or longer are possible. Trails include:

- The 37 km (23 mile) trip from Mount Norquay to Johnston's Canyon via Mystic Pass.
- The 54.4 km (33.8 mile) Palliser Pass route.
- The 26 km (16 mile) route from Johnston's Canyon to Pulsatilla Pass via Luellen Lake.
- Networks of trails in the Egypt Lake, Skoki Valley and Boulder Pass areas.
- Trails can be linked for longer trips. An interesting 67.6 km (42 mile) trip can be made by connecting the Dolomite Pass-Isabella Lake Trail with the Fish Lakes-North Molar Pass Trail via Pipestone Pass.

Supplies ▶ Backpacking supplies may be acquired in the town of Banff.

Guidebooks ▶ *The Canadian Rockies Trail Guide; The Canadian Rockies Access Guide; Banff-Assiniboine: A Beautiful World;* and *The World of Lake Louise.* (See end of chapter.)

More Information:
Banff National Park
PO Box 900
Banff, AB T0L 0C0
Telephone: (403) 762-1550
Fax: (403) 762-1551
Website: http://www.parkscanada.gc.ca/
E-mail: Banff_vrc@pch.gc.ca

3. Waterton Lakes National Park
In the Rocky Mountains in southwestern Alberta; 265 km (160 miles) southwest of Calgary

Waterton Lakes National Park covers 525 square km (203 square miles) of the Rocky Mountains in the southwestern corner of Alberta. On the western boundary is the Continental Divide; the United States border is on the south; and the rolling prairie grassland is on the northeastern boundary. Glacier National Park in Montana and Waterton Lakes in Alberta together form the Waterton-Glacier International Peace Park.

Waterton Park has 255 km (191 miles) of trails.

Forest Cover ▶ The transition zone forest between prairie and mountain has bands of trembling aspen, cottonwood, Douglas maple and other deciduous trees. On the mountain slopes the forest cover below the treeline at 2,100 metres (6,900 feet) is made up of Douglas fir, lodgepole pine, limber pine and white spruce. Engelmann spruce, white bark pine and alpine fir are found at higher elevations.

Wildlife, Birds and Fish ► Wildlife at middle elevations include moose, red squirrel, black bear and grizzly bear. At higher levels are bighorn sheep, mountain goats, mule deer, elk, golden-mantled ground squirrels, marmot and pikas. Swans, herons, gulls, waders and shore and marsh birds inhabit the park. During spring and autumn migrations ducks and geese rest in Waterton Lakes. The park's lakes contain pike, whitefish and several species of trout.

WALKS. Among the variety of walks in Waterton Park:

- The Bear's Hump Trail climbs 1.4 km (0.9 mile) to a panoramic view at the summit.
- The 0.7 km (0.3 mile) Red Rock Canyon Loop Trail explores a red-hued canyon.

HIKES. Among the park's hikes:

- The 2.9 km (1.8 mile) Lower Bertha Falls Trail provides good views down Waterton Lake.
- The Rowe Lakes Trail is a 6.2 km (3.8 mile) each-way route to sub-alpine meadows.
- Hikers reach the trailhead of the 8.7 km (5.4 mile) each-way Crypt Lake Trail by boat across Waterton Lake and take a natural tunnel widened by the park.
- The 8 km (5 mile) each-way trail from Summit Lake leads to the secluded Carthew Lakes.

BACKPACKING. Routes include:

- The Crypt Lake Trail, described above, which is also a suitable overnight trip.
- The 36 km (22 mile) Tamarack Trail in the western section of the park, on the Great Divide.
- From the Waterton Park townsite, a trail runs along Upper Wateron Lake and provides access to the 1,120 km (695 miles) of trails in

4,100 square km (1,584 square mile) Glacier National Park in Montana. Backpackers hiking into Glacier Park from Waterton Park must register with rangers at Goat Haunt Ranger Station.

Guidebooks ▶ *The Canadian Rockies Access Guide; Waterton and Northern Glacier Trails for Hikers and Riders; Short Hikes and Strolls in Waterton Lakes National Park*; and *Glacier National Park and Waterton Lakes National Park*. (See end of chapter.)

More Information:
Waterton Lakes National Park
Waterton Park, AB TOK 2M0
Telephone: (403) 859-2224
Fax: (403) 859-2650
TDD: (403) 859-2224
Website: http://www.parkscanada.gc.ca/
E-mail: angelene_mcintyre@pch.gc.ca

4. Kananaskis Country
Forests and meadows of the Rocky Mountain Foothills

Prairie and mountain plants and animals, alpine meadows, glaciers and snowfields are all compressed into this 4,000 square km (1,600 square mile) wilderness area southwest of Calgary. Within the alpine area are 17 peaks over 3,000 metres (10,000 feet)—including 3,400 metre (11,300 foot) Mount Joffre; the most southerly glaciers in Alberta's Rocky Mountains; and blue alpine lakes.

Wildlife, Birds and Fish ▶ Sheep, elk, moose, weasel, coyote, hares, pikas, marmots and squirrels may be seen as well as warblers, chickadees, Spruce grouse and Canada jay. Three Isles, Maude and Lawson lakes contain cutthroat trout.

Cathedral Provincial Park, British Columbia.

Tsusiat Falls, Pacific Rim National Park, British Columbia.

Mayer River, Queen Charlotte Islands, British Columbia.

Jasper National Park, Alberta.

Sulphur Mountain, Banff National Park, Alberta.

Glacier Trail, Jasper National Park, Alberta.

Hiking above Kluane Lake, Yukon.

Ogilvie Mountains, Yukon.

Hiking above Reptile Creek, Wernecke Mountains, Yukon.

Winter hiking, River Valley to Mokka Fiord, Axel Heiberg Island, Nunavut.

Tanquary Fiord, Ellesmere Island National Park, Northwest Territories.

Barrow Strait, Northwest Territories.

Spruce River Highlands Trail, Prince Albert National Park, Saskatchewan.

Strolling a country lane, Manitoba.

Limestone cliffs, Lake Manitoba, Manitoba.

Winter camping in Algonquin Provincial Park, Ontario.

Gatineau Park, Quebec.

Algonquin Provincial Park, Ontario.

Prince Edward Island National Park, Prince Edward Island.

Prince Edward Island National Park, Prince Edward Island.

Trail to Peskowesk Brook, Kejimkujuk National Park, Nova Scotia.

Cape Breton Highlands National Park, Nova Scotia.

Gros Morne National Park, Newfoundland.

Gros Morne Mountain, Gros Morne National Park, Newfoundland.

WALKS. Kananaskis Country has more than 15 interpretive trails; among them:

- The wheelchair- and stroller-accessible 1 km (0.6 mile) Spruce Road Trail.
- The wheelchair- and stroller-accessible Marl Lake Trail, with 1.6 km (1 mile) and 3.6 km (2.2 mile) sections.
- The 2.2 km (1.3 mile) Montane Trail, which loops through the montane forest.
- The 1 km (0.6 mile) Sibbald Flat loop, which offers a view of a Sundance site.
- The 2 km (1.2 mile) one-way Heart Creek Trail, which leads up a narrow creek canyon to a waterfall.
- The 0.5 km (0.3 mile) Barrier Lake Trail loop, which overlooks Barrier Lake and the Kananaskis Valley.

DAY-HIKES. The many day-hikes in Kananaskis Country include:

- The 6.6 km (4.1 mile) return Lower Lake Trail, which Skirts Lower Kananaskis Lake.
- The 10 km (6 mile) Elk Pass Trail, which leads to Elk Pass and the 15.6 km (9.6 mile) Upper Lake Trail loop along Upper Kananaskis Lake.

BACKPACKING. Kananaskis Country features a network of over 1,500 km (900 miles) of hiking trails, including:

- The 32 km (20 mile) Maude Lawson Trail along the Upper Kananaskis River to Lawson and Maude lakes and the North Kananaskis Pass.
- The 23 km (14 mile) Three Isle Lake Trail, which follows along Three Isle Creek to Three Isle Lake and the South Kananaskis Pass. Also possible: a circuit into British Columbia from North Kananaskis Pass to South Kananaskis Pass.

Supplies and Campfires ▶ Carry a stove. Campfires are permitted at only some of the campsites.

Guidebooks ▶ *Kananaskis Country Trail Guide* (vols. 1 and 2); *The Canadian Rockies Access Guide*; and *Short Walks for Inquiring Minds: Canmore and Kananaskis Country*. (See end of chapter.)

More Information:
Kananaskis Country
201 - 800 Railway Ave.
Canmore, AB T1W 1P1
Telephone: (403) 678-5508
Fax: (403) 678-5505
Website: http://www.gov.ab.ca/env/parks.html
E-mail: ray.andrews@gov.ab.ca

5. *Willmore Wilderness Park*
Wilderness north of Jasper Park; 142 km (85 miles) northwest of Hinton on Highway 40

In Willmore Wilderness Park the mountains are more rounded and the treeline lower than the national parks to the south. This makes it easier to hike along exposed mountain ridges. The park covers 4,597 square km (1,776 square miles) of the Front Ranges, Main Ranges and Foothills of the Rocky Mountains. It is the most northerly park in Alberta's Rocky Mountains.

Forest Cover ▶ Dominated by Engelmann spruce, lodgepole pine and alpine fir. Above the treeline between 1,860 and 1,950 metres (6,100 and 6,400 feet) are shrubs including dwarf willows, gooseberry and white, yellow and purple heathers.

Wildlife Birds and Fish ▶ The park is home to elk, woodland caribou, Rocky Mountain sheep, Rocky Mountain goats, black bears and grizzly bears. Numerous birds inhabit the area, among them ruffed grouse, spruce grouse, blue grouse, sparrows, robins and white-tailed ptarmigan. Anglers can fish for Dolly Varden, Rocky Mountain white-fish, Arctic grayling and rainbow trout.

BACKPACKING. Willmore Wilderness Park's 750 km (460 miles) of trails are situated in most of the valley systems and over most of the passes in the eastern portion of the park.

The park is linked with the North Boundary Trail in Jasper Park by trails along Rock Creek, Blue Creek, Smoky River, and a route along Chown Creek, over Bess Pass and Jackpine Pass.

There are cross-country travel routes along the high ridges and over many of the saddles and passes. It is also possible to hike along the Continental Divide on the park's western boundary. A topographic map is available at the park office (address below).

More Information:
Willmore Wilderness Park
Alberta Forest Service
Box 239, Shand Ave.
Grande Cache, AB T0E 0Y0
Telephone: (780) 827-3626
Website: A privately maintained website is at
http://www.ualberta.ca/ERSC/willmore/right.html

6. White Goat Wilderness Area
Wilderness on the southeastern boundary of Jasper National Park. From the Banff-Jasper Highway the area can be reached via the Norman Creek trail, then over Sunset Pass to Pinto Lake, connecting with the Cline River Trail; by the Nigel Pass Trail and over Cataract Pass; or by the trail along the north side of the Cline River from the David Thompson Highway.

The 445 square km (172 square mile) White Goat Wilderness Area lies in the Front Ranges and Main Ranges of the Rocky Mountains adjacent to the southern boundary of Jasper National Park and the eastern boundary of Banff National Park. The 3,000 metre (10,000 foot) mountain ranges containing alpine lakes and several major streams are separated by wide valleys.

Forest Cover ▶ Subalpine forest is dominated by white spruce, subalpine fir and lodgepole pine. Above the treeline at 2,100 metres (6,900 feet) are alpine meadows carpeted with grasses, sedges and brightly colored flowers. Crutose lichen appears on the rocks.

Wildlife and Birds ▶ Bighorn sheep, mountain goats, mountain caribou, wolves, mountain lions, coyote, elk, grizzly bears, black bears and a few wolverines and martens inhabit the wilderness area. Among the 100 to 120 species of birds observed in the area are Canada jay, ptarmigan, spruce grouse and Clarke's crow.

DAY-HIKES/BACKPACKING. Travel within the White Goat Wilderness Area is by foot only. The routes were old outfitters' trails. Bring maps and a compass. The wilderness area's 112 km (70 miles) of trails generally follow rivers and include:

• The 61 km (38 mile) Cline River route.
• The 21 km (13 mile) Cataract Creek route.
• The 30 km (19 mile) McDonald Creek route.

Guidebook ▶ The access routes are described in *The Canadian Rockies Trail Guide*. (See end of chapter.)

More Information:
White Goat Wilderness Area
Box 920
Rimbey, AB T0C 2J0
Telephone: (403) 843-2545
Website: www.gov.ab.ca/env/parks/wilderness/index.htm

7. Siffleur Wilderness Area

Wilderness on the northeastern boundary of Banff National Park. Reached from the David Thompson Highway on the Kootenay Plains; about 1 km (0.6 mile) south of Two O'Clock Creek campground. Access from Banff Park is by Dolomite Pass.

The 412 square km (159 square mile) Siffleur Wilderness Area is situated in the Front Ranges and Main Ranges on the northeastern boundary of Banff National Park.

Wildlife ▶ Elk, mountain goats and a few grizzly bears inhabit the area.

DAY-HIKES. Travel in the area is by foot only. Hiking trails are generally situated along rivers. Siffleur's hiking and backpacking opportunities include:

- The 28 km (17 mile) Siffleur River Valley route leading from the David Thompson Highway to Dolomite Pass in Banff Park. (This is the most popular route through the area.)
- The Siffleur Falls route leading 3.7 km (2.3 miles) from the Siffleur Falls parking lot (located off the David Thompson Highway) to the falls. An 11 km (6.5 mile) route goes to Landslide Lake, with good fishing opportunities.

BACKPACKING. Among the area's backpacking opportunities:

- A 54 km (32 mile) route goes along White Rabbit Creek and Ram River.
- A 30 km (18 mile) route goes along the Siffleur River to the Escarpment Lakes.

Guidebook ▶ Access from Banff Park by the Dolomite Pass is described in *The Canadian Rockies Trail Guide*. (See end of chapter.)

More Information:
Siffleur Wilderness Area
Box 920
Rimbey, AB T0C 2J0
Telephone: (403) 843-2545
Website: www.gov.ab.ca/env/parks/wilderness/index.htm

8. Ghost River Wilderness Area

In the Palliser Range, on the southeastern boundary of Banff National Park. Access is by foot only. Aylmer Pass provides access from Banff (see The Canadian Rockies Trail Guide*). From the east, the wilderness area is reached by hiking about 10 km (6 miles) along the Ghost River; to reach the Ghost River, drive 19 km (12 miles) along a secondary road off the Forestry Trunk Road in the Bow-Crow Forest Reserve.*

Surrounded by the 2,900 metre (9,500 foot) Palliser Range, the 153 square km (59 square mile) Ghost River Wilderness Area is almost a complete ecological unit. Travel within the wilderness area is by foot only.

Forest Cover ▶ The subalpine coniferous forest contains white spruce, Engelmann spruce, subalpine fir and lodgepole pine. Above the tree-line at 2,100 metres (6,900 feet) the alpine tundra is made up of grasses, sedges, lichens and colorful alpine flowers.

Wildlife and Birds. ▶ The park is inhabited by bighorn sheep, mountain goats, mountain caribou, wolves, mountain lions, coyote, elk, black bears and grizzly bears. A small number of wolverine and marten also inhabit the area. Among the more than 100 species of birds observed here are Canada jay, ptarmigan, spruce grouse and Clarke's crow.

DAY-HIKES. Among the hikes:

- The 2.7 km (1.6 mile) trek to Mockingbird Hill Lookout leads to views of the limestone cliffs of the Palliser Range.
- An 8 km (5 mile) route goes to the Ghost Lakes.
- A steep 4.5 km (2.8 mile) hike leads to the summit Black Rock Mountain.

BACKPACKING. There are more than 50 km (31 miles) of backpacking routes; among them:

- The 21 km (13 mile) Ghost River Trail connects with several trails along Ghost River tributaries and also links with the 18 km (11 mile) Aylmer Pass Trail into Banff National Park.

More Information:
Ghost River Wilderness Area
Box 920
Rimbey, AB T0C 2J0
Telephone: (403) 843-2545

Alberta Plateau

9. Waskahegan Trail
Loop trail around Edmonton

When completed, the 300 km (180 mile) Waskahegan will form a loop connecting Edmonton, Coal Lake, Battle River, Camrose, Miquelon Provincial Park, the Blackfoot Area, Elk Island National Park and Fort Saskatchewan.

The trail follows glacial meltwater channels and the natural and rural landscapes south of Edmonton.

From Edmonton, the trail follows Blackmud Creek through old Gwynne Outlet to glacial Lake Edmonton. It next goes along Saunders Lake and Coal Lake, and then south to Gwynne, via the Battle River Valley, which it follows into the town of Camrose. From Miquelon Provincial Park the trail goes north to the Ministik Waterfowl Sanctuary, Wanisai Lake and Elk Island National Park. From Elk Island Park, it turns west to Fort Saskatchewan and Lamoureux. North of Lamoureux the trail is planned to go through the Sturgeon Valley to St. Albert, and then west to the trail's starting point in Edmonton.

Most of the Waskahegan Trail crosses private land with some forested areas. Campsites and shelters are situated along the route. Water is not always available and should be carried.

OTHER HIKES. In addition to the routes described above, Elk Island National Park offers five day-hiking trails.

Supplies ▶ Food and fuel supplies may be acquired in Edmonton, Camrose and Fort Saskatchewan. Food may also be obtained at small stores in Gwynne and north of Miquelon Lake.

Guidebook ▶ A trail guidebook is available from the Waskahegan Trail Association. (See address below.)

More Information:
For more information on Elk Island Park:
Waskahegan Trail Association
PO Box 131
Edmonton, AB T5J 2G9

Elk Island National Park
Site 4, RR No. 1
Fort Saskatchewan, AB T8L 2N7
Telephone: (780) 992-2950
Fax: (780) 992-2951
Website: www.parkscanada.gc.ca/
E-mail: natlparks-ab@pch.gc.ca

10. Cypress Hills Interprovincial Park

Rising 750 metres (2,500 feet) above the surrounding prairie; on the Saskatchewan boundary

The Cypress Hills in eastern Alberta reach an elevation of 1,450 metres (4,800 feet). Alberta's 202 square km (78 square mile) Cypress Hill Park borders on Saskatchewan's Cypress Hills Interprovincial Park.

Green forests and grasslands of the Cypress Hills plateau contrast markedly with the dusty brown flatland prairie.

Forest Cover ► Lodgepole pine, a tree native to the Rockies, is found in the rocky soil at higher elevations of the plateau. White spruce and aspen poplar grow at lower elevations. There are 14 species of mountain and woodland orchids.

Wildlife, Birds and Fish ► Elk, moose, white-tailed deer, mule deer, coyote, muskrat, mink and beaver make the Cypress Hills their home. Among the birds seen are ruffed grouse, horned owls, hawks and many types of shoreline birds and waterfowl. Rainbow trout, brook trout, northern pike and yellow perch populate the park's lakes and streams.

WALKS/DAY-HIKES. Among the park's trails:

- The wheelchair- and stroller-accessible Soggy Bottom Trail, 1 km (0.6 miles), crosses a field, a forest and a marsh.
- The 3 km (1.8 mile) Shoreline Trail follows the south shoreline of Elkwater Lake.
- The 5 km (3.1 mile) Streamside Trail loop follows a stream through a spruce forest.

BACKPACKING. For backpackers:

- The 11 km (7 mile) trail from Elkwater to Spruce Coulee provides a backcountry campsite at the east end of Spruce Coulee.
- The 8 km (5 mile) Beaver Creek-Horseshoe Canyon loop offers an overnight stop at Nichol Springs campground.

Open fires are not permitted.

Supplies. ► Supplies are available in the town of Elkwater.

More Information:
Cypress Hills Provincial Park
Elkwater, AB T0J lC0
Telephone: (403) 893-3777
Fax:
Website: http://www.gov.ab.ca/env/parks/html
E-mail: infocent@env.gov.ab.ca

Trans Canada Trail—Alberta

In Alberta, the Trans Canada Trail will have both an east-west route (connecting Saskatchewan to British Columbia) and a north-south route (going north to the Northwest Territories from the east-west route).

The east-west route, more than 900 km (540 miles) long, will go from southeastern Alberta, through Calgary on part of the city's trail system, to Canmore, through Kananaskis Country and Banff National Park and to the British Columbia provincial boundary.

The north-south route will follow some of the old Calgary-Edmonton Trail between those two cities. It will continue north to Slave Lake, Peace River, Lac La Biche and Fort McMurray en route to the Northwest Territories.

More Information:

Alberta TrailNet
11759 Groat Rd.
Edmonton, AB T5M 3K6
Telephone: (780) 287-0795
Fax: (780) 243-0530
Website: http://www.tctrail.ca/alberta.htm

Guidebook Sources

Some of these books have been published by:

Rocky Mountain Books
#4 Spruce Center SW
Calgary, AB T3C 3B3
Telephone: (403) 249-9490
Toll-free: 1-800-566-3336
Website: http://www.rmbooks.com.
E-mail: tonyd@rmbooks.com

Banff-Assiniboine: A Beautiful World. Don Beers. A guide to trails in the Palliser Pass to Castle Junction area of Banff National Park and the core area of Mount Assiniboine Provincial Park. Rocky Mountain Books.

The Canadian Rockies Access Guide. John Dodd and Gail Helgason. Includes hikes in Banff, Jasper, Waterton Lakes, Kootenay and Yoho national parks and Kananaskis Country. (Lone Pine Publishing, Suite 206, 10426 - 81 Ave., Edmonton, AB T6E 1X5, Telephone: (780) 433-9333, Fax: (780) 433-9646, Website: http://www.lonepinepublishing.com)

The Canadian Rockies Trail Guide. Brian Patton and Bart Robinson. (Book and Art Den, PO Box 1420, Banff, AB T0L 0C0, Telephone: (403) 762-4126)

David Thompson Highway: A Hiking Guide. Jane Ross and Daniel Kyba. Describes hikes between Nordegg and Banff National Park. Rocky Mountain Books.

Glacier National Park and Waterton Lakes National Park. Vicky Spring. Rocky Mountain Books.

Hiking the Historic Crowsnest Pass. Jane Ross and William Tracy. Rocky Mountain Books.

Jasper-Robson: A Taste of Heaven. Don Beers. A guide to trails in Jasper National Park and Mount Robson Provincial Park. Rocky Mountain Books.

Kananaskis Country Trail Guide, volumes 1 and 2. Gillian Daffern. Rocky Mountain Books.

Scrambles in the Canadian Rockies. Alan Kane. Rocky Mountain Books.

Short Hikes and Strolls in Waterton Lakes National Park. Waterton Natural History Association (Box 145, Waterton Park, AB T0K 2M0, Telephone/Fax: (403) 859-2624).

Short Walks for Inquiring Minds: Canmore and Kananaskis Country. Gillean Daffern. Rocky Mountain Books.

Waterton and Northern Glacier Trails for Hikers and Riders. Waterton Natural History Association (Box 145, Waterton Park, AB T0K 2M0, Telephone/Fax: (403) 859-2624).

The World of Lake Louise. Don Beers. A hiking guide to the Lake Louise area of Banff National Park. Rocky Mountain Books.

12

Northwest Territories

The Northwest Territories cover more than 1.17 million square km (about 450,000 square miles)—larger than the combined area of France, Italy and the United Kingdom. The territories lie above Saskatchewan, Alberta and eastern British Columbia, and between Yukon and Nunavut. The territories offer opportunities to experience the remote wilderness, consisting of two geographical regions: the taiga, a boreal forest belt circling the subarctic zone; and the tundra, a rocky Arctic region.

In the summer, the sun shines up to 24 hours a day. The weather is similar to that of the Prairie Provinces, but with slightly lower temperatures. The mean maximum for July is about 21°C (69°F), and the mean minimum is 10°C (50°F).

Supplies ▶ Food and hiking supplies in the North are more expensive than in southern Canada, and choice is limited. If traveling to the Northwest Territories it's best to bring supplies.

NORTHWEST TERRITORIES

1. Wood Buffalo National Park
2. Nahanni National Park Reserve
3. Canol Heritage Trail

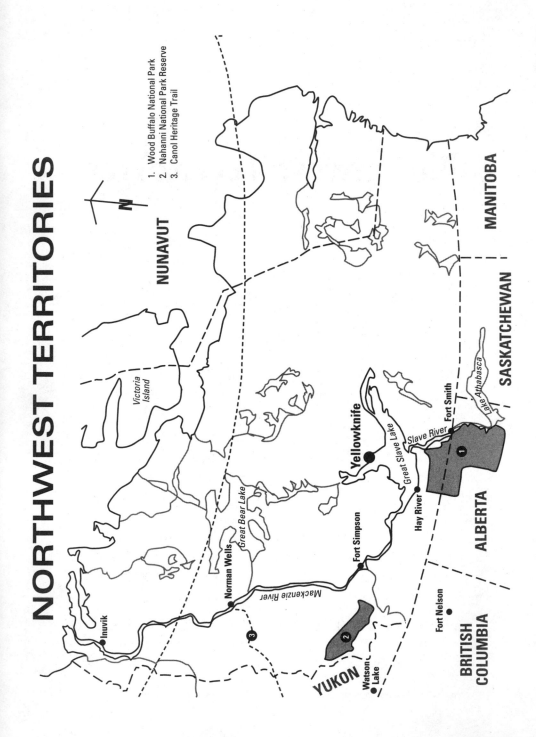

Northwest Territories Tourist Information
NWT Arctic Tourism
PO Box 610
Yellowknife, NT X1A 2N5
Toll-free telephone: 1-800-661-0788 or (867) 873-7200
Fax: (867) 873-4059
Website: www.nwttravel.nt.ca
E-mail: arctic@nwttravel.nt.ca

1. Wood Buffalo National Park
Largest free-roaming bison herd in the world. The park may be reached via the Mackenzie Highway to Hay River and Highway 5 to Fort Smith; or by air to Fort Smith, 36 km (22 miles) from the park.

Straddling the boundary between the Northwest Territories and the province of Alberta, this 44,807 square km (17,300 square mile) park was created in 1922 to protect the last remaining herd of wood bison. There are now 4,000 bison in the park. The major part of this wilderness area is the flat, glacial-outwash plain known as the Alberta Plateau. The Birch Mountains in the southwest of the park and the Caribou Mountains in the west are erosion plateaus left by glaciers. The park has several sinkholes characteristic of karst topography. Some parts of the salt plains drained by the Salt River contain no plant life, the result of the high salt content of the ground.

Forest Cover ▶ The park's forest is typical of the boreal forest zone and is dominated by white and black spruce, jack pine and tamarack.

Wildlife, Birds and Fish ▶ Moose, wolves, lynx and black bears inhabit the area. Wood Buffalo Park is the only known nesting ground of the endangered whooping crane. Hawks, eagles, owls and ravens are present throughout the park. Anglers can fish for pike, pickerel, goldeye and trout in the park's lakes and streams.

WALKS. For walkers:

- The wheelchair- and stroller-accessible first section of the 0.75 km (0.5 mile) Karstland Loop interpretive trail explores karst terrain, notably active sinkholes.
- The 0.5 km (0.3 mile) Salt Plains Access Trail explores salt-encrusted terrain—saline springs, salt mounds and vegetation that is salt tolerant.
- The 1.3 km (0.8 mile) Salt River Meadows Trail travels a meadow of wildflowers, along a saline stream.

DAY-HIKES. For hikers:

- The Salt River Trail through karst terrain (caves, salt meadows, sinkholes and underground streams) includes the 7.5 km (4.6 mile) North Loop and the 9 km (5.5 mile) South Loop.
- The 13 km (8 mile) Lane Lake Trail explores a chain of five sinkhole lakes fed by underground springs.

BACKPACKING. For backpackers:

- The 6 km (3.7 miles) Rainbow Lakes Trail leads to a primitive campsite at the Rainbow Lakes—a series of deep, clear sinkhole lakes.
- The 12 km (7.5 mile) Sweetgrass Station Trail is a bison path to vast meadows and remains of bison corrals from the 1950s.

More Information:
Wood Buffalo National Park
Box 750
Fort Smith, NT X0E 0P0
Telephone: (867) 872-7900
Fax: (867) 872-3910
TDD: (867) 872-3727
Website: http://www.parkscanada.gc.ca/
E-mail: wbnp_info@pch.gc.ca

2. Nahanni National Park Reserve

*Hot springs and alpine tundra. Accessible by air or water. The
park is 145 km (90 miles) west of Fort Simpson, Northwest
Territories, and 1,046 km (650 miles) northwest of Edmonton.
Fort Simpson and Watson Lake, Yukon, are the major jumping-off
and supply points for Nahanni and have facilities for chartering
aircraft. Both centers may be reached by all-weather highways
and by air.*

Created in 1971, Nahanni Park is a 4,766 square km (1,840 square
mile) wilderness area in the southwest corner of the Northwest Territories. The South Nahanni River flows 300 km (186 miles) through the
park, from the Ragged Range of the Selwyn Mountains to the Franklin
Mountains near the southeast park boundary. Here is the Splits, a 48 km
(30 mile) stretch of river up to 3 km (2 miles) wide and divided into
many shallow channels. At Virginia Falls, the South Nahanni River
plummets 90 metres (300 feet).

The park features sulphur hot springs at the lower mouth of the
First Canyon; the Wild Mint Mineral Springs near Flat River; and Rab-
bitkettle Hotsprings in the northwest portion of the park. Alpine tundra is found above the timberline, which is at an elevation of between
1,050 and 1,200 metres (3,500 to 4,000 feet).

Forest Cover ▶ Dense growth of white spruce and balsam poplar are
found in the valley bottoms. The general lowland forest contains open
stands of white spruce and trembling aspen.

WILDLIFE ▶ Moose, beaver, woodland caribou, Dall sheep, black bear,
white-tailed deer and mule deer inhabit the park.

DAY-HIKES/BACKPACKING. Opportunities include:

- The 10 km (6 mile) one-way Glacier Trail hike, leading to the Ragged Range and the Cirque of the Unclimbables.
- The 8 km (5 mile) one-way Sunblood Mountain route, leading to the mountain's peak.
- The 4 km (2.5 mile) one-way Marengo Falls hike through mossy spruce and muskeg terrain to the falls, which cascade 30 metres (100 feet) over limestone ledges.
- The 4 km (2.5 mile) one-way Prairie Creek hike, which crosses an alluvial fan in the Deadman Valley.
- The 10 km (6 mile) one-way hike along Dry Canyon Creek at the eastern end of the Deadman Valley, which leads up a steep walled canyon to the Nahanni Plateau.
- The 15 km (9 mile) one-way Ram Creek hike, leading to the Tlogotsho Plateau.
- The 10 km (6 mile) one-way Lafferty Creek route, leading from the South Nahanni River up a narrow canyon.

Supplies ▶ Hikers should bring their supplies with them. A list of aircraft charter companies and river outfitters may be obtained from the park office.

More Information:
Nahanni National Park
PO Box 348
Fort Simpson, NT X0E 0N0
Telephone: (867) 695-3151
Fax: (867) 695-2446
TDD: (867) 695-3841
Website: http://www.parkscanada.gc.ca/
E-mail: Nahanni_Info@pch.gc.ca

3. Canol Heritage Trail

Second World War pipeline route across Mackenzie Mountains.
Norman Wells is accessible by air from Edmonton and Yellowknife.
Ross River may be reached by summer road from Whitehorse.

The Canol Heritage Trail extends 355 km (220 miles) through Mackenzie Mountains wilderness, from Norman Wells on the Mackenzie River to Macmillan Pass on the Yukon border. The Backbone Range to the west averages 2,100 metres (6,900 feet) above sea level, with some peaks soaring higher than 2,400 metres (8,000 feet). The Canyon Range in the eastern Mackenzie Mountains is characterized by many canyons carved by streams.

The trail follows the route of the Canol Road and pipeline built during the Second World War to move oil from the fields at Norman Wells to Whitehorse and the Alaska Highway. It was part of the American war effort to protect Alaska from attack. The project was completed in 1945, before the end of the war but too late to be of any use. The pipeline was scrapped and the road abandoned.

Hiking the Canol Heritage Trail requires extra care in planning and should be attempted only by experienced backpackers. Supplies should be acquired beforehand. Local outfitters offer guided trips.

More Information:
NWT Resources Wildlife & Economic Development
PO Box 130
Norman Wells, NT X0E 0V0
Telephone: (867) 587-3500
Fax: (867) 587-2204
Website: A privately maintained website of information on the Canol Heritage Trail is at http://internet.ggu.edu/~jvorderstrass/canolban.htm

Trans Canada Trail—Northwest Territories

The planned route of the Northwest Territories section of the multi-use Trans Canada Trail will come north from Fort McMurray, Alberta. It will go through the southwest part of the Northwest Territories and will then follow historic water routes to Norman Wells, where it will take the Canol Heritage Trail to the Yukon. From Dawson City in the Yukon, the Trans Canada Trail will follow the Dempster Highway and come back into the Northwest Territories to Inuvik and Tuktoyaktuk and the Arctic Ocean. A link from the main trail to the city of Yellowknife on Great Slave Lake is being considered.

More Information:
NWT Trail Council
c/o NWT Recreation and Parks Association
Box 841
Yellowknife, NT X1A 2N6
Telephone: (867) 920-5647
Fax: (867) 669-6791
Website: http://www.tctrail.ca/nwt.htm

13

Nunavut

Nunavut means "our land" in Inuktitut, the Inuit language. The Inuit, meaning "the people, those who are living today," make up 85 percent of Nunavut's population. Nunavut covers 1.9 million kilometres (770,000 square miles) of land and water. It includes Baffin Island with towering mountains capped with ice, U-shaped valleys and hanging glaciers. Also part of Nunavut is the Arctic archipelago of islands—including Ellesmere Island, located opposite Greenland—stretching almost to the North Pole. Nunavut also includes part of what was formerly mainland Northwest Territories, where low-rounded Canadian Shield hills stretch from the Arctic coast east to Hudson Bay. The tundra is covered with tiny flowers. In summer there are about 20 hours of daylight.

Southern Baffin Island experiences short, cool summers. July is the warmest month, with a mean high of 10°C (50°F) and a mean low of 2°C (35°F). Only 12 to 25 cm (5 to 10 inches) of rain fall during June, July and August.

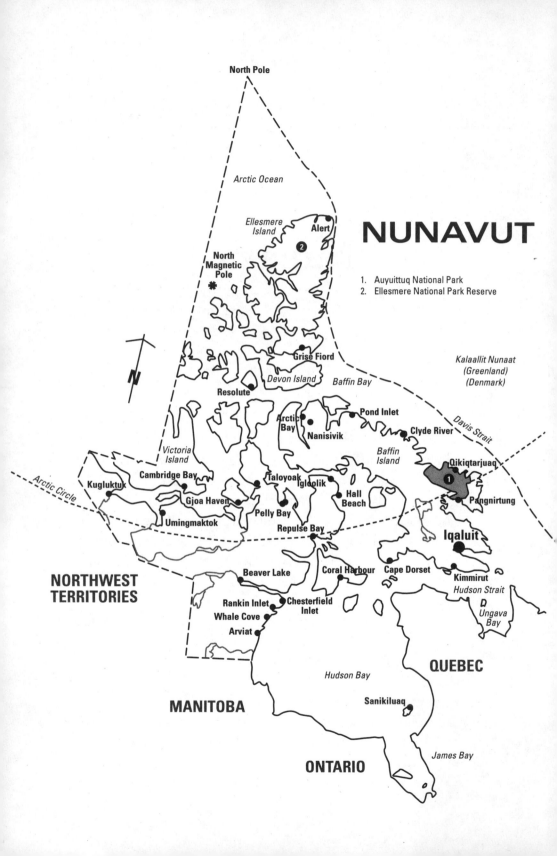

<u>*Nunavut Tourist Information*</u>
Nunavut Tourism
PO Box 1450
Iqaluit, Nunavut X0A 0H0
Toll-free telephone (in North America): 1-800-491-7910
Toll-free telephone (outside North America): (867) 979-6551
Fax: (867) 979-1261
Website: http://www.nunatour.nt.ca/home.html
E-mail: nunatour@nunanet.com

1. Auyuittuq National Park

Inuktitut for "the place which does not melt." Auyuittuq Park is located 2,400 km (1,500 miles) northeast of Montreal. Reaching the park involves flying to Iqaluit and then onto Pangnirtung or Broughton Island.

Located on the Cumberland Peninsula of Baffin Island, Auyuittuq National Park lies on the Arctic Circle. From May through July, Auyuittuq has 24 hours of daylight. A large part of the 21,470 square km (8,290 square mile) park is on the Penny Highlands, the extreme northern part of the Precambrian Canadian Shield. Peaks in the area reach 2,100 metres (6,900 feet) above sea level. The Penny Ice Cap covers 6,000 square km (2,300 square miles) and is a remnant of the last Ice Age. Coronation Glacier, a river of ice 32 km (20 miles) long, is the largest of the glaciers spawned by the ice cap.

Pangnirtung Pass is a U-shaped valley carved by glaciers over hundreds of thousands of years. The pass forms a 97 km (60 mile) long, ice-free trough through the mountains joining Cumberland Sound with Davis Strait. Along the park's coast the glaciers have carved spectacular fiords with sheer cliffs up to 900 metres (3,000 feet) high.

Vegetation ▶ Only hardy lichens, mosses and Arctic heather are found on the park's barren highlands. Cotton grass, Labrador tea, sedges and the dwarf willow grow on the valley floors. Arctic flowers such as white mountain avens, yellow Arctic poppy and purple saxifrage are in bloom during June and July, and the barren, rocky terrain is ablaze with color.

Wildlife, Birds and Marine Life ▶ The sparse tundra vegetation supports a small number of mammals, including the lemming, weasel, Arctic fox, polar bear, and barren ground caribou. Marine animals that can be seen off the coast include ringed, harp and bearded seals, narwhals and white whales, and Atlantic walruses.

Among the 40 species of birds that may be observed are Canada geese, ptarmigan, snowy owls, eider ducks, ravens and glaucous gulls. The peregrine falcon and gyrfalcon are two rare birds found in the park.

BACKPACKING. Careful planning is essential. Backpackers in Auyuittuq should be experienced, have equipment designed for Arctic conditions, and be self-sufficient.

- Pangnirtung Pass Trail begins at Overlord, the park entrance on the Pangnirtung Fiord, follows the east bank of the Weasel River, and goes around Glacier Lake and Summit Lake. At 400 metres (1,300 feet) above sea level, Summit Lake is the highest point in the pass. The trail returns to Overlord on the west side of the river. The route traverses sandy slopes, gravel fans, and mossy and wet tundra, and it crosses moraine and glacial creeks. The 103 km (64 mile) round trip averages about 47 hours of hiking. Some hikers begin at Broughton Island and hike the full length of the pass from north to south. The main trail is also the starting point of unmarked routes to the glaciers on both sides of the pass. Nine emergency shelters equipped with first-aid supplies and two-way radios are located in Pangnirtung Pass.

More Information:
Auyuittuq National Park Reserve
Box 353
Pangnirtung, Nunavut X0A 0R0
Telephone: (867) 473-8828
Fax: (867) 473-8612
Website: http://www.parkscanada.gc.ca/
E-mail: Nunavut_Infor@pch.gc.ca

2. Ellesmere National Park Reserve

Canada at the top of the world. Reaching the park involves flying to Resolute Bay in the Northwest Territories, and continuing by charter aircraft to Lake Hazen or Tanquary Fiord.

Covering 37,775 square km (14,590 square miles) of northern Ellesmere Island, this park is situated in the eastern high Arctic. Icefields 900 metres (3,000 feet) cloak the Grant Land Mountains that cover the northern part of the park. The ice is a remnant of the last continental glacier that covered North America ten thousand years ago. Several peaks of the Grant Land Range are over 2,500 metres (8,250 feet) tall. Mount Barbeau at 2,616 metres (8,633 feet) is the highest mountain in eastern North America. Glacial valleys and fiords cut into the park's ocean coastline.

Wildlife ▶ Polar bears, musk ox, wolves and foxes inhabit the park.

DAY-HIKES/BACKPACKING. Routes and opportunities:

• Most hikers do the long-distance trek from Tanquary Fiord to Lake Hazen via the Very and MacDonald river valleys.
• There are also possibilities for shorter overnight hikes and day-hikes from base camps in the Rollrock and Redrock valleys near Tanquary Fiord, or from camps in Glacier and Blister Creek valleys near Hazen Camp.

More Information:
Ellesmere Island National Park Reserve
Box 353
Pangnirtung, Nunavut X0A 0R0
Telephone: (867) 473-8828
Fax: (867) 473-8612
Website: http://parkscanada.pch.gc.ca/parks/nwtw/Auyuittuq/
E-mail: Nunavut_Infor@pch.gc.ca
Information on charter companies and outfitters offering organized trips
is available from the park.

14

Saskatchewan

One usually thinks of Saskatchewan as a province of rolling wheat fields, and so it is. But it is also a province of forest and lake and muskeg, rich in wildlife and exciting for hikers. Most of the northern third of the province, an area of 233,010 square km (90,000 square miles) of Saskatchewan's total area of 651,651 square km (251,700 square miles), lies on the Canadian Shield underlain with Precambrian rock and covered with a northern coniferous forest of black spruce, jack pine, larch and poplar. The area has many lakes and rivers, wide areas of muskeg and swamp, forest and outcroppings of rock.

Most of the southern two-thirds of the province is a great plain sloping gradually from an elevation of 900 metres (3,000 feet) in the southwest to 450 metres (1,500 feet) in the northeast. Exceptions are the Cypress Hills in the southwest corner of the province, and the Missouri Coteau, the long narrow escarpment extending from south-central Saskatchewan into northeastern Alberta. This separates the

SASKATCHEWAN

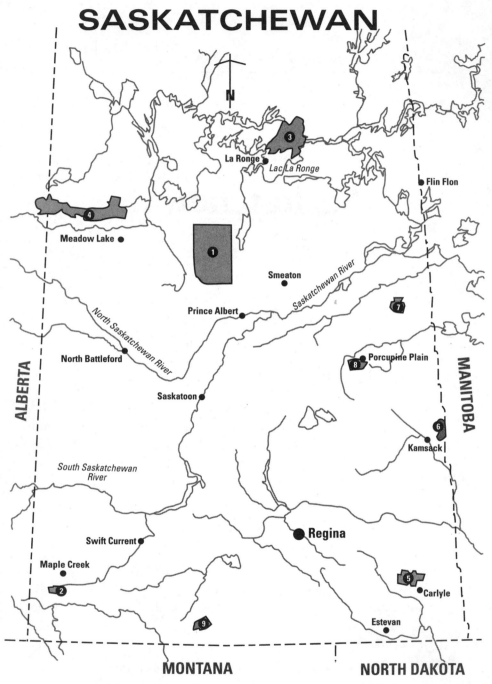

N

ALBERTA

MANITOBA

MONTANA

NORTH DAKOTA

La Ronge

Lac La Ronge

Flin Flon

Meadow Lake

Smeaton

Saskatchewan River

North Saskatchewan River

Prince Albert

North Battleford

Porcupine Plain

Saskatoon

Kamsack

South Saskatchewan River

Regina

Swift Current

Maple Creek

Carlyle

Estevan

1. Prince Albert National Park
2. Cypress Hills Interprovincial Park
3. Lac La Ronge Provincial Park
4. Meadow Lake Provincial Park
5. Moose Mountain Provincial Park
6. Duck Mountain Provincial Park
7. Wildcat Hill Provincial Park
8. Greenwater Lake Provincial Park
9. Grasslands National Park

Saskatchewan Plain—the second prairie steppe—and the Alberta Plateau, which is the third prairie steppe. The moraine-covered Missouri Coteau consists of rolling hills rising 60 to 150 metres (200 to 500 feet) above the Saskatchewan Plain.

The transition zone between the prairie of the south and the northern forest region is known as the park belt. This region contains many lakes and rivers and a forest consisting of white poplar, white spruce, black spruce and jack pine.

Saskatchewan has a continental climate with short, hot summers and long, cold winters. During the summer the average temperature varies from 10°C (50°F) at sunrise to 24°C (75°F) in the afternoon. Average annual precipitation is 28 to 51 cm (11 to 20 inches), half of that occurring during June, July and August.

Most of Saskatchewan's hiking opportunities are located in the park belt, though hiking routes exist in all parts of the province.

Saskatchewan Tourist Information
Tourism Saskatchewan
1922 Park St.
Regina, SK S4P 3V7
Toll-free telephone (Canada and the United States): 1-877-237-2273
Website: www.sasktourism.com

Hostels
Hostelling International—Saskatchewan
2014 - 14th Ave.
Regina, SK SRP 0X5
Telephone: (306) 791-8160

1. *Prince Albert National Park*

Forest, parkland and prairie; from the city of Prince Albert, north on Highway 2 for 77 km (49 miles), then left on Highway 264 for 13 km (8 miles) to Waskesiu Lake in Prince Albert Park

Prince Albert Park is a transition zone. It has plant life characteristic of the three floral zones—boreal forest, aspen parkland and prairie grassland—that lie within its boundaries.

Forest Cover ▶ Boreal forest—broken by several lakes and numerous streams—covers more than half the park with white spruce, black spruce and jack pine.

Wildlife and Birds ▶ Among the animal life inhabiting the park are badgers in the prairie area, elk in the aspen parkland and wolf in the boreal forest. White-tailed deer, mule deer, moose, black bear, woodland caribou and a herd of free-roaming bison are also found.

The park is home to a colony of white pelicans. Great blue herons inhabit the marshes, pileated woodpeckers live in the forest and waterfowl are found on the lakes. Other birds that may be seen are the common loon, gray jay, black-billed magpie and common raven.

WALKS. Among the park's walking trails:

- The Waskesiu River Trail leads 0.5 km (0.3 mile) on a boardwalk and 1.5 km (0.9 mile) on ground along the riverbank. Wheelchair- and stroller-accessible, the trail is also accessible for people with visual disabilities.
- The 2 km (1.2 mile) Mud Creek self-guiding nature trail loops along the south shore of Waskesiu Lake.

- The Kingsmere River Trail is a 1.5 km (0.9 mile) one-way walk to the shores of Kingsmere Lake.

DAY-HIKES. Hikes include:

- The King Fisher Trail, a 13 km (8 mile) loop where mineral licks and a variety of animal tracks may be seen.
- The 27 km (16 mile) one-way Freight Trail, which follows the historic route used by horse-drawn wagons and sleighs to transport furs and supplies between Prince Albert and Waskesiu.

BACKPACKING. For backpackers:

- The Grey Owl Trail is a 20 km (12.4 mile) route each way along Kingsmere Lake and across rolling terrain to Ajawaan Lake and the cabin of Grey Owl, the famous conservationist who lived here in the 1930s. The trail passes several backcountry campsites.
- The Fish, Hunters and Elk Trail circuit is a 41 km (25 mile) route suitable for a three-day backpacking trip.

Guidebooks ▶ *Prince Albert National Park Trail Guide* and *Saskatchewan Trails: A Guide to Nature Walks and Easy Hikes*. (See end of chapter.)

More Information:
Prince Albert National Park
Box 100
Waskesiu Lake, SK S0J 2Y0
Telephone: (306) 663-4522
Fax: (306) 663-5424
Website: http://www.parkscanada.gc.ca/
E-mail: PANP_INFO@pch.gc.ca

2. Cypress Hills Interprovincial Park

Highest point in Saskatchewan; the park's Center Block is 164 km (102 miles) southwest of Swift Current

Situated in the southwestern corner of the province, the Cypress Hills form a dissected flat-topped plateau rising 600 metres (2,000 feet) above the surrounding prairie. The plateau extends in an east-west direction for about 130 km (80 miles), with a width ranging from 24 to 40 km (15 to 25 miles). The hills reach 1,370 metres (4,500 feet), the highest point in Saskatchewan, and offer a panoramic view of the surrounding prairie.

The 144 square km (55 square mile) park is divided into two sections: the Center Block, which is the core area; and the West Block, 24 km (15 miles) to the west.

Plant life mixes the prairie vegetation of the surrounding plains with the montane vegetation that is characteristic of the Rocky Mountain Foothills, 320 km (200 miles) to the west.

Wildlife and Birds ▶ Elk, moose, mule deer and white-tailed deer are common. Among the 246 bird species that may be observed are double-crested cormorant, trumpeter swan, red-necked grebe, great blue heron, western tanager, white-breasted nuthatch, and mountain chickadee.

WALKS. The park's Center Block offers:

- The 1.2 km (0.7 mile) Whispering Pines interpretive trail.
- The 1.6 km (1 mile) Highland interpretive trail.
- 25 km (15.5 miles) of cross-country skiing and hiking trails.
- The Trans Canada Trail crosses 10 km (6 miles) of the Center Block.

DAY-HIKES/BACKPACKING. The Western Block offers:

- 31 km (19 miles) of hiking trails in addition to fireguard trails. Topographical maps are needed.
- The Trans Canada Trail crosses 15 km (9 miles) of the West Block.

Guidebook ▶ *Saskatchewan Trails: A Guide to Nature Walks and Easy Hikes.* (See end of chapter.)

More Information:
Cypress Hills Interprovincial Park
Box 850
Maple Creek, SK S0W 1N0
Telephone: (306) 662-4411
Reservations: (306) 662-4459
Website: http://www.serm.gov.sk.ca/parks/
E-mail: Cypress.Hills.Interprov.Park.erm@govmail.gov.sk.ca

3. Lac La Ronge Provincial Park
Precambrian Shield wilderness; 240 km (150 miles) north of the city of Prince Albert

This wilderness park in northern Saskatchewan's Precambrian Shield is covered with a dense forest and surrounded by many lakes including Lac La Ronge.

Wildlife, Birds and Fish ▶ White-tailed deer, moose, wolf, lynx, beaver, muskrat and snowshoe hare are some of the mammals that may be observed. Birds include the raven, ruffed grouse, spruce grouse, great horned owl, red-winged blackbird, bald eagle, pelican and common loon. Rainbow trout, lake trout, northern pike and walleye are found in the park's lakes.

WALK. For walkers:

- The Nemeiben Lake interpretive trail is a 1.5 km (0.9 mile) loop through boreal forest and Canadian Shield landscape.

DAY-HIKES/BACKPACKING. For hikers and backpackers:

- The 15 km (9.5 mile) one-way Nut Point Hiking Trail traverses muskeg, rock ridges and several stands of jack pine and leads to Nut Point at the tip of a peninsula jutting into Lac La Ronge. Return is by the same route.

Guidebook ▶ *Saskatchewan Trails: A Guide to Nature Walks and Easy Hikes.* (See end of chapter.)

More Information:
Lac La Ronge Provincial Park
Box 5000
La Ronge, SK S0J 1L0
Telephone: (306) 425-4234
Reservations: 1-800-772-4064
Fax: (306) 425-2580
Website: http://www.serm.gov.sk.ca/parks/
E-mail: k.weatherbee.erm@govmail.gov.sk.ca

4. Meadow Lake Provincial Park
On the Missouri Coteau escarpment; 195 km (117 miles) north of North Battleford

The 1,658 square km (645 square mile) area of Meadow Lake Park lies almost entirely in the valley of the Waterhen River in the Missouri Coteau. The eastward-facing escarpment that rises 60 to 150 metres (200 to 500 feet), the Missouri Coteau separates the second and third prairie steppes. The park's rolling terrain encompasses moraines, kames and eskers—geological structures created by glacial effects.

Forest Cover ► A transition zone near the Mustus Lakes separates the park into northern and southern sections of the boreal forest. Jack pine, birch, aspen, poplar and white spruce predominate in the southern section. The northern section is covered with black spruce and jack pine.

Wildlife, Birds and Fish ► Black bears, coyote, gray wolves, lynx, moose, elk and white-tailed deer are among the mammals that inhabit the park. Great blue herons, California gulls, ring-billed gulls, pelicans, golden eagles and bald eagles are seen in the park. The lakes and rivers contain a wide variety of fish, including whitefish, walleye, pike, rainbow trout, brook trout and cohoe salmon.

WALKS. For walkers:

- The 1.8 km (1.1 mile) White Birch Trail loops through a mixed forest and bog.
- The 2 km (1.2 mile) Kimball Lake Trail travels past a burned area —note the beaver activity—to Kimball Lake Beach.

DAY-HIKES. For hikers:

- The Vivian Lake Trail offers 1.5 km (0.9 mile) and 7 km (4.3 mile) loops through a mature spruce stand.

BACKPACKING. For backpackers:

- The Mustus Chain Trail is a 20 km (12 mile) loop around Mustus Lake. It offers an overnight shelter at the halfway point.

Supplies ► Camping supplies may be obtained at stores located in and just outside the park.

Guidebook ▶ *Saskatchewan Trails: A Guide to Nature Walks and Easy Hikes*. (See end of chapter.)

More Information:
Meadow Lake Provincial Park
PO Box 70
Dorintosh, SK S0M 0T0
Telephone: (306) 236-7680
Fax: (306) 236-7679
Website: http://www.serm.gov.sk.ca/parks/
E-mail: meadow.lake.prov.park.erm@govmail.gov.sk.ca

5. *Moose Mountain Provincial Park*
Knob and kettle terrain; 137 km (82 miles) northeast of Weyburn

Covering 388 square km (150 square miles) in the southeastern plains region of the province, Moose Mountain Park is a thick forest of white birch and aspen poplar on an elevated plateau that contrasts with the surrounding grassland region. The park's "knob-and-kettle" terrain has a topographic relief of 90 to 120 metres (300 to 400 feet); more than 1,200 small lakes are found in the depressions.

Wildlife and Birds ▶ Mammals inhabiting the area include white-tailed deer, elk, moose, mink, beaver, coyote, porcupine and snowshoe hare. Among the many songbirds are the veery, ovenbird and northern waterthrush. Other birds that have been observed include the great blue heron, turkey vultures and various waterfowl.

WALKS. The park's walking trails include:

- The 2.1 km (1.3 mile) Birch Forest interpretive trail, which leads through a mature white birch forest and offers good bird-watching.
- The 0.9 km (0.5 mile) Lakeview Trail, which follows the lakeshore and provides views of waterfowl, shorebirds and other wildlife. It is wheelchair- and stroller-accessible for half its distance.

DAY-HIKES. For hikers:

- The Beaver Lake Trail features 3.6 km (2.2 mile) and 6 km (3.7 mile) loops through a mature deciduous forest.
- The Little Kenosee Trail network is accessible via the Blue Heron Trail.

BACKPACKING. The park has 32 km (20 miles) of trails, with two rest shelters. There are also cutlines and old access roads that are suitable for backpacking. A topographical map is needed for hiking these routes and may be purchased at the park office.

Supplies ▶ Supplies may be purchased at stores in and near the park.

Guidebook ▶ *Saskatchewan Trails: A Guide to Nature Walks and Easy Hikes.* (See end of chapter.)

More Information:
Moose Mountain Provincial Park
Box 220
Kenosee Lake, SK S0C 2S0
Telephone: (306) 577-2600
Reservations: (306) 577-2611
Website: http://www.serm.gov.sk.ca/parks/
E-mail: heather.tessier.erm@govmail.gov.sk.ca

6. Duck Mountain Provincial Park

On the Manitoba Escarpment; 104 km (62 miles) northeast of Yorkton

Lying on the Duck Mountain Upland of the Manitoba Escarpment with elevations reaching 750 metres (2,500 feet), Duck Mountain Park covers 240 square km (93 square miles) adjacent to the Manitoba border and is the most southerly park in Saskatchewan's forest and lake belt.

Forest Cover ▶ The heavy, mixed forest comprises aspen, spruce, jack pine, balsam fir, black spruce and tamarack.

Wildlife ▶ The park is home to an abundance of wildlife, including bear, deer, moose, elk and beaver.

WALKS. Walking trails include:

- The wheelchair- and stroller-accessible 1 km (0.6 mile) Boreal Forest Trail, which explores the life cycle of a boreal forest.
- The 2 km (1.2 mile) Woodland Nature Trail, which explores the mixed Duck Mountain forest and offers good birdwatching.
- The 4.4 km (2.7 mile) Pelly Point Nature Trail, a wilderness route to Pelly Point.

DAY-HIKES/BACKPACKING. For hikers and backpackers:

- The 12.5 km (7.8 mile) loop from Sergeant Lake to Moose Lake Trail explores old-growth forests and kettle lakes.
- The Trans Canada Trail crosses 17 km (10.5 mile) of the park from the Saskatchewan-Manitoba border to Green Lake.

Supplies ▶ Groceries and camping supplies are available in the park.

Guidebook ▶ *Saskatchewan Trails: A Guide to Nature Walks and Easy Hikes*. (See end of chapter.)

More Information:
Duck Mountain Provincial Park
Box 39
Kamsack, SK S0A 1S0
Telephone: (306) 542-5500
Fax: (306) 542-5512
Reservations: (306) 542-5513
Website: http://www.serm.gov.sk.ca/parks/
E-mail: duck.mtn.pp.erm@govmail.gov.sk.ca

7. Wildcat Hill Provincial Park

Between the first and second prairie steppes; 40 km (24 miles) north of the town of Hudson Bay

Located in northeastern Saskatchewan, the 217 square km (85 square mile) Wildcat Hill Wilderness Area encompasses the Pasquia Hills, which are part of the Manitoba Escarpment—the rise between the first and second prairie steppes. The northern and eastern slopes rise steeply —approximately 540 metres (1,800 feet) from the muskeg of the Manitoba Lowlands—and reach an elevation of 822 metres (2,700 feet) at their highest point. Steep canyons, fast-flowing rivers, and dense forests are part of the landscape. The park is home to a wide variety of wildlife.

DAY-HIKES/BACKPACKING. Recommended for experienced backpackers only:

• A 16 km (10 mile) hike to the park, which crosses rugged terrain on an undeveloped trail.

More Information:
Saskatchewan Environment and Resources Management
Box 430
Porcupine Plain, SK S0E 1H0
Telephone: (306) 865-2274
Website: http://www.serm.gov.sk.ca/parks/

8. Greenwater Lake Provincial Park
Rolling foothills; 110 km (66 miles) southeast of Melfort

Greenwater Park occupies 202 square km (78 square miles) of the great rolling foothills of the Pasquia Hills.

Forest Cover ▶ The park has a boreal forest of trembling aspen and white spruce along with stands of white birch, balsam poplar and black spruce.

Wildlife and Fish ▶ White-tailed deer, elk, moose, black bear and mule deer inhabit the park. Northern pike, walleye, perch, rainbow trout and tiger trout are found in the park's lakes.

WALK. For walkers:

• The Highbush Nature Trail, a 4 km (2.5 mile) hike, parallels Greenwater Creek through a mature mixed forest of aspen and spruce. One may take a shorter loop of 1.5 km (0.9 miles).

DAY-HIKES/BACKPACKING. The park offers 25 km of cross-country trails (with two trail shelters) and more than 100 km (60 miles) of snowmobile trails (four shelters along the trails). Topographical maps are necessary; available at park office.

Supplies ▶ Supplies may be purchased at stores in and adjacent to the park.

More Information:
Greenwater Lake Provincial Park
Box 430
Porcupine Plain, SK S0E 1H0
Telephone: (306) 278-2972
Fax: (306) 278-3545
Reservations: (306) 278-2389
Website: http://www.serm.gov.sk.ca/parks/
E-mail: alex.dunlop.erm@govmail.gov.sk.ca

9. Grasslands National Park

Original mixed-grass prairie of North America; in southwestern Saskatchewan, between Val Marie and Killdeer. The West Block is accessible by one dry weather road; the East Block is accessible only in dry weather.

The area was used by Sitting Bull and his Sioux followers as a refuge from the United States army after the Battle of Little Big Horn in 1876. A few homesteaders tried farming here, but could not make a go of it. The surrounding area was then used for ranching operations.

The park has two separate blocks covering a total of 450 square km (175 square miles). The Frenchman River Valley, a glacial meltwater channel with deeply dissected plateaus, coulees and erosion features, is in the park's West Block. The park's East Block overlooks the Killdeer badlands of the Rock Creek area and the Wood Mountain uplands. Grasslands is the only park protecting original mixed-grass prairie. There are no services or facilities in the park, nor are there campgrounds. Primitive camping is allowed away from the road.

Wildlife and Birds ▶ Pronghorn antelope and prairie rattlesnake inhabit the park, along with sage grouse, ferruginous hawk and prairie falcon.

WALK. For walkers:

- The Two Trees Trail is a self-guiding trail.

DAY-HIKES. For hikers:

- There is hiking in the Frenchman Valley and in the coulees. Old trails once used by ranchers offer a way to explore the prairie and view wildlife.

Guidebooks ▶ *Prairie Winds and Silver Sage* and *Saskatchewan Trails: A Guide to Nature Walks and Easy Hikes.* (See end of chapter.)

More Information:
Grasslands National Park
PO Box 150
Val Marie, SK S0N 2T0
Telephone: (306) 298-2257
Fax: (306) 298-2042
TDD: (306) 298-2217
Website: http://www.parkscanada.gc.ca/
E-mail: grasslands_info@pch.gc.ca

Trans Canada Trail—Saskatchewan

From Duck Mountain Provincial Park, the Trans Canada Trail leads west through Kamsack, Canora, Good Spirit Provincial Park, Yorkton and Melville; then along Crooked and Katepwa lakes, and Fort Qu'Appelle, Regina and Lumsden to Nicolle Flats. At Nicolle Flats the trail branches.

The south branch will wind through Moose Jaw, Gravelbourg, Lafleche, Mankota and the area near Grasslands National Park, and then continue through Val Marie, Shaunavon, Eastend and Cypress

Hills Interprovincial Park, where it will enter Alberta. The northern branch will go through Buffalo Pound Provincial Park, Tugaske, Douglas Provincial Park, Mistusinne, Elbow, Saskatoon, Borden, Radisson, Maymont, The Battlefords, Meota, Vawn and Paradise Hill, and then link with the Alberta section of the trail.

Among the completed sections are 17 km (10.5 miles) in Duck Mountain Provincial Park, 12 km (7 miles) in Douglas Provincial Park and 15 km (9 miles) in Cypress Hills Interprovincial Park.

More Information:
Saskatchewan Parks and Recreation Association
210 - 33003 Hillsdale St.
Regina, SK S4S 6W9
Telephone: (306) 780-9262
Fax: (306) 780-9257
Website: www.tctrail.ca/saskatchewan.htm

Guidebook Sources

Prairie Winds and Silver Sage. Describes trails in Grasslands National Park. Val Marie, SK: Friends of Grasslands (Box 83, Val Marie, SK S0N 2T0, E-mail: friends.grasslands@sk.sympatico.ca).

Prince Albert National Park Trail Guide. Shanna D. Frith. Waskesiu Lake, SK: Friends of Prince Albert National Park (Box 11, Waskesiu Lake, SK S0J 2Y0, Telephone: (306) 663-5213, Fax: (306) 663-5424, E-mail: Friends_panp@pch.gc.ca).

Saskatchewan Trails: A Guide to Nature Walks and Easy Hikes. Robin and Arlene Karpan. Saskatoon, SK: Parkland Publishing (501 Mount Allison Place, Saskatoon, SK S7H 4A9, Telephone/Fax: (306) 242-7731, Website: www.skyport.com/parkland/books, E-mail: parkland@skyport.com).

15

Manitoba

Despite the image of bland, comfortable wheat fields, more than half of Manitoba is as rugged as it was in the days of the fur-trading voyageurs. Only the southern and southwestern areas, representing less than two-fifths of Manitoba's 649,839 square km (251,000 square miles), is flat prairie farmland. The three-fifths of the province to the east and south-east of Lake Winnipeg lie within the Precambrian Shield and is characterized by very rugged terrain with numerous lakes, wooded ridges, and rocks protruding from a surface denuded of soil by glacial action.

The highest hills in the province are along the Manitoba Escarpment, which forms the edge between the Manitoba Plain—the first prairie steppe—and the Saskatchewan Plain—the second prairie steppe. The escarpment extends from the Pembina Mountains near the United States boundary and northward to the Pasquia Hills just south of the Saskatchewan River, and encompasses the Tiger Hills, Riding Mountain, Duck Mountain and Porcupine Mountain. At an elevation of

MANITOBA

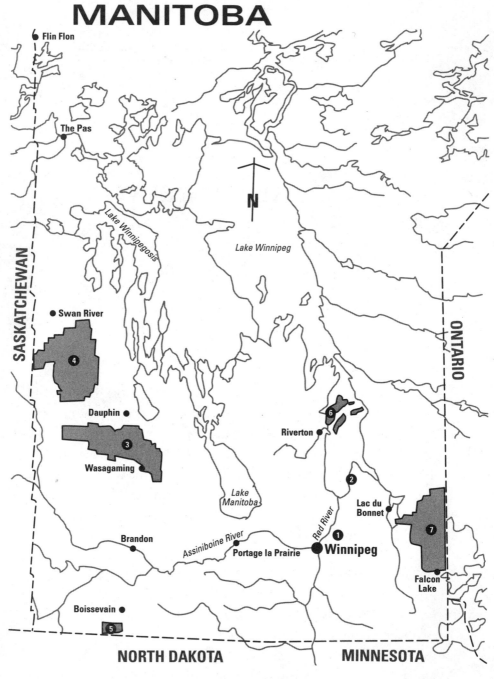

Flin Flon

The Pas

SASKATCHEWAN

Lake Winnipegosis

Lake Winnipeg

N

Swan River

4

Dauphin

3

Wasagaming

Lake Manitoba

Brandon

Assiniboine River

Portage la Prairie

Red River

Winnipeg

1

2

Riverton

6

Lac du Bonnet

7

Falcon Lake

ONTARIO

Boissevain

5

NORTH DAKOTA

MINNESOTA

1. Birds Hill Provincial Park
2. Grand Beach Provincial Park
3. Riding Mountain National Park
4. Duck Mountain Provincial Park
5. Turtle Mountain Provincial Park
6. Hecla Provincial Park
7. Whiteshell Provincial Park

831 metres (2,727 feet) above sea level, Mount Baldy in the Duck Mountains is the highest point in Manitoba.

Manitoba has the most temperate climate of the three Prairie Provinces. Summer temperatures range from 10°C (50°F) at night to about 24°C (75°F) during the day. Average annual precipitation across the province varies from 41 to 53 cm (16 to 21 inches), most of it falling during the summers.

Manitoba Tourist Information
Travel Manitoba
155 Carlton St., 7th Floor
Winnipeg, MB R3C 3H8
Telephone in Winnipeg: (204) 945-3777
Toll-free telephone (United States and rest of Canada): 1-800-665-0040
Website: www.travelmanitoba.com

Hostels
Hostelling International—Manitoba
194-A Sherbrook St.
Winnipeg, MB R3C 4M2
Telephone: (204) 784-1131
Website: http:/www.hostellingintl.ca/database/Manitoba/

1. Birds Hill Provincial Park
Prairie grassland and sandy beaches; from Winnipeg, take Highway 59 north for 24 km (15 miles)

Located close to Winnipeg, Birds Hill Park features a trembling aspen and bur oak forest, prairie grassland, and an artificial lake with sandy beaches. White-tailed deer inhabit the park. The 35 square km (13 square mile) park is a popular camping base for visitors to Winnipeg.

WALKS. Among the park's self-guiding nature trails:

- The 3.5 km (2.1 mile) Cedar Bog Trail travels through grasslands of aspen and oak, and descends to a cedar bog.
- The 1 km (0.6 mile) Bur Oak Trail explores large meadows; tall eastern white cedars are inhabited by white-tailed deer.
- The 1.8 km (1.1 mile) Nimowin Trail focuses on the meaning of "peace." (Nimowin is Cree for "peaceful").

DAY-HIKES. Among the park's hikes:

- The 7.5 km (4.6 mile) Carriageway Trail.
- The 16 km (10 mile) Bridle Path Trail.
- The 7.8 km (4.8 mile) Lime Kiln Trail.
- The 6.5 km (4 mile) Aspen Trail.

More Information:
Manitoba Natural Resources
Box 22, 200 Saulteaux Crescent
Winnipeg, MB R3J 3W3
Telephone: (204) 222-1982
Toll-free telephone (provincial parks information): 1-800-214-6497
Fax: (204) 222-4858
Reservations: 1-888-482-2267
Website: http://www.gov.mb.ca/natres/parks/

2. Grand Beach Provincial Park
A natural sand beach on the shores of Lake Winnipeg; from Winnipeg, take Highway 59 north for 80 km (50 miles) and Highway 12 east for 6 km (3.7 miles).

Grand Beach Park is on Lake Winnipeg, Canada's sixth largest lake. The 25 square km (9.6 square mile) park, popular for swimming and sailing, offers several trails.

WALKS. Walks include:

- The Ancient Beach self-guiding trail, a 3.1 km (1.9 mile) walk that follows the beach of ancient Lake Agassiz, the inland lake that covered most of southeastern Manitoba and disappeared 8,000 years ago. Lake Winnipeg is 3 km (1.8 mile) west.
- The 1 km (0.6 mile) Wild Wings Trail, which explores Grand Beach Marsh and winds through cattails and willows.
- The 1.1 km (0.7 mile) Spirit Rock Walking Tour, which provides views of Lake Winnipeg and explores glacial erratics.

DAY-HIKES. The 30 km (19 miles) of backcountry trails offer six trails, ranging from 1.1 km (0.7 mile) to 13.3 km (8.3 miles).

More Information:
Grand Beach Provincial Park
Box 220
Grand Beach, MB R0E 0T0
Telephone: (204) 754-2212
Toll-free telephone (provincial parks information): 1-800-214-6497
Fax: (204) 754-8977
Reservations: 1-888-482-2267
Website: http://www.gov.mb.ca/natres/parks/

3. Riding Mountain National Park

Rolling plateau rising above the prairie; from Winnipeg, take Highway 1 west to Highway 16 north, then Highway 16 to Highway 10 and go north to Wasagaming.

Riding Mountain Park occupies 2,977 square km (1,150 square miles) of the Manitoba Escarpment, a rolling plateau that rises 450 metres (1,500 feet) above the surrounding prairie. At an elevation of 750 metres (2,460 feet), Riding Mountain is the third highest point in Manitoba.

The park's 40 trails, totaling 400 km (250 miles), explore Riding Mountain's three major environments: the Manitoba Escarpment and the hardwood forest at its base; the northern boreal forest of evergreens and moss-filled bogs; and the open prairies and aspen forests of the Western Highland.

Forest Cover ▶ The forest area is made up of white spruce, black spruce, jack pine, balsam fir, tamarack, trembling aspen and white birch. The base of the escarpment, the park's lowest and warmest region, is covered with a deciduous forest of hardwoods, shrubs, vines and ferns.

Wildlife and Fish ▶ Black bear, elk, moose and white-tailed deer are among the larger mammals in the park. Beaver may be seen in almost every pond. One may fish the lakes for northern pike, walleye, whitefish, lake trout, rainbow trout and brook trout.

WALKS. Among the park's walks:

- The wheelchair- and stroller-accessible 1 km (0.6 mile) or 2.6 km (1.6 mile) Lakeshore Walk winds along Clear Lake to Deep Bay.
- The wheelchair- and stroller-accessible 1.9 km (1.1 mile) return Ominnik Marsh Trail extends along a boardwalk through a marsh.
- The 1 km (0.6 mile) loop Ma-ee-gun Trail travels through a forest of white spruce.
- The 2.2 km (1.3 mile) Burls and Buttersweet Trail, a return walk, travels through an eastern hardwood forest at the base of the Manitoba Escarpment.
- The 3.4 km (2.1 mile) Arrowhead Trail, a return path, explores features remaining from the last Ice Age.

DAY-HIKES. Hikes include:

- The 6.4 km (3.9 mile) Gorge Creek, a one-way hike that descends 320 metres (1,050 feet) along Dead Ox and Gorge creeks through the shale of the Manitoba Escarpment.

- The 9.2 km (5.7 mile) return Moon Lake Trail, along which various animal tracks may be seen.
- The Oak Ridge Trail, with 3 km (1.8 mile) and 6.4 km (3.9 mile) loops, which leads through oak groves and meadows to a view of the Manitoba Escarpment.

BACKPACKING. Riding Mountain Park's trail network includes 15 backpacking trails for trips ranging from overnight to six days. Primitive campsites are located at regular intervals. Among the trails:

- The 7.7 km (4.8 mile) North Escarpment Trail, which follows the edge of the Manitoba Escarpment, going over the park's highest point.
- The 31.8 km (19.7 mile) South Escarpment Trail, offering views of the McFadden Valley.
- The 17.9 km (11.1 mile) Grasshopper Valley Trail, which follows the shore of Audy Lake and crosses the semi-open meadows and fescue grass prairie, a remnant of the original prairie.
- The 73 km (45 mile) Central Trail—the park's longest trail—across the western half of Riding Mountain. Examples of the vegetation range from white spruce stands to open rolling grasslands. It provides access to seven other trails.

Supplies ► Supplies may be obtained at stores in Wasagaming.

More Information:
Riding Mountain National Park
Wasagaming, MB R0J 2H0
Telephone: (204) 848-7275
Toll-free telephone: 1-800-707-8480
Fax: (204) 848-2596
TDD: (204) 848-2001
Website: http://www.parkscanada.gc.ca/
E-mail: rmnp_info@pch.gc.ca

4. Duck Mountain Provincial Park

Site of Mount Baldy, Manitoba's highest point; 400 km (250 miles)
northwest of Winnipeg. From Winnipeg, north on Highway 6 to
Highway 68 and then Highway 5 to Dauphin; from Dauphin,
Highway 5 west to PR366 and north to the park.

Lying on the rolling landscape of the Manitoba Escarpment, Duck
Mountain Park includes 831 metre (2,727 foot) Mount Baldy, the highest point in the province. The park covers 1,424 square km (550 square
miles) of forests, lakes, river valleys, wetlands and streams.

Forest Cover ▶ The boreal forest consists of white spruce, jack pine,
balsam, aspen and birch.

Wildlife and Fish ▶ The park environment supports a major elk herd,
moose, white-tailed deer, black bear, fox, lynx, coyote and timber wolf.
The lakes and streams contain brook, speckled, rainbow, brown and
lake trout, kokanee salmon, splake, muskellunge, pickerel, jackfish,
whitefish, walleye and yellow perch. The park is a favorite place for
anglers. Several lakes have been stocked with species not native to the
area.

WALKS. For walkers:

- The 1.1 km (0.6 mile) Shining Stone self-guiding trail follows the
  shore of a peninsula that juts into West Blue Lake.
- The 1.2 km (0.7 mile) Copernicus Hill Hiking Trail climbs to a hill
  with a northward view.

DAY-HIKES/BACKPACKING. Opportunities include:

- The 5.5 km (3.4 mile) return Blue Lakes Hiking Trail, which travels from level ground to rolling hills.
- The 3.8 km (2.3 mile) return Glad Lake Hiking Trail, featuring a few
  steep slopes.

- The 4.5 km (2.8 mile) return Shell River Valley Trail, which leads through forest, past elk beds and to a point for viewing the Shell River Valley.

More Information:
Duck Mountain Provincial Park
PO Box 640
201 - 4th Ave. South
Swan River, MB R0L 1Z0
Telephone: (204) 734-3429
Toll-free telephone (provincial parks information): 1-800-214-6497
Fax: (204) 734-4210
Reservations: 1-888-482-2267
Website: http://www.gov.mb.ca/natres/parks/

5. Turtle Mountain Provincial Park
Higher than surrounding prairie; from Brandon, Highway 10 south for 100 km (60 miles)

Situated in the southwest corner of the province on the North Dakota border, 185 square km (71 square mile) Turtle Mountain Park is at a higher elevation than and has a different environment from the surrounding flat prairie. The park has 39 km (24 miles) of trails.

Forest Cover ▸ Trees include aspen, Manitoba maple, elm, black poplar, ash and birch.

Wildlife ▸ Beaver, mink and muskrat are indigenous to the park.

WALK. For walkers:

- The Disappearing Lakes interpretive trail, 1.5 km (0.9 mile) along a boardwalk, explores the life of a lake and how it eventually disappears.

DAY-HIKES. For hikers:

- The 2.5 km (3.1 mile) Adam Lake loop is the start of four other trails ranging from 5 to 15 km (3 to 9 miles). All explore the park's forests, lakes and potholes.

BACKPACKING. For backpackers:

- The James Lake Trail is a 15 km (9 mile) route with a backcountry cabin and shelter.

Supplies ▶ Supplies may be obtained in Boissevain, 20 km (12 miles) north of the park.

More Information:
Turtle Mountain Provincial Park
Parks Branch, Box 820
Boissevain, MB R0K 0E0
Telephone: (204) 534-2578
Toll-free telephone (provincial parks information): 1-800-214-6497
Fax: (204) 534-6858
Reservations: 1-888-482-2267
Website: http://www.gov.mb.ca/natres/parks/

6. Hecla Provincial Park

Largest island in Lake Winnipeg; from Winnipeg, north 140 km (87 miles) on Highway 8

Hecla Island, covering 158 square km (61 square miles), is the largest island in Lake Winnipeg and the only one of the park's seven islands accessible by causeway. Rugged cliffs dominate the northern shore, while most of the eastern shore is made up of open fields. The ground cover on Hecla Island is usually moist, so rubber boots may be needed. Open fires are prohibited in the interior.

The park has 60 km (37 miles) of trails.

Forest Cover ▶ The interior is covered with a dense forest of spruce, aspen, balsam, jack pine and tamarack. The southern part of the island is a series of marshes containing rushes, cattails, duckweeds and water grasses.

Wildlife and Birds ▶ Moose and deer come to feed on Hecla's water grasses. The park's marshes are on the central North American flyway, and 50,000 northern migrant birds make them their summer home. Among the species observed are Canada geese, snow geese, blue geese, pelicans, sandhill cranes, whistling swans, herons, bitterns, cormorants and 15 varieties of ducks. The predatory bald eagle and golden eagle, plus a multitude of hawks, also inhabit the island.

WALKS. Of note:

- The 1 km (0.6 mile) Hecla Village Trail features remnants dating back to the island's Icelandic settlers.

DAY-HIKES. Opportunities include:

- The 10 km (6 mile) West Quarry Trail, also favored by moose, which has viewing towers and boardwalks.
- The five trails in the Grassy Narrows Marsh, ranging from 0.5 to 10.6 km (0.3 to 6.5 miles), which explore marshes and a nesting area for Canada geese and other waterfowl.

BACKPACKING. For backpackers:

- Two routes may be hiked, including a 60 km (37 mile) trail on the eastern side of the island.

More Information:
Hecla Provincial Park
Parks Branch, Box 70
Riverton, MB R0C 2R0
Telephone: (204) 279-2369
Toll-free telephone (provincial parks information): 1-800-214-6497
Fax: (204) 378-5274
Reservations:1-888-482-2267
Website: http://www.gov.mb.ca/natres/parks/

7. Whiteshell Provincial Park

*Primitive Precambrian Shield forest; from Winnipeg, Highway 1
east 126 km (78 miles) to Falcon and West Hawk*

Lying on the Ontario border, Whiteshell Park covers 2,719 square km
(1,058 square miles) of Precambrian Shield forests, rushing rivers, and
deep lakes.

Wildlife, Birds and Fish ▶ Moose, fox, coyote, deer, black bear, beaver,
bald eagle, turkey vultures, spruce grouse, ruffed grouse and Canada
geese may be observed in the park. The primitive forest is dotted with
more than 200 lakes and streams containing Northern pike, trout and
walleye. Wild rice grows in the bays of some of the lakes.

WALKS. Opportunities include:

- Several self-guiding trails, among them the 2.2 km (1.3 mile) Falcon Creek Trail loop, explore the influence of human beings on
  Whiteshell over the past 80 years.
- The McGillivray Falls Trails offer a 4.6 km (2.8 mile) or 2.8 km (1.7
  mile) walk to a small Precambrian Shield drainage basin.
- The 8.2 km (5 mile) Pine Point Trail explores boreal forest, waterfalls and rapids along the Whiteshell River.

DAY-HIKES. Hiking opportunities:

- The Hunt Lake Trail is a 12.6 km (7.8 mile) loop that leads north to Indian Bay and returns along the east shore of West Hawk Lake.
- The Amisk Trail is a 4.8 km (3 mile) return route to the Rennie River below Inverness Falls.
- The Bear Lake Trail is a 6 km (3.7 mile) route along rock ridges through jack pine stands.

BACKPACKING. For backpackers:

- The 60 km (37 mile) Mantario Hiking Trail is a three- to six-day hike that traverses the Precambrian wilderness and skirts the shores of several lakes. Campsites are located at regular intervals.

More Information:
Whiteshell Provincial Park
Parks Branch
Rennie, MB R0E 1R0
Telephone: (204) 369-5246
Toll-free telephone (provincial parks information): 1-800-214-6497
Fax: (204) 369-5341
Reservations: 1-888-482-2267
Website: http://www.gov.mb.ca/natres/parks/

Trans Canada Trail—Manitoba

The Manitoba section of the Trans Canada Trail includes the 22 km (13 mile) South Whiteshell Trail from Falcon Lake to West Hawk Lake to Caddy Lake, the 8 km (5 mile) Forks to Kildonan Park Trail, and the 180 km (108 mile) Rossburn Subdivision Line from Neepawa to Russell.

In the Interlake region between Lake Winnipeg and Lake Manitoba, the Trans Canada Trail plans to develop trails on abandoned rail lines, including the old Winnipeg to Gypsumville line and the Gross Isle to Fisher Branch line, and along the old Gimli and Riverton rail line along Lake Winnipeg's western shore.

More Information:
Manitoba Recreational Trail Association
204 - 825 Sherbrook St.
Winnipeg, MB R3A 1M5
Telephone: (204) 786-2688
Fax: (204) 786-0860
Website: www.tctrail.ca/manitoba.htm

16

Ontario

Ontario has hiking opportunities in every part of the province. They range from easy trails close to cities, to rugged wilderness treks. The Bruce Trail, completed in 1967, along the Niagara Escarpment from Queenston to Tobermory, was the first long-distance hiking trail in Canada. Since then, hiking trails totaling hundreds of kilometres have been developed. Many trails pass close to towns where supplies are available, making it possible to take extended trips. In Northern Ontario, trails explore rugged wilderness. Most of Ontario's provincial and national parks have self-guided trails for short walks. Most of the parks described here have longer hiking paths as well.

The geographic division between Northern and Southern Ontario is a line lying along the Mattawa River, Lake Nipissing and the French River. Most of the 932,000 square km (360,000 square miles) of Northern Ontario is underlaid by the Precambrian rock of the Canadian Shield. About one-third of the 129,500 square km (50,000 square mile)

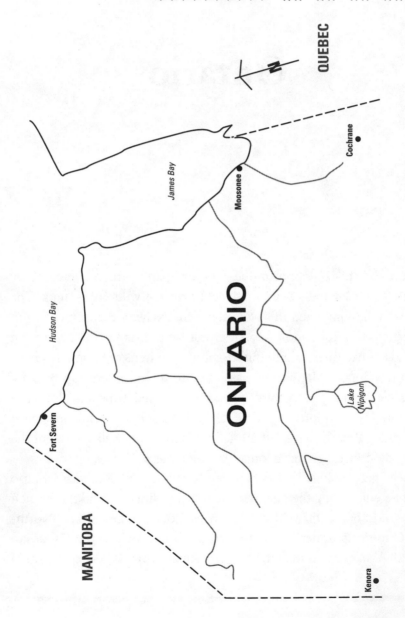

1. Toronto Region Conservation Areas
2. Waterfront Trail
3. Bruce Trail
4. Oak Ridges Trail
5. Grand Valley Trail
6. Avon Trail
7. Thames Valley Trail
8. Speed River Trail, Redail Line Trail, and other trails maintained by the Guelph Hiking Trail Club
9. Elora Cataract Trailway
10. Elgin Hiking Trail
11. Maitland Trail
12. Point Pelee National Park
13. Rideau Trail
14. Gatineau Park
15. Algonquin Provincial Park
16. Ganaraska Trail
17. Frontenac Provincial Park
18. Bon Echo Provincial Park
19. Charleston Lake Provincial Park
20. Killarney Provincial Park
21. Halfway Lake Provincial park
22. Esker Lakes Provincial Park
23. Wakami Lake Provincial Park
24. Voyageur Trail
25. Lake Superior Provincial Park
26. Pukaskwa National Park
27. Sleeping Giant Provincial Park
28. Quetico Provincial Park

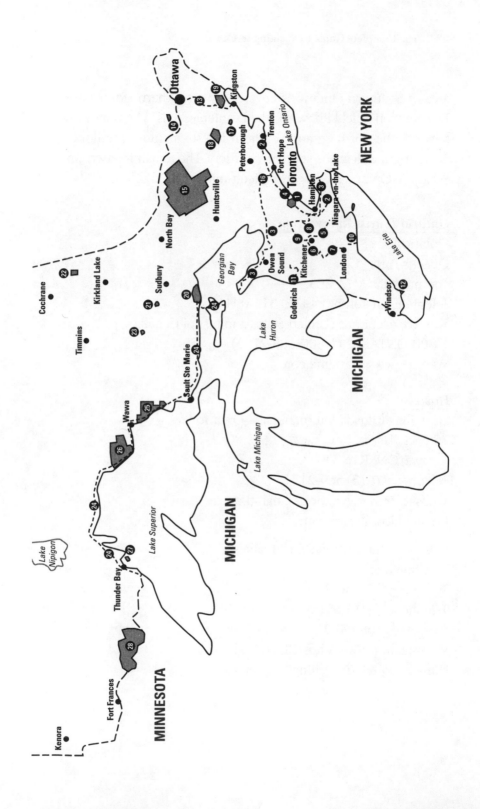

area of Southern Ontario is covered by a southern extension of the Precambrian Shield known as the Frontenac Axis. The transition zone between the northern and southern forests includes the flora of the northern as well as the southern portion. The remaining two-thirds of Southern Ontario are largely agricultural land and forests.

Ontario Tourist Information
Ontario Travel
Queen's Park
Toronto, ON M7A 2E5
Telephone in Toronto: (416) 314-0944
Toll-free telephone (United States and rest of Canada):
1-800-ONTARIO (1-800-668-2746)
Website: www.travelinx.com

Hostels
Hostelling Canada International—Ontario East
75 Nicholas St.
Ottawa, ON K1N 7B9
Telephone: (613) 569-2131
Website: http://www.hostellingintl.on.ca/
E-mail: hicoe@magi.com

Hostelling International Great Lakes
76 Church St.
Toronto, ON M5C 2G1
Telephone: (416) 363-0697
Fax: (416) 368-6499
Website: http://www.hostellingint-gl.on.ca
E-mail: thostel@hostellingint-gl.on.ca

Toronto Area and Southwestern Ontario

1. Toronto Region Conservation Areas
Trails in and near Canada's largest city

Near Toronto are conservation areas offering a variety of trails. Many offer interpretive programs:

- The **Kortright Centre for Conservation**, which covers 4 square km (1.5 square miles) near Kleinburg, features 12 km (7.4 miles) of trails through forests, along a pond, and past a sugarshack. Also near Kleinburg, the 0.9 square km (0.3 square mile) Boyd Conservation Area offers a nature trail.
- The 4.5 square km (1.7 square mile) **Albion Hill Conservation Area**, located 8 km (5 miles) north of Bolton, offers 30 km (18 miles) of trails through rolling terrain covered by hardwood bush and open parkland.
- West of Whitchurch-Stouffville is **Bruce's Mill Conservation Area**, named for its 120-year-old restored mill. The area features 12 km (7.4 miles) of trails through 0.9 square km (0.3 square miles) of mixed and hardwood forest.
- **Palgrave Forest and Wildlife Area**, 10 km (6 miles) north of Bolton, covers 2.2 square km (0.8 square miles) of the Oak Ridges Moraine. Over 16 km (10 miles) of trails wind through the forest.
- The **Greenwood Conservation Area**, covering 2.8 square km (1 square mile) north of Ajax, offers nature trails through woodlots, reforested areas and open spaces.
- **Within Toronto** are trails along river valleys and ravines including the Humber, Don and Rouge rivers and Highland Creek.

Guidebooks ▸ The walks within Toronto are described in *Great Country Walks Around Toronto* and *The Hike Ontario Guide to Walks Around Toronto*. (See end of chapter.)

More Information:
Toronto and Region Conservation Authority
5 Shoreham Drive
Toronto, ON M3N 1S4
Telephone: (416) 661-6600
Website: www.trca.on.ca

2. Waterfront Trail
Multi-use trail along the shore of Lake Ontario

The Waterfront Trail, which offers walking, bicycling, in-line skating and jogging, stretches more than 325 km (200 miles) along the shore of Lake Ontario from Niagara-on-the-Lake to Quinte West. It passes through 22 cities, including St. Catharines, Hamilton, Toronto and Oshawa. It links numerous waterfront natural areas, parks, promenades and marinas.

Guidebooks ▶ The *Waterfront Trail Guidebook* and *Waterfront Trail Mapbook*. (See end of chapter.)

More Information:
Waterfront Regeneration Trust
207 Queen's Quay West, Box 129
Toronto, ON M5J 1A7
Telephone: (416) 943-8080
Fax: (416) 943-8068
Website: www.waterfronttrust.com
E-mail: webmaster@wrtrust.com

3. Bruce Trail

Footpath along Niagara Escarpment

The Bruce Trail, the longest and best-known footpath in Ontario, winds its way for 736 km (457 miles) along the Niagara Escarpment from Queenston on the Niagara River near Niagara Falls to Tobermory on the tip of the Bruce Peninsula in Georgian Bay. In 1990, the United Nations declared the Niagara Escarpment a UNESCO World Biosphere Reserve, recognizing it as a unique ecological environment.

The trail is the nearest long-distance footpath to the Toronto area. And though it passes close to some of Southern Ontario's heavily populated areas, walkers catch only occasional glimpses of urbanization. The Bruce Trail traverses a number of conservation areas, provincial parks and one national park, which provide convenient access for hikers who want to walk, day-hike or backpack on the trail. Though extended backpacking trips can be taken, there are gaps without camping facilities or shelters.

From the southern terminus at Queenston Heights Park along the Niagara Parkway, the Bruce Trail leads through the fruit lands of the Niagara Peninsula, passes the historic Welland Canal, and crosses the Dundas Valley in the Royal Botanical Gardens near the city of Hamilton.

From Mount Nemo Conservation Area, the trail begins to climb along the escarpment; it passes through the Crawford Lake Conservation Area, traverses the ski slopes at Glen Eden and the Kelso Conservation Area, and crosses Highway 401 near Milton. North of the highway, the trail goes through Hilton Falls Conservation Area and continues north to Limehouse Conservation Area near Georgetown, and to Terra Cotta Conservation Area.

The trail winds northward through the Caledon Hills and the Hockley Valley, traversing Forks of the Credit Provincial Park near Belfountain, Glen Haffey Conservation Area, and Scott's Falls Provincial Park.

In the Dufferin Hi-Lands section, Mono Cliffs Provincial Park and Boyne Valley Provincial Park are crossed by the trail. Near Collingwood are the high bluffs and wide valleys of the Blue Mountain ski resort area. In this section, the Bruce Trail traverses Nottawasaga Bluffs Conservation Area, Devil's Glen Provincial Park and Petun Conservation Area.

In the Beaver Valley, a deep wedge in the Niagara Escarpment, the Bruce Trail goes through Old Baldy Conservation Area and along the valley's east rim, and then along the west rim to the Owen Sound area. From Wiarton, the trail follows the Georgian Bay shore—considered the footpath's most spectacular section—much of it on high cliffs through Bruce Peninsula National Park.

Guidebooks ▶ *The Bruce Trail Guide* is available from the Bruce Trail Association. *Country Walks: The Niagara Escarpment* is a guide to day-hikes on the Bruce Trail and other trails on the Niagara Escarpment. (See end of chapter.)

More Information:
Bruce Trail Association
PO Box 857
Hamilton, ON L8N 3N9
Telephone: (905) 529-6821
Toll-free telephone: 1-800-665-HIKE
Fax: (905) 529-6823
Website: http://www.brucetrail.org

4. Oak Ridges Trail
Ice-age remnants north of Toronto

When completed, the Oak Ridges Trail will stretch 230 km (143 miles) along the Oak Ridges Moraine from the Niagara Escarpment east to the Northumberland Forest. More than 100 km (60 miles) has been completed through Caledon, King, Aurora, Whitchurch-Stouffville, Uxbridge and Scugog. The 58 km (36 miles) portion from Uxbridge to the Long Sault Conservation Area in the Scugog area is the longest completed section of trail.

The Oak Ridges Moraine reaches up to 300 metres (1,000 feet). Located approximately 60 km (37 miles) north of Lake Ontario, the ridge of land was formed from materials carried by the massive ice sheets during the last Ice Age.

More Information:
Oak Ridges Trail Association
P. O. Box 28544
Aurora, ON L4G 6S6
Toll-free telephone: 1-877-319-0285
Website: www.orta.on.ca/
E-mail: orta@interlog.com

5. Grand Valley Trail
Along Grand River flood plain

This 250 km (155 mile) trail stretches from Rock Point Provincial Park on Lake Erie to the town of Alton. The route goes along the Grand River flood plain, woodlots and rolling hills. The area, a historic part of Southern Ontario, includes Mennonite and Scottish settlements.

Camping is available at the Elora Gorge, Conestoga, Pinehurst and Brant conservation areas, and at Rock Point Provincial Park.

More Information:
Grand Valley Trail Association
Box 40068
75 King St. South
Waterloo, ON N2J 4V1
Telephone: (519) 745-5252
Website: http://www.gvta.on.ca

6. Avon Trail
Links Thames Valley and Grand Valley trails

The Avon Trail connects the Thames Valley Trail at St. Mary's with the Grand Valley Trail at Conestoga, near Kitchener. The 100 km (60 mile) route goes to Wildwood Lake and then in a northeasterly direction to Stratford. From there, the trail follows the Avon River and Silver Creek toward Amulree. Continuing in a northeasterly direction, the trail runs close to Wellesley and through Elmsville and the Waterloo Farmers Market. After following Martin Creek and part of the Conestoga River, it meets the Grand Valley Trail in the village of Conestoga.

The trail meanders along streams and through woodlands and farm fields, sometimes following backroads. A 10 km (6 mile) side trail runs from the main trail into the city of Stratford.

More Information:
Avon Trail Association
PO Box 21148
Stratford, ON N5A 7V4
Website: www.avontrail.ca/

7. Thames Valley Trail
Path along Thames River linking Elgin and Avon trails

Beginning south of the city of London, this trail follows the Thames River starting at a link with the Elgin Trail at Southdel Road at the boundary of Elgin and Middlesex counties. The trail extends upstream through the town of Delaware, Komoka Provincial Park, and London. It then goes along the north branch of the Thames River through Fanshawe Conservation Area to the town of St. Mary's. Most of the 109 km (65 mile) trail is on private rural land. Camping along the trail is available at the Fanshawe, Sharon Creek and Wellwood conservation areas; the Scouts Canada campsite in London; and the privately owned Riverview campground.

At St. Mary's, the Thames Valley Trail meets the Avon Trail. Camping is available in Wildwood Park on the Avon Trail. There are also 25 km (15 miles) of side trails.

More Information:
Thames Valley Trail Association
c/o Grosvenor Lodge
1017 Western Rd.
London, ON N6G 1G5
Telephone: (519) 645-2845
Fax: (519) 645-0981
Website: http://info.london.on.ca/environment/tvta.html

8. Speed River Trail, Radial Line Trail, and Other Trails Maintained by the Guelph Hiking Trail Club
Guelph area

The Speed River Trail follows the Speed River for 25 km (16 miles) from Guelph through Cambridge to Riverside Park near Preston, where a side trail links with the Grand Valley Trail. Most of the trail goes through meadows. There are also sections of cedar and hardwood bush where Canada geese, herons and other wildlife abound. There are no campsites.

The Guelph Radial Trail runs from 28 km (17 miles) from Guelph to Limehouse, where it connects with the Bruce Trail. From Guelph to Georgetown it follows the route of the old Radial electric railway and passes through meadows and bush. The trail has a few steep sections. There are no campsites.

Other trails maintained by the Guelph Hiking Trail Club are the 8 km (4.9 mile) Arkell loop trail (through a variety of forests and meadows); the 4 km (2.4 mile) Starkey loop (leading to the area's highest point of land); and a portion of the 19 km (11 mile) section of the Guelph-Grand River section of the Trans Canada Trail.

More Information:
Guelph Hiking Trail Club
PO Box 1
Guelph, ON N1H 6J6
Telephone: (519) 822-3672

9. Elora Cataract Trailway
Links watersheds of Grand and Credit rivers

This 47 km (29 mile) trailway goes from Elora Gorge on the Grand River to the Cataract at the Forks of the Credit River, where it links with the Bruce Trail. Following an abandoned CP rail right of way, this multi-use route links parks and communities in south-central Ontario.

More Information:
Elora Cataract Trailway Association
PO Box 99
Fergus, ON N1M 2W7
Telephone: (519) 843-3650
Fax: (519) 843-6907
Website: www.trailway.org

10. Elgin Hiking Trail

Near Lake Erie

The Elgin Hiking Club maintains two trail sections, a total of 38.5 km (23 miles) in length. The main trail winds along the creek valleys, ravines, woodlots and hillsides of Kettle Creek, from a link with the Thames Valley Trail at Southdel Road at the boundary of Middlesex and Elgin counties, to Port Stanley on Lake Erie. A side trail goes east from Union on the main trail to Shaw's Dairy. There is no camping on the trail. Overnight camping is available at Dalewood Conservation Area near the trail.

The trails cross private land. Hikers should be prepared to show a current membership card of a trail organization.

Guidebook ▶ Trail guides are available from stores in St. Thomas and London, and from the Elgin Hiking Trail Club.

More Information:
Elgin Hiking Trail Club
c/o Kettle Creek Conservation Authority
RR 8
St. Thomas, ON N5P 3T3
Telephone: (519) 631-1270

11. Maitland Trail

Through uninhabited wild river valley, Goderich area

The 40 km (25 mile) Maitland Trail winds through wilderness along the north side of the Maitland River valley, from Goderich to the Auburn area. Hiking the entire trail takes two to three days. There is camping along the trail at Falls Conservation Area in the hamlet of Benmiller.

More Information:
Maitland Trail Association
PO Box 443
Goderich, ON N7A 4C7

Free map of the Maitland Trail (and other trails in Huron County):
Huron County Planning and Development
Courthouse Square
Goderich, ON N7A 1M2
Telephone: (519) 524-2188
Fax: (519) 524-5677
Website: www.hurontourism.on.ca
E-mail: htinfo@hurontourism.on.ca

12. Point Pelee National Park

*The most southerly point on the Canadian mainland; about 50 km
(30 miles) from Windsor*

Well known for its spring and fall migration of birds and autumn
migration of monarch butterflies, Point Pelee Park is on a triangle of
land jutting into Lake Erie. In the park's 20 square km (8 square miles)
are forests, fields, a marsh and 20 km (12 miles) of beaches. Individual camping is not available. Group camping is available for educa-
tional and not-for-profit groups, but must be reserved in advance.

Forest Cover ▶ Situated in the region known as the Carolinian zone, the
park has more than 70 species of trees, including many southern trees.
In the park's open areas are red cedars, cottonwoods, willows, hop trees
and honey locusts. The park's mature jungle-like forests are so dense
that light can barely penetrate. Vines—such as wild grape, Virginia
creeper and poison ivy—hang from tall trees. Southern trees found in
the park include the hackberry, black walnut, chinquapin oak, swamp
white oak, tuliptree, red mulberry, blue ash and sassafras. Sugar maple,
basswood, oak and white pine, typical of Ontario mixed-wood forests,
are also found in the park.

Wildlife and Birds ▶ Thousands of monarch butterflies stop at Point Pelee during their autumn migration south to Mexico. The park has 27 species of reptiles and 20 species of amphibians—the most in Canada. On the surface of the marsh are frogs, turtles, muskrats, snakes and various insects, including dragonflies and damselflies. There are 50 species of spiders and insects that are not found elsewhere in Canada. The park's fields are inhabited by deer, cottontail rabbits, butterflies, coyotes, lizards and snakes. More than 370 species of birds have been sighted here during migrations. Point Pelee is the most northern area of the breeding range of Acadian flycatchers, Carolina wrens, blue-gray gnatcatchers, red-bellied woodpeckers and yellow-breasted chats.

WALKS/DAY-HIKES. The park's 12 km (7.5 miles) of trails includes hiking, self-guiding interpretive trails and trails that lead to the beach:

- The 1.4 km (0.85 mile) Marsh Boardwalk explores Point Pelee's cat-tail marsh. At either end is an observation tower overlooking the marsh.
- The 4 km (2.5 mile) Centennial Biking/Hiking Trail leads from the Marsh Boardwalk through hackberry dry forest and provides access to West Beach.
- The 1.25 km (0.75 mile) DeLaurier Trail along open fields, red cedar savannah, swamp forest and old canals leads to a partly restored homestead dating from the 1840s.
- The 1 km (0.6 mile) Tilden's Woods Trail explores horsetails, mature swamp forest and red cedar savannah and provides access to East Beach.
- The 0.5 km (550 yard) Botham Tree Trail is a self-guiding interpretive trail exploring the Carolinian dry forest.
- The 2.75 km (1.75 mile) self-guiding Woodland Nature Trail explores swamp and dry Carolinian forest, red cedar savannah and grassland.

Guidebook ▶ *The Hike Ontario Guide to Walks in Carolinian Canada.* (See end of chapter.)

More Information:
Point Pelee National Park
407 Robson St., R.R. #1
Leamington, ON N8H 3V4
Telephone: (519) 322-2365
Park info line (recorded message updated daily during spring and fall migration): (519) 322-2371
Fax: (519) 322-1277
Website: http://www.parkscanada.gc.ca
E-mail: Pelee_Info@pch.gc.ca

Eastern Ontario

13. Rideau Trail
Through Rideau country

The Rideau Trail stretches 388 km (241 miles) between Kingston and Ottawa. Located in the broad corridor surrounding the historic Rideau Canal, the trail begins on the shores of Lake Ontario at the marshes of the Little Cataraqui, and then heads north to Sydenham and through bush country—along the shores of Gould Lake and in Frontenac Park—to the Perth Road. Foley Mountain Conservation Area at Westport and Murphy's Point Provincial Park are traversed, as are the towns of Perth and Smiths Falls. The trail then passes through the Richmond Farming district and the Ottawa/Carleton Conservation Centre. It enters Ottawa at Bells Corners and follows the Ottawa River Parkway to Richmond Landing.

Most of the trail is easy walking through meadows, bush and farmland. Campsites are located near the trail. A map kit is available.

More Information:
Rideau Trail Association
Box 15
Kingston, ON K7L 4V6

Telephone: (613) 542-5414
Fax: (613) 544-0340
Website: www.ncf.carleton.ca/RTA
E-mail: jean@kingston.net

14. Gatineau Park
North of the Ottawa River

Gatineau Park in Quebec offers walking and hiking trails close to the city of Ottawa. (See Chapter 17, Quebec.)

15. Algonquin Provincial Park
On the southern edge of the Canadian Shield, midway between Ottawa and Sudbury; a three-hour drive from Toronto—north, and then east

Created in 1893, Algonquin Park is the oldest provincial park in Ontario. The 7,725 square km (2,983 square mile) park is a land of rounded hills, rocky ridges, spruce bogs, fast-flowing rivers and thousands of lakes, ponds and streams.

Forest Cover ▶ The hills of the western two-thirds of the park are covered with hardwood forests of sugar maple, beech and yellow birch, with groves of hemlock and scattered giant white pine. White pine, red pine and jack pine predominate in the drier and sandier eastern part of Algonquin. Situated in the transition zone between southern broadleaf forests and northern coniferous forests, the park is the home of wildlife of both forest types.

Wildlife, Birds and Fish ▶ Wolf, moose and fisher, all northern animals, populate the park, as do such southern species as raccoon and white-tailed deer. Among the northern birds are the raven, gray jay and spruce grouse. Southern birds include the rose-breasted grosbeak, wood thrush and scarlet tanager. The lakes are populated by lake trout and brook trout.

WALKS. The park offers interpretive footpaths:

- The 0.8 km (0.5 mile) Lookout Trail leads to a magnificent view of the park.
- The 1.9 km (1.1 mile) Peck Lake Trail loop explores the ecology of a small Algonquin lake.
- The 2 km (1.2 mile) Beaver Pond Trail explores beaver pond ecology.
- The 1.5 km (0.9 mile) Spruce Bog Trail explores the flora and fauna of a typical northern bog.
- The 2.1 km (1.3 mile) Two Rivers Trail leads to a pine-clad cliff.
- The 3.5 km (2.1 mile) Hemlock Bluff Trail explores the results of research in the park.

DAY-HIKES. Hiking trails include:

- The 5.1 km (3.1 mile) Booth's Rock Trail, which leads to vistas of Algonquin scenery and returns along an abandoned railway.
- The 11 km (6.8 mile) Mizzy Lake Trail, which visits nine ponds and small lakes, with good opportunities to view wildlife.
- The 7.7 km (4.6 mile) Track and Tower Trail loop, which features a lookout and traces some of the park's history.
- The 5.6 km (3.4 mile) Bat Lake Trail, which features a hemlock stand, a lookout and an acidic lake.
- The 10 km (6 mile) Centennial Ridges Trail, a demanding hike to five cliffs, offering outstanding scenery.

BACKPACKING. Algonquin Park's backpacking trails wind through the forest and along lakes and rivers. These trails have backcountry campsites:

- The Western Uplands Backpacking Trail has three loops: a 32 km (20 mile) hike to Maggie Lake, Oak Lake and Ramona Lake; a 55 km (34 mile) route to Clara Lake, Tern Lake and Rainbow Lake; and a

71 km (44 mile) trek to Islet Lake, Brown Lake and Rainbow Lake.

• The Highland Backpacking Trail has two loops: a 19 km (11.8 mile) trail around Provoking Lake; and a 35 km (21.7 mile) hike around Head Lake.

• The Eastern Pines Trail, on the park's east side, has 6 and 15 km (3.7 and 9.3 mile) loops.

Quotas ▶ Limits on the number of people allowed on backpacking trails have been set to alleviate overcrowding. Contact the park office.

Supplies ▶ Supplies may be obtained at several stores and outfitters within the park. Cans and bottles are banned from the interior.

Guidebook ▶ *Exploring Algonquin Park* by Joanne Kates. Includes descriptions of the park's trails. (See end of chapter.)

More Information:
Algonquin Provincial Park
Box 219
Whitney, ON K0J 2M0
Telephone: (705) 633-5572
Toll-free telephone: Ministry of Natural Resources, 1-800-667-1940
Website: www.algonquinpark.on.ca
Reservations for campgrounds and interior camping permits: toll-free
1-888-ONT-PARK (1-888-668-7275), or visit www.ontarioparks.com/

16. Ganaraska Trail

From Lake Ontario to the Bruce Trail

Created in 1969, the 500 km (310 mile) Ganaraska Trail begins in Port Hope along the Ganaraska River near Lake Ontario; it continues to the Bruce Trail at Glen Huron near Collingwood and then to Midland and Wasaga Beach.

The route crosses varied terrain: from Lake Ontario north it goes through the sand hills of the Ganaraska Forest, the lakes and drumlin fields of the Kawarthas, and the rugged wilderness of the Canadian Shield. Then it goes west, through the rolling hills of Simcoe County and along the shores of Georgian Bay.

About 257 km (160 miles) of trail have been completed. A little less than a quarter of the route remains to be blazed. Provincial parks and conservation areas with camping facilities are located adjacent to most sections of the trail. Emily Provincial Park at Omemee and Bass Lake Provincial Park at Orillia are recommended.

More Information:
Ganaraska Trail Association
12 King St.
Box 19
Orillia, ON L3V 1R1
Telephone: (905) 729-4545
Fax: (905) 729-4646
Website: http://www3.sympatico.ca/hikers.net/
E-mail: ck281@torfree.net

17. Frontenac Provincial Park
Lakes and forests on southern Canadian Shield; about 40 km (25 miles) north of Kingston

Frontenac Provincial Park is on the Frontenac Axis—the southernmost part of the Canadian Shield. Frontenac Park covers 70 square km (27 square miles) of diverse lake, forest and rugged terrain.

Forest Cover ▶ Rolling hills covered by deciduous forests lie in the northwest corner of the park. The middle section of the park is a transitional zone of broken ridges covered by mixed forests of pine, poplar, birch and red maple. The southern third of the park is a low area of sparse vegetation and numerous beaver dams.

Wildlife and Birds ▶ White-tailed deer, black bear, beaver, coyotes, red fox, otter, mink, weasel and raccoons are among the mammals that inhabit the park. Many birds may be seen here; among them, eagle, turkey vulture, red-tailed hawk, cliff swallow, loon, osprey, heron, kingbird, warbler, vireo, red-shouldered hawk and ruffled grouse.

WALKS. For walkers:

- The 1 km (0.6 mile) Arab Lake Gorge interpretive trail follows a boardwalk and explores the gorge's geology and ecology.

DAY-HIKES/BACKPACKING. For hikers and backpackers:

- A network of over 160 km (100 miles) of trails provides access to most of the park's backcountry for day-hikes, overnight trips, or longer outings. You can do loops ranging from 1.5 to 21 km (0.9 to 13 miles). The Moulton Gorge, the Arkon Lake Bog and the Black Lake homestead are all worth exploring. The Rideau Trail (described above) is incorporated into the southern part of the park's trail system.

More Information:
Frontenac Provincial Park
PO Box 11
Sydenham, ON K0H 2T0
Telephone: (613) 376-3489
Toll-free telephone: Ministry of Natural Resources, 1-800-667-1940
Website: http://www.ontario parks.com/
Reservations: toll-free 1-888-ONT-PARK (1-888-668-7275), or visit www.ontarioparks.com/

18. Bon Echo Provincial Park
Cliffs drop to Mazinaw Lake; on Highway 41, midway between Belleville and Renfrew, 10 km (6 miles) north of the village of Cloyne

The scenic highlight of this 66 square km (25 square mile) park in eastern Ontario is Mazinaw Rock. This 1.5 km (0.9 mile) long spectacular cliff—the result of faulting—drops 100 metres (328 feet) to Mazinaw Lake. The name Bon Echo refers to the acoustical properties of Mazinaw Rock. Scattered along the rock at canoe level are scores of Indian pictographs.

Bon Echo is located on the Frontenac Axis, the narrow southern extension of the Canadian Shield. Both northern and southern plants and wildlife are found within the park.

Forest Cover ▶ The mixed forest cover is made up of northern spruce, pine conifer, southern maple, beach and oak trees.

Wildlife ▶ Northern animals include timber wolves, snowy owls and moose; prairie warblers, grey squirrels and the five-lined skink are among the southern animals.

WALKS. Walks include:

- The 4.8 km (3 mile) Shield Trail, an interpretive walk on a part of the old Addington Road through rugged Canadian Shield landscape.
- The 1.4 km (0.8 mile) High Pines Trail, which leads past tall pines, hemlock groves and seasonal ponds to a view of Bon Echo Rock.
- The 1 km (0.6 mile) Bon Echo Creek Trail, which follows a winding creek bed as it enters lower Mazinaw Lake.

DAY-HIKES/BACKPACKING. For hikers and backpackers:

- The park features the Abes and Essens Trail, which consists of three loops: a 4 km (2.4 mile) loop around Chutes Lake; and two 9 km (5.5 mile) loops around Essens Lake. A hike around all three loops is about 17 km (10.5 miles) and may be done as a long day-hike or an overnight backpacking trip. The trail has five interior campsites, all situated near lakes. An interior camping permit is required. Call in advance for reservations.

More Information:
Bon Echo Provincial Park
RR #1
Cloyne, ON K0H 1K0
Telephone: (613) 336-2228
Toll-free telephone: Ministry of Natural Resources, 1-800-667-1940
Website: http://www.ontarioparks.com/
Reservations: toll-free 1-888-ONT-PARK (1-888-668-7275), or visit
www.ontarioparks.com/

19. Charleston Lake Provincial Park

*On the southern extension of Canadian Shield; exit from Highway
401 east of Gananoque, which is east of Kingston—go north
through the village of Lansdowne*

Charleston Lake Park occupies 8.5 square km (2 square miles) on the
Frontenac Axis, the southerly extension of the Canadian Shield. The
park combines a northern land form with a southern climate. More
than 30 prehistoric sites and Indian pictographs are located in the
park.

Wildlife and Birds ▶ Wildlife typical of both regions inhabit the area.
Loons, black rat snakes, great blue herons, turkey vultures, ducks and
geese may be observed.

WALKS. For walkers:

- The Sandstone Island Trail explores a prehistoric campsite and
  abandoned farm remains.
- The Quiddity Trail includes a 256 metre (840 foot) boardwalk and
  a lookout over Charleston Lake.
- The Hemlock Ridge interpretive trail explores the park's forests.

DAY-HIKES/BACKPACKING. For hikers and backpackers:

- The Westside hiking trail system provides access to Tallow Rock Bay and Captain's Gap on the park's secluded west side, where there are wilderness campsites. Quartzite ridges permit excellent views of Charleston Lake and surrounding area.

More Information:
Charleston Lake Provincial Park
RR 4
Lansdowne, ON K0E IL0
Telephone: (613) 659-2063
Toll-free telephone: Ministry of Natural Resources, 1-800-667-1940
Website: http://www.ontarioparks.com/
Reservations: toll-free 1-888-ONT-PARK (1-888-668-7275), or visit www.ontarioparks.com/

Northeastern Ontario

20. Killarney Provincial Park
White quartzite mountains and turquoise lakes; on the north shore of Georgian Bay, southwest of Sudbury—entrance is on Highway 637

The white quartzite La Cloche Mountains and clear lakes that vary in color from ink blue to turquoise make up this 485 square km (188 square mile) park located on the shores of Georgian Bay. Visibility in the lakes, which are found high on the ridges as well as in the valleys, ranges from 9 to 20 metres (30 to 65 feet). Many artists, including members of the Group of Seven, have painted scenes of the park.

Forest Cover ▶ The park is in a transition zone, lying between northern and southern forest types.

Wildlife and Birds ▶ Deer, moose, bears, timber wolves, coyotes and bobcats are among the mammals that inhabit the forest. Ruffed grouse, white-throated sparrows, barred owls, blue herons and common loons are among the resident birds.

WALKS. The park offers three self-guided nature trails:

• Cranberry Bog; Chikanishing; and Granite Ridge are loop routes, each of which can be walked in under three hours.

DAY-HIKES/BACKPACKING. The park features:

• The La Cloche Silhouette Trail—a 100 km (60 mile) loop through a variety of terrain that includes hemlock forests, beaver meadows and crystal clear lakes. The trail climbs to the summit of Silver Peak, which towers 360 metres (1,200 feet) above Georgian Bay. The trail also provides access to the exposed ridges for which Killarney is well known.

Supplies ▶ Outfitters in the town of Killarney and the city of Sudbury supply hiking needs. Cans and bottles are banned from the interior.

More Information:
Killarney Provincial Park
Killarney, ON P0M 2A0
Telephone: (705) 287-2900
Toll-free telephone: Ministry of Natural Resources, 1-800-667-1940
Website: http://www.ontarioparks.com/
Reservations: toll-free 1-888-ONT-PARK (1-888-668-7275), or visit www.ontarioparks.com/

21. Halfway Lake Provincial Park
Covered by an ancient glacier; along Highway 44, approximately 90 km (54 miles) northwest of Sudbury

High rolling hills, valleys with glacial soils, and eskers, kames and moraines on the uplands remain from the last Ice Age.

Forest Cover ▶ Giant white pines dominate the forest. Jack pine is the most common tree. Black spruce and tamarack are found in moist lowland areas, while white birch, maple and trembling aspen grow in the drier upland areas.

Wildlife and Birds ▶ Mammals common to Northern and Southern Ontario are found here. Moose are often seen. Other wildlife inhabiting the park include wolf, lynx, beaver, rabbit, chipmunk, squirrel and groundhog. Black bear are found in the park's remote areas. More than 90 species of birds have been identified. Herons, osprey and broad-winged hawks nest in the park. In the spring, migrating Canada geese may be seen. Also to be observed are pine warbler, evening grosbeak and barn swallow.

WALKS/DAY-HIKES. Of note:

- The 4 km (2.4 mile) and 8 km (4.8 mile) loop trails begin at Raven Lake and wind through rugged Canadian Shield terrain.

BACKPACKING. For backpackers:

- A 30 km (18 mile) loop trail to Three Island Lake and Crystal Lake has ten backcountry campsites along the shores of the park's lakes. These are also used by canoe-campers.

More Information:
Halfway Lake Provincial Park
199 Larch St.
Suite 901
Sudbury, ON P3E 5P9
Telephone: (705) 965-2702 (May to September); (705) 688-3161 (October to April)
Toll-free telephone: Ministry of Natural Resources, 1-800-667-1940
Website: http://www.ontarioparks.com/
Reservations: toll-free 1-888-ONT-PARK (1-888-668-7275), or visit www.ontarioparks.com/

22. Esker Lakes Provincial Park

Eskers, erratics and kettle lakes from last Ice Age; 37 km (23 miles) northeast of Kirkland Lake

Located in northeastern Ontario near the Quebec border, this 32 square km (12 square mile) park is characterized by long, winding serpentine ridges called eskers, great boulders known as erratics, and kettle lakes. These features were formed as a result of the last Ice Age.

Forest Cover and Berries ▶ The northern forest contains white birch, black spruce and jack pine. In the woods, you can pick raspberries, saskatoon berries, red currants, pin cherries and blueberries.

Wildlife, Birds and Fish ▶ The park is home to numerous large mammals, including moose, wolves and bears. Among the many species of birds in the park are the great blue heron, hermit thrush, red-eyed vireo, loon and grouse. The lakes contain speckled trout, northern pike and yellow perch.

WALKS. For walkers:

- The Lonesome Bog Trail is a 1.5 km (0.9 mile) walk circling Sausage Lake that explores the bog ecology of a dying lake.
- The 1 km (0.6 mile) Prospector's Trail skirts Lake Panagapka and passes old mining equipment.

DAY-HIKES/BACKPACKING. For hikers and backpackers:

- The Trapper's Trail explores a rolling esker, glacial erratics and an ancient Ojibwa trapping ground. It has three interlocking loops of 6.4 km (3.9 miles), 13 km (8 miles) and 20 km (12 miles), making it suitable for day-hiking or overnight trips. Rest shelters are located along the trail.

More Information:
Esker Lakes Provincial Park
PO Box 129
Swastika, ON P0K 1T0
Telephone: (705) 568-7677 (May to September); (705) 642-3222 (off-season)
Toll-free telephone: Ministry of Natural Resources, 1-800-667-1940
Website: http://www.ontarioparks.com/
Reservations: toll-free 1-888-ONT-PARK (1-888-668-7275), or visit www.ontarioparks.com/

23. Wakami Lake Provincial Park

On the divide between the Arctic and Atlantic oceans; 145 km (90 miles) northeast of Sault Ste. Marie along Highway 667, which is off Highway 129

Lying on the height of land separating rivers flowing to the Arctic Ocean and those flowing toward the Great Lakes and the Atlantic Ocean, the 88 square km (34 square mile) Wakami Lake Park encompasses Wakami Lake. Wakami is an Ojibwa name meaning "water is clear and still."

Forest Cover ▶ The forest is in a transition zone, between the northern boreal forest and the southern Great Lakes-Saint Lawrence forest.

Wildlife, Birds and Fish ▶ The park is inhabited by moose, mink, marten, fox, timber wolf, weasel, beaver and black bear. Birdlife includes bald eagles, ospreys, pileated woodpeckers, merlins, hawks and owls. Hikers fishing from the shore of Wakami Lake can catch walleye, pike and whitefish.

WALKS. Walks include:

• The 2 km (1.2 mile) Transitional Forest Trail, a loop route through a forest transitional zone.

- The Beaver Meadow Discovery Trail, a 2.4 km (1.5 mile) path that shows how beavers' activities have altered the forest.
- The Hidden Bog Trail, which is accessed at the 3 km (1.8 mile) point on the Height of Land Hiking Trail. Hidden Bog is a 1 km (0.6 mile) route along a northern bog on which vegetation is slowly growing across the acidic water.

DAY-HIKES/BACKPACKING. For hikers and backpackers:

- The 75 km (46 mile) Height of Land Hiking Trail goes around the shores of Wakami Lake. The hike takes four or five days. The western shore is the height of land—the watershed divide between the Arctic and Atlantic oceans. Along the route are remnants of early commercial activity. There are 20 campsites along the trail, all located on the shores of the lake.

More Information:
Wakami Lake Provincial Park
190 Cherry St.
Chapleau, ON P0M IK0
Telephone: (705) 864-1710
Toll-free telephone: Ministry of Natural Resources, 1-800-667-1940
Website: http://www.ontarioparks.com/
Reservations: toll-free 1-888-ONT-PARK (1-888-668-7275), or visit www.ontarioparks.com/

24. Voyageur Trail
Wilderness Trail along Lake Superior's shores

When completed, the Voyageur Trail will extend from South Baymouth on Manitoulin Island along the top of Lake Huron, through Sault Ste. Marie and then north along the shore of Lake Superior to Thunder Bay —a total distance of approximately 1,100 km (700 miles).

Approximately 500 km (310 miles) of the trail have been completed in bits and pieces along the north shore. The longest completed section runs from Elliot Lake (Highway 108), west to just past Sault Ste. Marie. Another section runs from Schreiber to Terrace Bay, and to Rossport. The coastal hiking trails in Pukaskwa National Park and Lake Superior Provincial Park (both described below) are affiliated with the Voyageur Trail.

The Voyageur Trail is a wilderness trail, and some remote or little-used sections may be in poor condition as a result of fallen trees or regrowth of vegetation. Always carry a map, compass and guidebook. The website includes information on the condition of each section of the trail.

Access ▶ In addition to road access, a ferry service operated by the Ontario Northland Marine Services connects South Baymouth with the Bruce Trail at Tobermory.

Supplies ▶ The website provides links to businesses along the trail.

More Information:
Voyageur Trail Association
PO Box 20040
150 Churchill Blvd.
Sault Ste. Marie, ON P6A 6W3
Telephone: (705) 253-5353
Toll-free telephone: 1-877-393-4003 (select message #9999)
Website: http://www3.sympatico.ca/voyageur.trail
E-mail: voyageur.trail@sympatico.ca

25. Lake Superior Provincial Park
On the rugged eastern shore of Lake Superior; along Highway 17
—south of Wawa and north of Sault Ste. Marie

Lake Superior Provincial Park features some of Ontario's most rugged landscapes. This 1,550 square km (600 square mile) park ranges from 180 metres (600 feet) above sea level at the Lake Superior shore to 600 metres (2,000 feet) at the peak of its hills.

The park offers more than 130 km (80 miles) of hiking trails.

Forest Cover ▶ The forest is part of the transition zone between southern deciduous and northern boreal forest. The hilltops are covered with yellow birch and sugar maple. Spruce, balsam fir and tamarack grow in the lowlands. This mixing of forests is dramatic in the fall. The colors are usually at their peak during the third week of September. The golds of the birch, aspen and tamarack persist well into October.

Wildlife, Birds and Fish ▶ The park's wildlife represent a mix of northern and southern species including moose, black bear, wolf and lynx, and smaller mammals. More than 130 species of birds have been recorded in the park, which is on a migration corridor. Brook trout and lake trout may be caught in the park's lakes. Rainbow trout spawn in the stream flowing into Lake Superior.

WALKS. Walking opportunities include:

- The 0.4 km (0.2 mile) Agawa Rock Pictographs Trail, which leads to the site of rock paintings.
- The 2 km (1.2 mile) Crescent Lake Trail, which loops through a stand of maple, birch and white pine.
- The 1.6 km (1 mile) Trapper's Trail, which loops along a floating boardwalk from where you can see wetland wildlife.
- The 6 km (3.7 mile) return Pinguisibi Trail, which leads along the waterfalls and rapids of the Sand River.

DAY-HIKES. These include:

- The Orphan Lake Trail, which leads 8 km (5 miles) to a cliff overlooking Orphan Lake and climbs to lookouts over Lake Superior.
- The 10 km (6 mile) Awausee Trail, which climbs the Awausee and offers views of the Agawa River Valley, Agawa Mountain and Lake Superior.
- The 5 km (3 mile) loop Nokomis Trail, which leads to a lookout over Old Woman Bay.

BACKPACKING. Two outstanding trails for backpackers:

- The most spectacular of the park's trails is the 60 km (37 mile) Coastal Trail. This is a challenging route along the high cliffs and rocky beaches of Lake Superior. It takes five to seven days to hike the whole trail. Access points make it possible to spend anywhere from a few hours to a full week on this trail. A shuttle service can be arranged in Wawa or Montreal River Harbour.

- The 24 km (15 mile) return Towab Trail leads to the 25 metre (82 foot) cascade of Agawa Falls, the park's highest waterfall.

Supplies ▸ Supplies may be obtained in Wawa, Montreal Harbour or Sault Ste. Marie.

More Information:
Lake Superior Provincial Park
PO Box 267
Wawa, ON P0S IK0
Telephone: (705) 856 2284
Toll-free telephone: Ministry of Natural Resources, 1-800-667-1940
Fax: (705) 856-1333
Website: http://www.ontarioparks.com/
Reservations: toll-free 1-888-ONT-PARK (1-888-668-7275), or visit www.ontarioparks.com/

26. Pukaskwa National Park

Primitive wilderness on Lake Superior. The park is near the town of Marathon, 305 km (189 miles) east of Thunder Bay and 406 km (252 miles) west of Sault Ste. Marie. Take Highway 17—the Trans Canada Highway—and turn off onto Highway 627, which is 10 km (6 miles) east of Marathon. Take Highway 627 for 15 km (9 miles) to the park.

Pukaskwa is a primitive wilderness area on 1,878 square km (725 square miles) of hilly Canadian Shield between the Pic and Pukaskwa rivers on the northeast shore of Lake Superior. Tip Top Mountain, the highest summit in the park, with an elevation of 630 metres (2,066 feet), is 450 metres (1,500 feet) above Lake Superior. The park's coastline is 80 km (50 miles) of exposed headlands, islands and islets, shoals, sand beaches, boulder beaches and coves. Lake Superior modifies the weather, and the coastal sections have cooler summers.

Forest Cover ▶ Arctic alpine plants grow here. Spruce, fir, cedar, birch and aspen cover the interior.

Wildlife, Birds and Fish ▶ Moose, wolf, black bear and woodland caribou inhabit the park's boreal forest. Birdlife includes ravens, hawks, loons, chickadees, kinglets, nuthatches and warblers. The park's rivers contain speckled trout, yellow pickerel, pike and sturgeon. Lake trout, rainbow trout, coasters and whitefish thrive in Lake Superior.

WALKS. For walkers:

- The 2 km (1.2 mile) Southern Headland Trail traces the history of volcanic rocks and ancient sea beds that formed the Canadian Shield.
- The 3.5 km (1.5 mile) Halfway Lake Trail explores a rock-rimmed lake in the boreal forest and reveals how a northern forest has been changed by Lake Superior.
- The 2 km (1.2 mile) Beach Trail winds along a boardwalk through sand dunes and sandy beaches. Don't miss the Pic River Dunes— the largest sand dunes on Lake Superior's north shore.

DAY-HIKES. For hikers, there is:

- A day-hike on the Coastal Hiking Trail for 7.6 km (5 miles) one-way from Hattie Cove to the White River Suspension Bridge. From the bridge is a view of the rushing torrents of Chigamiwinigum Falls.

BACKPACKING. For backpackers:

- The Coastal Hiking Trail meanders south over the rugged Shield terrain for 60 km (37 miles) along the Lake Superior shore. The northern section of the trail is well used and generally clear, but the southern half is more remote and rugged. Average time to walk to the North Swallow end and return is 10 to 14 days. Many hikers take a boat down and then hike back.

Supplies ▶ The nearest stores are in Marathon, 20 km (12 miles) away.

More Information:
Pukaskwa National Park
Heron Bay, ON P0T 1R0
Telephone: (807) 229-0801
Fax: (807) 229-2097
Website: http://www.parkscanada.gc.ca/
E-mail: ont_pukaskwa@pch.gc.ca

Northwestern Ontario

27. Sleeping Giant Provincial Park

Peninsula looks like giant when viewed from Thunder Bay. East of Thunder Bay; from Highway 11/17, go south on secondary road 587.

Sleeping Giant Park lies on the 40 km long and 13 km wide (25 by 8 mile) Sibley Peninsula, which juts southward into Lake Superior near Thunder Bay. The western shore of the 263 square km (101 square mile) park is dominated by cliffs rising over 240 metres (800 feet). The eastern lowlands of the peninsula rise gradually from Lake Superior. The highlands in the middle are characterized by deep valleys, sheer cliffs and fast-flowing streams. The high cliffs at the southwest end of the park are known as the Sleeping Giant, after an Ojibwa Indian legend.

Forest Cover ▶ The Great Lakes mixed forest is composed of poplar, white spruce, birch, white pine, red pine and cedar. Cloudberry, arctic bistort and butterwort are among the plants found here and elsewhere along the north shore of Lake Superior that otherwise do not appear south of Hudson Bay.

Wildlife, Birds and Fish ▶ Moose, wolf, lynx, deer and bear inhabit the forest. Several species of gulls, ducks and ruffed grouse may be seen. Pike, pickerel, bass, brook trout and rainbow trout may be caught in the park's lakes and streams.

WALKS. Interpretive trails at Sleeping Giant Park include:

- Sibley Creek Trail, which traverses a former timber-cutting area.
- Joe Creek Trail, which often has woodland flowers along the path.
- Thunder Bay Bogs Trail, which explores the effects of glaciation.

DAY-HIKES/BACKPACKING. The park has 64 km (40 miles) of interconnecting hiking trails:

- The 40 km (25 mile) Kabeyun Trail follows the western and southern shores of the peninsula and circles the Sleeping Giant and offers good views in all directions. The longest distance between campsites is 13 km (8 miles). The several connecting trails enable hikers to do trips from one to five days.
- The park's eight other hiking trails provide access to the interior.

Supplies ▶ Supplies may be obtained in Thunder Bay; or in the town of Pass Lake, which borders the park.

More Information:
Sleeping Giant Provincial Park
Pass Lake, ON P0T 2M0
Telephone: (807) 977-2526
Toll-free telephone: Ministry of Natural Resources, 1-800-667-1940
Website: http://www.ontarioparks.com/
Reservations: toll-free 1-888-ONT-PARK (1-888-668-7275), or visit
www.ontarioparks.com/

28. Quetico Provincial Park
Dramatic cliffs, waterfalls and lakes; off Highway 11, about 160 km (100 miles) west of Thunder Bay and extending south to the Minnesota border

Quetico covers more than 4,660 square km (1,800 square miles) of Canadian Shield wilderness in northwestern Ontario. The rugged landscape is characterized by waterfalls, lakes and majestic cliffs. Among the park's highlights are its numerous Indian pictograph sites. Many of the rock paintings are on the cliff faces. The park, although perhaps best known for its wilderness canoeing, offers good hiking opportunities.

Forest Cover ▶ Northern trees include black spruce, jack pine, trembling aspen and white birch. There are some southern trees, among them oak, elm, silver maple and yellow birch.

Wildlife, Birds and Fish ▶ Moose, wolves, black bears, red squirrels, chipmunks, beaver and mink inhabit the park. As well, more than 90 species of birds nest in Quetico, among them bald eagles, osprey, common loons and barred owls. The many lakes offer good opportunities for catching trout, bass, yellow pickerel and northern pike.

WALKS. Five interpretive trails, beginning at the Dawson Trail Campground near the French Lake area, range from 1.5 km (0.9 miles) to 2.5 km (1.5 miles):

- The wheelchair- and stroller-accessible 0.8 km (0.5 mile) Pickerel River Trail is a boardwalk trail that explores the river's edge and lets you feel temperature changes, hear the sounds of the forest, and smell the soil and vegetation.
- The 2.5 km (1.5 mile) Beaver Meadows Trail loops through a variety of forest habitats.
- The 2.4 km (1.4 mile) return French Falls Trail winds along the French River as it cascades over rocky terrain in a series of waterfalls.
- The 0.8 km (0.5 mile) Pickerel Point Trail explores aquatic, plant and animal life along the Pickerel River. At Pickerel Point you may see bald eagles, great blue heron kingfisher or osprey.
- The 2.5 km (1.5 mile) loop Whiskey Jack Trail extends along a boardwalk through forested lowland covered in various moss species.

DAY-HIKES. For hikers:

- The 5 km (3 mile) French Portage Trail follows the route of a portage used by European explorers and fur traders. For a short while, the route was used by settlers on their way to Manitoba's Red River area.

BACKPACKING. For backpackers:

- The 10 km (6 mile) return Pines Hiking Trail travels along the Pickerel River through the interior to beaches on Pickerel Lake. You can hike this trail for overnight camping.

Supplies ▶Supplies may be obtained nearby in Atikokan. Cans and bottles are banned from the interior.

More Information:
Quetico Provincial Park
108 Saturn Ave.
Atikokan, ON P0T lC0
Telephone: (807) 597-2735
Toll-free telephone: Ministry of Natural Resources, 1-800-667-1940
Website: http://www.ontarioparks.com/
Reservations: toll-free 1-888-ONT-PARK (1-888-668-7275), or visit
www.ontarioparks.com/

Trans Canada Trail—Ontario
*Multi-use recreational trail across eastern, southwestern and
northern Ontario*

The Ontario section of the Trans Canada Trail is more than 3,500 km
(2,175 miles) long. From Quebec, it enters Ontario at Ottawa and heads
southwest to the Niagara Escarpment near Toronto. Branch lines from
Niagara Falls and Windsor will connect with the main trail. The route
will then go north toward North Bay and then west through Sudbury
and along the north shore of Lake Superior to Thunder Bay. It will then
go west past Kenora to Manitoba.

The multi-use Trans Canada Trail will link hiking trails, snowmobile trails, old railway right-of-ways and—in Northern Ontario—
forestry roads and pipeline corridors. Trails that will be part of the Trans
Canada Trail include the Voyageur Trail, the Elora Cataract Trailway
and the Elmira to Guelph Trailway.

More Information:
Ontario Trails Council
232A Guelph St.
Suite 203
Georgetown, ON L7G 4B1
Telephone: 1-800-ON TRAIL (668-7245)
Fax: (905) 873-7452
Website: www.tctrail.ca/ontario.htm
E-mail: admin@ontariotrails.on.ca

Trans Canada Trail National Office
43 Westminster Ave. North
Montreal West
Quebec H4X 1Y8
Telephone: 1-800-465-3636
Fax: (514) 485-4541
Website: www.tctrail.ca
E-mail: info@tctrail.ca

Guidebook Sources

Country Walks: Cottage Country. Anne Craik. Erin, ON: Boston Mills Press. Website: www.boston-mills.on.ca

Country Walks: The Niagara Escarpment. Ross McLean, Anne Craik and John Sherk. Erin, ON: Boston Mills Press. Website: www.boston-mills.on.ca

Exploring Algonquin Park. Joanne Kates. Describes the park's hikes. Vancouver, BC: Greystone Books (Douglas and McIntyre Publishing Group).

Great Country Walks Around Toronto. Elliott Katz. A guide to public transit accessible walks in the natural areas along Toronto's rivers and ravines, and on the shores of Lake Ontario. Toronto, ON: Firefly Books.

The Hike Ontario Guide to Walks in Carolinian Canada. Erin, ON: Boston Mills Press. Website: www.boston-mills.on.ca

The Hike Ontario Guide to Walks Around Toronto. Brad Cundiff. Erin, ON: Boston Mills Press. Website: www.boston-mills.on.ca

Ontario Provincial Parks Trail Guide. Allen MacPherson. Erin, ON: Boston Mills Press. Website: www.boston-mills.on.ca

The Waterfront Trail Guidebook. (Waterfront Regeneration Trust, 207 Queen's Quay West, Box 129, Toronto, ON M5J 1A7. Telephone: (416) 943-8080. Fax: (416) 943-8068. Website: www.waterfronttrust.com. E-mail: webmaster@wrtrust.com)

Waterfront Trail Mapbook. (MapArt Publishing Corporation, 70 Bloor St. E., Oshawa, ON L1H 3M2. Telephone: (905) 436-2525. Fax: (905)723-6677. Website: www.mapart.com)

17

Quebec

Jacques Cartier, the French explorer, climbed the wooded slopes of Mount Royal on Montreal Island in 1535 and gazed at the magnificent vista before him. This sense of discovery, along with the province's beauty and joie de vivre, can be enjoyed in Quebec.

Quebec's area of 1,667,926 square km (643,819 square miles) is twice the size of Texas and greater than the combined areas of France, Germany and Spain. Its three main geological regions are the Canadian Shield, stretching north of the St. Lawrence River to Hudson Bay; the Appalachian region south of the St. Lawrence; and the St. Lawrence Lowlands between the Canadian Shield and the Appalachian region.

The Canadian Shield forms an immense rolling plateau with a coniferous forest and many rivers and lakes. Quebec's Appalachian region, an extension of the Appalachian Mountain chain of the eastern United States, is a succession of plateaus and plains. The Chic-Choc Mountains in the Gaspé, with an average height of 900 metres (3,000

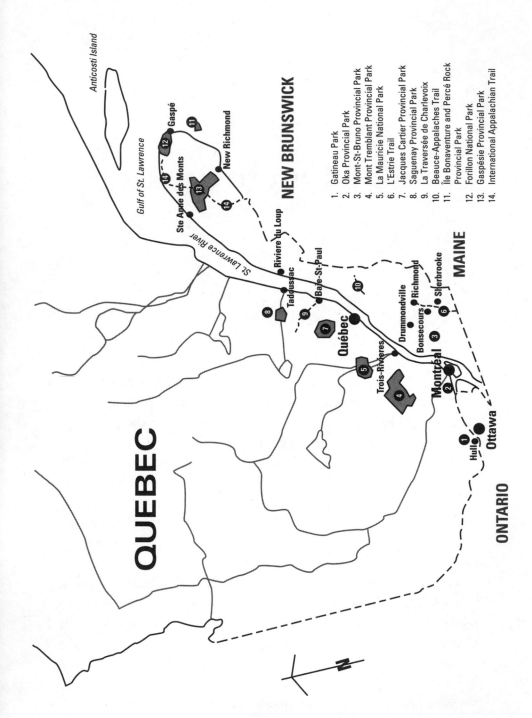

QUEBEC

Anticosti Island

Gulf of St. Lawrence

NEW BRUNSWICK

Gaspé

New Richmond

Ste Anne des Monts

Rivière du Loup

St. Lawrence River

Baie-St-Paul

Tadoussac

Québec

Trois-Rivières

Drummondville

Richmond

Bonsecours

Sherbrooke

MAINE

Montréal

Hull

Ottawa

ONTARIO

1. Gatineau Park
2. Oka Provincial Park
3. Mont-St-Bruno Provincial Park
4. Mont Tremblant Provincial Park
5. La Mauricie National Park
6. L'Estrie Trail
7. Jacques Cartier Provincial Park
8. Saguenay Provincial Park
9. La Traversée de Charlevoix
10. Beauce-Appalaches Trail
11. Île Bonaventure and Percé Rock
    Provincial Park
12. Forillon National Park
13. Gaspésie Provincial Park
14. International Appalachian Trail

feet), are a continuation of the 600 to 900 metre (2,000 to 3,000 foot) Sutton, Stoke and Megantic ranges of the Eastern Townships region southeast of Montreal.

Most of Quebec experiences a temperate climate, with hot summers and cold winters. Average rainfall during the summer months is approximately 11 cm (4 inches) per month. Quebec's mild autumn temperatures provide comfortable hiking weather, while the forests are a dazzling kaleidoscope of blazing colors; the backcountry is at its peak of beauty and should not be missed.

Quebec Tourist Information
Tourisme Quebec
PO Box 979
Montreal, QC H3C 2W3
Toll-free telephone: 1-877-BONJOUR (266-5687)
Fax: (514) 864-3838
Website: http://www.tourisme.gouv.qc.ca
E-mail: info@tourisme.gouv.qc.ca

Hostels
Tourisme Jeunesse
4545 avenue Pierre De Coubertin
Box 1000, Station M
Montreal, QC H1V 3R2
Telephone: (514) 252-3117
Toll-free telephone (Quebec and Ontario): 1-800-461-8585
Fax: (514) 252-3119
Website: http://www.tourismej.qc.ca/images/infos.htm
E-mail: info@tourismej.qc.ca

Ottawa/Hull Area

1. Gatineau Park
Wooded hills north of Ottawa

Situated just north of the Ottawa-Hull area, Gatineau Park covers 356 square km (138 square miles) of wooded mountains and lakes at the confluence of the Ottawa and Gatineau rivers.

WALKS/DAY-HIKES. These include:

- The 3 km (1.8 mile) Larriault Trail, which begins near Lake Mulvihill, winds along the 250 metre (820 foot) high Eardley Escarpment overlooking the Ottawa Valley and skirts a waterfall.
- The 2.5 km (1.5 mile) King Mountain Trail interpretive path from Black Lake to the top of King Mountain provides good views of the Ottawa Valley and is the site of Canada's first triangulation point, a reference mark for surveying.
- The Lusk Cave Trail, which leads 5 km (3.1 miles) to a marble cave, is considered rare in the hard rock of the Canadian Shield. From the cave you can return to the road or continue another 9 km (5.5 miles) to Taylor Lake.

More Information:
Gatineau Park
National Capital Commission
40 Elgin St., Suite 202
Ottawa, ON KIP 1C7
Telephone: (819) 827-2020
Website: www.capcan.ca

Montreal Area

2. Oka Provincial Park
On Lac des Deux Montagnes, 50 km (31 miles) from Montreal

Situated on the north shore of Lac des Deux Montagnes, Oka Park's 23.7 square km (9.2 square miles) offer a variety of trails and a sandy beach. The park is also traversed by a 30 km (18 mile) bicycle path stretching from St-Eustache to the town of Oka. The area is famous for Oka cheese made by Trappist monks of La Trappe monastery, located just outside the park.

WALKS/HIKES. The park has 30 km (18 miles) of trails:

* The 2.5 km (1.5 mile) Montée du Calvaire leads to a lookout on Le Calvaire d'Oka. Along the trail are several chapels that date back to 1739.
* The 5 km (3.1 mile) Colline Trail leads to the summit of Monteé du Calvaire and explores local ecology.
* The 9 km (5.5 mile) Grand Baie ecological trail features a floating walkway and skirts the shores of a bay of Lac des Deux Montagnes.

More Information:
Oka Provincial Park
2020 chemin Oka
Oka, QC J0N 1E0
Telephone: (450) 479-8365
Toll-free telephone: 1-888 PARC OKA (727-2652)
Fax: (450) 479-6250
Website: http://www.sepaq.com
E-mail: parc.oka@sepaq.com

3. Mont-St-Bruno Provincial Park

Rising from surrounding flat terrain; 20 km (12 miles) east from downtown Montreal

Mont-St-Bruno, 198 metres (650 feet) above sea level and standing out against the surrounding flat terrain, is a geographic phenomenon known as a monteregian hill. Other examples are Montreal's Mont Royal and nearby Mont-St-Hilaire and Rougemont.

Mont-St-Bruno Provincial Park's 6 square km (2.3 square miles) encompasses five lakes, a mixed hardwood forest, apple trees and a variety of birdlife. An old flour mill remains from its early settlement.

WALKS/HIKES. The park's network of 30 km (18 miles) of trails offers:

- Seven suggested circuits, ranging from 4.6 to 9.1 km (2.0 to 5.6 miles). Along the trails are a nature center at a restored mill (le vieux moulin); the remnants of glaciers from the last Ice Age; and look-outs offering good views.

More Information:
Mont-St-Bruno Provincial Park
55 Île Sainte-Marguerite
Box 310
Boucherville, QC J4B 5J6
Telephone: (450) 653-7544
Fax: (450) 670-2747
Website: http://www.sepaq.com/
E-mail: parc.st-bruno@sepaq.com

Laurentian Mountains

4. Mont Tremblant Provincial Park
In the Laurentians, 140 km (87 miles) north of Montreal

Created in 1894, Mont Tremblant Park covers 1,492 square km (580 square miles) of rolling hills, forests, lakes and streams in the northern Laurentian Mountains. At 967 metres (3,175 feet), Mont Tremblant is the highest peak in the Laurentians. Highlights include 15 metre high (50 foot) Diable Falls and 17 metre high (55 foot) Aux Rats Falls.

Forest Cover ► The mountains are covered with sugar maple, yellow birch, beech, fir, spruce and white birch.

Wildlife, Birds and Fish ► Moose, white-tailed deer, beaver, red foxes, black bears and wolves inhabit the park. More than 190 bird species have been seen in this park. The park's lakes and rivers contain northern pike, walleye, speckled trout and lake trout.

WALKS. The park's self-guiding nature trails include:

- The 2.7 km (1.6 mile) Lac des Femmes Trail, which explores geographic features of the Laurentians.
- The 1.5 km (0.9 mile) Lac aux Atocas Trail, which leads to various waterways.
- The 1.6 km (1 mile) L'Envol Trail, which traverses the park's maple and yellow birch forest.

DAY-HIKES. Most of the park's day-hikes lead to panoramic viewpoints:

- The 3.3 km (2 mile) La Roche Trail and the connecting 2.5 km (1.5 mile) La Corniche Trail lead to views of the Lac Monroe Valley.

BACKPACKING. Mont Tremblant Park offers 85 km (53 miles) of back-packing trails:

- The 51 km (31 mile) Grand Randonee Trail, a circuit from Lac Monroe to La Cachée, may be hiked as a loop or as a one-way trek (22 or 29 km; 13.6 or 18 miles). There are four shelters along the trails in addition to backcountry campsites.

- A 37 km (23 mile) trail in the park's La Pimbina area goes from Lac aux Rats and skirts Lac des Sables.

Supplies ▶ Supplies may be purchased in St-Faustin or St-Donat.

More Information:
Mont Tremblant Park
Chemin du lac Superieur
Lac Superieur, QC J0T 1P0
Telephone: (819) 688-2281
Fax: (819) 688-6369
Website: http://www.sepaq.com/
E-mail: parc.mont-tremblant@sepaq.com

5. La Mauricie National Park
Low rounded hills, narrow valleys and many small lakes; 60 km (37 miles) north of Trois-Rivières, 200 km (124 miles) northeast of Montreal and 190 km (118 miles) west of Quebec City

This 536 square km (208 square mile) park straddles the Laurentian Plateau and the St. Lawrence Lowlands. The Laurentians were rounded by glaciers during the Ice Age, and moraine deposits are now widely scattered in the park.

Forest Cover ▶ The transition forest consists of northern coniferous trees and the deciduous forests of the St. Lawrence Lowlands.

Wildlife, Birds and Fish ▶ The park is inhabited by moose, deer, black bear, wolf, coyote, lynx, fox and beaver. More than 143 species of birds have been observed in here, with 116 species nesting in the park. Anglers may fish the park's lakes for speckled trout, lake trout, northern pike and small-mouth bass.

WALKS. For walking:

- The 0.5 km (0.3 mile) Ruisseau Bouchard Trail is wheelchair- and stroller-accessible.
- The 3 km (1.8 mile) return Lac-Gabet Trail crosses a sugar maple stand to a blind where moose and other wildlife may be observed.
- The 1.5 km (0.9 mile) loop Lac Etienne Trail crosses several aquatic habitats, from where great blue herons, beavers and moose may be observed.
- The 2.1 km (1.3 mile) Les Cascades Trail follows a stream with cascades, crossing a marsh, an area hit by a tornado, and a maple forest.

DAY-HIKES. Day-hiking trails in La Mauricie Park include:

- The 6 km (3.7 mile) Plantation Circuit.
- The 14 km (8.6 mile) Bouchard-Pimbina-Benoit-Isaie Lakes Trail.
- The 6.4 km (3.9 mile) Bouchard and Pimbina Lakes Trail.
- The 17 km (11 mile) Les Deux-Cirques Trail, which has several steep climbs and leads to waterfalls of the ruisseau du Fou.

BACKPACKING. For backpackers:

- The 45 km (28 mile) Isaie and à La Pêche Lakes Trail is a three-day route along the shores of several lakes.

Supplies ▶ Food supplies are available in St. Jean-des-Piles and Grand Mère. Topographical maps may be obtained at the park office.

More Information:
La Mauricie National Park
794 5th St.
PO Box 758
Shawinigan, QC G9N 6V9
Telephone: (819) 536-3232
Fax: (819) 536-3661
TDD: (819) 536-2638
Reservations: (819) 533-7272
Website: www.parkscanada.gc.ca/
E-mail: parcscanada-que@pch.gc.ca

Eastern Townships

6. L'Estrie Trail
Path through the Eastern Townships

Offering scenic views of the Eastern Townships, Le Sentier de l'Estrie is a 150 km (90 mile) route in the Appalachian Mountains in this region southeast of Montreal. The trail begins at Kingsbury near Richmond. From Kingsbury, the trail leads south along Rivière au Saumon and Gulf Brook and over the 465 metre (1,975 foot) Mont des Trois Lacs. The trail then goes through the 58 square km (22 square mile) Mount Orford Provincial Park, passing over the 858 metre (2,815 foot) Mount Orford, then over Mount Glen, Mount Echo and Mount Sutton. The trail has campsites.

Supplies ▶ Supplies may be purchased in towns near the route.

More Information:
Les Sentiers de l'Estrie
PO Box 93
Sherbrooke, QC J1H 5H5
Telephone: (450) 297-0654
Website: http://www.interlinx.qc.ca/sentier
E-mail: Sentier@interlinx.qc.ca

For information on Mount Orford Park:

3321 chemin du Parc
Canton d'Orford, QC J1X 3W3
Telephone: (819) 843-9855
Fax: (819) 868-1259
Website: http://www.sepaq.com/
E-mail: parc.mont-orford@sepaq.com

Quebec City Area

7. Jacques Cartier Provincial Park
*Peaks rise above swift-flowing Jacques River; 40 km (25 miles)
north of Quebec City*

Wooded peaks rise 450 metres (1,500 feet) above the swift-flowing
river in the spectacular Jacques Cartier Valley. The park's 670 square
km (260 square miles) include the plateaus bordering the valley where
the river flows through gorges up to 600 metres (2,000 feet) deep.

The park has more than 100 km (60 miles) of trails.

Forest Cover ▶ The park's forest of coniferous trees is surrounded by
stands of white birch.

Wildlife and Fish ▶ The park is home to moose, caribou, black bear, wolf and lynx. Speckled trout are found in the lakes and streams; salmon and brook trout spawn here as well.

WALKS. Walking trails include:

- The 1.7 km (1.1 mile) L'Aperçu Trail, which explores the valley's natural life and history.
- The 0.8 km (0.5 mile) Le Petit Portage Trail, which leads to scenic rapids on the Jacques Cartier River.
- The 1.6 km (1 mile) Le Confluent Trail, which explores the confluence of the Jacques Cartier and Sautauriski rivers.

DAY-HIKES. Hiking opportunities include:

- The 5 km (3 mile) Le Perdeau Trail around Lac Buvard.
- The 8 km (5 mile) Les Loups Trail, with views of the confluence of the Sautauriski and Jacques Cartier rivers.
- The 4.3 km (2.6 mile) Les Cascades Trail.

BACKPACKING. For backpackers:

- The 12.1 km (7.5 mile) Le Draveur Nord Trail and the 15 km (9 mile) Le Draveur Sud follow the shoreline of the Jacques Cartier River. Shelters and primitive campsites are available.

More Information:
Jacques Cartier Provincial Park
9530 rue de La Faune
Charlesbourg, QC G1G 5H9
Telephone: (418) 644-8844
Fax: (418) 622-3014
Website: http://www.sepaq.com/
E-mail: parc.jacques-cartier@sepaq.com

8. Saguenay Provincial Park

Fiord gouged by glaciers of last Ice Age; 250 km (155 miles) northeast of Quebec City

The park features the dramatic scenery of the Saguenay River flowing through a 1,500 metre (4,900 foot) wide valley, with cliffs rising 500 metres (1,600 feet) above the water. Covering 283 square km (110 square miles) on both sides of the river, the park stretches from Baie des Ha! Ha! near Chicoutimi to the confluence with the St. Lawrence River at Tadoussac. Near Tadoussac, at the lower Saguenay, is a fiord gouged by glaciers of the last Ice Age.

The park has nearly 100 km (60 miles) of hiking trails.

Marine Life ▶ The Saguenay River, up to 600 metres (2,000 feet) deep, is the breeding ground of the beluga whale. Near the river's confluence with the St. Lawrence River other marine life may be seen—porpoises and finback, humpback, pilot and blue whales. At Tadoussac there are sand dunes and beaches.

WALK. For walkers:

- The Méandres Trail is a 1.6 km (1 mile) loop along the Rivière Éternité.

DAY-HIKE. For hikers:

- The Statue Trail is an approximately four-hour return hike to 518 metre high (1,700 feet) Cap Trinité. Here, a large statue of the Virgin Mary, built in 1881, overlooks a panoramic view of the Saguenay Valley.

BACKPACKING. For backpackers:

- The 25 km (15 mile) Capes Trail leads from near where Rivière Éternité flows into Baie Éternité, travels along the ridge of mountains (many views of the Saguenay Valley), and ends at the village of L'Anse Saint Jean. Along the trail are backcountry campsites and two huts. Reservations are required for the huts.

More Information:
Saguenay Provincial Park
3415 boul de la Grande-Baie Sud
La Baie, QC G7B 1G3
Telephone: (418) 544-7388
Fax: (418) 697-1550
Website: http://www.sepaq.com/
E-mail: parc.saguenay@sepaq.com

9. La Traversée de Charlevoix
Route through mountainous wilderness; northeast of Quebec City, on the St. Lawrence's north shore

This "traverse of the Charlevoix" is a 100 km (60 mile) wilderness hike through the rugged Charlevoix region on the north shore of the St. Lawrence River. Located north of the towns of Saint-Urbain and La Malbaie, the trail goes from Grands-Jardins Park to Hautes-Gorges Park and is surrounded by mountains that reach 850 metres (2,800 feet). Along the route are six log cottages.

More Information:
La Traversée de Charlevoix
841 rue Saint-Édouard
PO Box 171
Saint-Urbain, QC G0A 4K0
Telephone: (418) 639-2284
Fax: (418)639-2777
Website: http://www.charlevoix.net/traverse/imraid/eraid.htm
E-mail: traverse@charlevoix.net

10. Beauce-Appalaches Trail
Northern extension of Appalachian Mountains

This 31 km (19 mile) trail is situated in the Beauce region, a northern extension of the Appalachian Mountains southeast of Quebec City. From the town of Ste-Marie-de Beauce on the Chaudière River, the trail goes east past the town of Saint-Édouard de Frampton and crosses the Etchemin River. The trail covers agricultural terrain and mixed forests of maple, cedar and pine. Hiking the entire trail—along which are five shelters and several campsites—takes about three and a half days.

More Information:
Association touristique Chaudière-Appalaches
800 Autoroute Jean Lesage
Saint-Nicholas, QC G7A 1C9
Telephone: (418) 831-4411
Fax: (418) 831-8442
Website: www.chaudapp.qc.ca

Gaspé Peninsula

11. Île Bonaventure and Percé Rock Provincial Park

Two famous Quebec landmarks; 800 km (500 miles) northeast of Quebec City

Percé Rock is near the town of Percé. Île Bonaventure, 3.5 km (2.1 miles) offshore in the Gulf of St. Lawrence, is reached by boat from Percé. The park covers 5.8 square km (2.2 square miles).

Percé Rock, one of Quebec's most popular tourist attractions, has been immortalized by many artists. Stretching 510 metres (1,673 feet) long, 100 metres (328 feet) wide and 70 metres (230 feet) high, the rock derives its name from the 30 metre wide (98 foot tall) archway pierced in it by the sea. At low tide you can walk to Percé Rock. At other times, there are boat tours.

Forest Cover ▶ The island has a conifer forest and many wildflowers.

Birds ▶ The 4.1 square km (1.6 mile) Île Bonaventure is known for its migratory bird population. More than 200,000 birds nest here, among them 50,000 gannets—believed to be the world's largest colony of this species.

WALKS. Île Bonaventure has four nature trails:

- The 2.8 km (1.7 mile) Colonies Trail is suited for seniors, young children and groups.
- The 3.5 km (2.1 mile) Mousses Trail offers opportunities for viewing flora.
- The 3.7 km (2.2 mile) Paget Trail explores wooded areas and fields.
- The Chemin du Roy Trail leads 4.9 km (3 miles) along cliffs, past Baie des Marigots and near historic houses.

More Information:
Île Bonaventure and Percé Rock Provincial Park
4 rue du Quai
PO Box 310
Percé Rock, QC G0C 2L0
Telephone: (418) 782-2240
Fax: (418) 782-2241
Website: http://www.sepaq.com/
E-mail: parc.bonaventure @sepaq.com

12. Forillon National Park

Dominated by limestone cliffs; at the eastern end of the Gaspé

At the eastern end of the scenic Gaspé Peninsula, which separates the Gulf of St. Lawrence and the Baie de Gaspé, is the 244 square km (95 square mile) Forillon National Park. The peninsula's eastern coast is dominated by 180 metre (600 foot) limestone cliffs, while the southern shore facing the Baie de Gaspé has pebble beaches and small coves interspersed with rocky headlands. The hills in the interior reach almost 540 metres (1,800 feet).

Forest Cover ▶ The park features deciduous trees and arctic alpine plants.

Wildlife, Birds and Marine Life ▶ White-tailed deer, moose, red fox, black bear, Canada lynx and beaver inhabit the interior. Harbor seals and several species of whales may be observed in the waters near the park. More than 220 species of birds visit the park each year.

WALKS. Walks include:

- The Prelude to Forillon interpretive trail, which is wheelchair- and stroller-accessible and set up for people with visual impairments. The 0.67 km (0.4 mile) loop, which appeals to all the senses, focuses on the park's theme: Harmony among Human Beings, the Land and the Sea.
- Une Tournée dans Les Parages, a 3 km (1.8 mile) interpretive trail in the Grand-Grave area, which includes exhibits on farming and fishing at the turn of the century.
- The 1 km (0.6 mile) La Chute Trail, which leads to a secluded waterfall.

DAY-HIKES. For hikers:

- The 9.1 km (5.6 mile) Le Mont Saint-Alban Trail circles the summit and offers good views.
- The 8 km (4.9 mile) Les Graves explores the Bay of Gaspé coast (pebble beaches) and sites that are centuries old, and provides views of seals and whales.

BACKPACKING. For backpackers:

- The 15.8 km (10 mile) Les Lacs Trail, which leads to the park's highest peak and to several small lakes, has wilderness campsites. It also leads to the park's section of the International Appalachian Trail, described below.
- The 17.9 km (11 mile) Les Crêtes Trail travels along some of Forillon's mountain peaks from the Penouille area to Petit Gaspé, and offers good views of the peninsula.

Supplies ► These can be obtained in the surrounding villages of Gaspé, Cap aux Os and Cap des Rosiers.

More Information:
Forillon National Park
122 Gaspé Boulevard
PO Box 1220
Gaspé, QC G4X 1A9
Telephone: (418) 368-5505
Campground reservations: (418) 368-6056
TDD: (418) 463-6769; toll free (from Canada and U.S.): 1-800-464-6769
Website: http://www.parkscanada.gc.ca/
E-mail: parcscanada-que@pch.gc.ca

13. Gaspésie Provincial Park
Highest peak in southern Quebec; 510 km (317 miles) northeast of Quebec City

This 802 square km (310 square mile) park encompasses the Chic-Chocs Mountains, a northern extension of the Appalachian chain. The highest mountains of this range are known as the McGerrigle Group of peaks; hikers will see tundra on the 1,270 metre (4,166 foot) Mont Jacques Cartier, the highest peak in southern Quebec. Mont Albert is a moonlike plateau; precipitous slopes form a 20 square 8 km (8 square mile) table at an elevation of 1,151 metres (3,775 feet).

Forest Cover ▶ At the base of the mountains is a boreal forest. On the upper slopes is a thin forest, where the trees are under 2.5 metres tall. Alpine tundra, thick shrubs, moss, lichen and alpine flowers are found at the summit. Peat bogs are on the valley floors. On the mountain slopes are mixed stands of spruce and birch.

Wildlife ▶ Caribou, moose, deer, black bear and beaver inhabit the park.

WALKS. For walkers:

* The 1.4 km (0.8 mile) Le Roselin Trail (each way) leads to Lac aux Américains.
* The 5.2 km (3.2 mile) Les Cailloux Trail (each way) climbs Mont Richardson.

DAY-HIKES. For hikers:

* A 16 km (10 mile) trail on Mont Albert loops across the plateau.
* A 4.7 km (2.9 mile) trail on Mont Jacques Cartier ascends to and loops around the summit.
* A 12.4 km (7.7 mile) loop trail in the Lac Cascapedia area climbs Pic du Brûlé.

BACKPACKING. For backpackers:

* Trails for overnight or longer trips lead from Mont Jacques Cartier's day-hiking trails, along Lac aux Américains and then to the Mont Albert area.
* A network of backpacking trails winds from the Lac Cascapedia area west over a number of mountain summits to Mount Logan. Shelters and backcountry campsites are located along the trails.

More Information:

Gaspésie Provincial Park
124 1st Ave. West
PO Box 550
Ste-Anne-des-Monts, QC G0E 2G0
Telephone: (418) 763-3301
Fax: (418) 763-7810
Website: http://www.sepaq.com/
E-mail: parc.gaspesie@sepaq.com

14. International Appalachian Trail
Northern extension of Appalachian Trail to the Gaspé

On the North American mainland, the northeastern end of the Appalachian Mountains plunges to the Atlantic Ocean at Cap Gaspé at the eastern tip of Quebec's Gaspé Peninsula. The 1,000 km (600 mile) International Appalachian Trail links the northern end of the Appalachian Trail at Mount Katahdin, Maine, to Cap Gaspé. The Quebec section of the trail begins at the New Brunswick boundary near Matapedia, heads north through the Matapedia Valley and the Matane Reserve to Mount Logan in Gaspésie Provincial Park, and then goes east in the park to Mont Jacques Cartier—southern Quebec's highest peak. The trail then goes along the north side of the Gaspé Peninsula and through Forillon National Park, where it ends at Cap Gaspé.

More Information:
International Appalachian Trail
27 Flying Point Rd.
Freeport, ME 04032
Website: http://www.internationalat.org/
E-mail: sia-iat@cgmatane.qc.ca

Trans Canada Trail—Quebec
Multi-use recreational trail through Quebec countryside

Quebec's 3,000 km (1,800 mile) section of the Trans Canada Trail will join many of the province's diverse scenic regions. Linking the Ontario and New Brunswick sections, the trail will go through mountainous regions, flat countryside, wooded forests and picturesque villages, and along rivers and lakes. Hikers will walk through maple sugar groves, cross historic covered bridges and climb to mountain summits.

More Information:
Conseil québécois du STC
17460 avenue St. Onge
St. Hyacinthe, QC J2T 3A9
Telephone: (450) 774-0597
Fax: (450) 774-3137
Website: www.sentier.ca/quebec.htm

Trans Canada Trail National Office
43 Westminster Ave. North
Montreal West, QC H4X 1Y8
Telephone: 1-800-465-3636
Fax: (514) 485-4541
Website: www.tctrail.ca
E-mail: info@tctrail.ca

Guidebook Sources

The Adventurer's Guide to the Magdalen Islands. George Fischer. Describes beach and cliff hikes and bicycling routes in this archipelago of islands in the Gulf of St. Lawrence north of Prince Edward Island. Halifax, NS: Nimbus Publishing (PO Box 9301, Station A, Halifax, NS B3K 5N5, Telephone: (902) 455-4286 or 1-800-NIMBUS-9 (646-2879).

Hiking in Quebec. Yves Séguin. Montreal, QC: Ulysses Travel Guides (4176 St-Denis, Montreal, QC H2W 2M5, Website: http://www.ulysse.ca).

18

New Brunswick

The link between the Atlantic Provinces and the rest of Canada, New Brunswick has an area of 73,432 square km (28,354 square miles) and is part of the Acadian Highland, a rolling plateau intersected by ridges of great hills in both the north and south, with elevations reaching over 600 metres (2,000 feet). The Gaspésie Hills and the northern Appalachian Highlands separate the province from Central Canada. About 88 percent of New Brunswick is covered with forest nurtured by heavy rainfall. The Acadian mixed forest of birch, red spruce, balsam fir and sugar maple covers all but the province's northwestern corner, which has a boreal forest of white spruce, black spruce and jack pine. New Brunswick has 2,250 km (1,400 miles) of coastline on the Bay of Fundy, Northumberland Strait, Gulf of St. Lawrence and Chaleur Bay.

The interior of New Brunswick has a continental climate of hot summers and very cold winters, while the coast has more temperate weather due to the moderating influence of the ocean.

NEW BRUNSWICK

1. Dobson Trail
2. Fundy National Park
3. Fundy Footpath
4. Kouchibouguac National Park
5. Mount Carleton Provincial Park
6. Anchorage Provincial Park
   (Grand Manan Island)
7. Campobello Island
8. International Appalachian Trail

New Brunswick Tourist Information

Tourism New Brunswick

PO Box 5000

Fredericton, NB E3B 5C3

Toll-free telephone (in New Brunswick): 1-800-442-4442

Toll-free telephone (rest of Canada and the United States): 1-800-561-0123

Website: http://www.tourismnbcanada.com

Hostels
Hostelling International—New Brunswick
890 Mitchell St.
Fredericton, NB E3B 6C5
Telephone: (506) 454-9326
Website: http://www.hostellingintl.ca/database/NewBrunswick/

1. Dobson Trail
Rugged landscape from Moncton to Fundy National Park

This 58 km (36 mile) wilderness trail between the city of Moncton and Fundy National Park was named after Dr. Arthur Dobson, who developed the idea and directed its completion. The Dobson Trail traverses the rugged landscape approaching the coast of the Bay of Fundy and is located on privately owned and leased Crown woodlands. The route goes near marshes and through Acadian mixed forest and open fields. Points of interest include the lookoff at Prosser Ridge, the Hayward Pinnacle and an abandoned gold mine.

An Appalachian-type shelter is situated on the trail; camping at other locations along the route is off the trail, near springs and brooks. The trail crosses several good back roads, but it does not pass any towns or go close to stores that carry supplies. Provisions must be carried or cached at road crossings. Blackwood Lake is the best fishing spot on the trail. Trout may be caught in the brooks along the trail, but tend to be small. A fishing permit is required.

At the Fundy Park boundary, the Dobson Trail links with the park's Laverty Falls Trail.

More Information:
Dobson Hiking Trail
71 Derby St.
Moncton, NB E1C 6Y8
Telephone: (506) 855-5089

2. Fundy National Park

Majestic cliffs and world's highest tides; from Saint John or Freder-icton, take the Trans Canada Highway to 17 km (11 miles) east of Sussex, then take Highway 114 for 25 km (16 miles) to the park.

Skirting the Bay of Fundy for 13 km (8 miles) and extending inland for 15 km (9 miles) over a rolling forested plateau, Fundy National Park is 207 square km (80 square miles) of virtual wilderness. The area is famous for its tides, which reach 16 metres (53 feet) and are among the highest in the world. The coastline is characterized by a line of majestic cliffs that range in height from 9 to 60 metres (30 to 200 feet) and are divided at intervals by deep valleys with streams that flow into the Bay of Fundy. The plateau, a remnant of an ancient mountain range, averages 300 metres (1,000 feet) above sea level and is cut by valleys with steep rocky walls and waterfalls.

Fundy Park has 104 km (65 miles) of trails.

Forest Cover ▶ Acadian mixed forest covers the park's valleys and rounded hills. Along the coast, the effects of cool summers have pro-duced forest cover of red spruce and balsam, with some yellow and white spruce. The plateau, with warmer summers, is covered with sugar maple, beech and yellow birch.

Wildlife, Birds and Fish ▶ Moose, white-tailed deer, beaver and snow-shoe hare are some of the mammals that can be observed. A large num-ber of bobcat inhabit the park, but are rarely seen.

The shoreline of the Bay of Fundy is along a migration route, and in the spring and autumn large numbers of migrating birds stop at the park. Of the 185 species of birds observed, 87 nest in the park. Birds that can be seen include the common loon, red-throated loon, great blue heron, bald eagle, spruce grouse and ruffed grouse.

Anglers can find speckled trout in almost all the park's streams and lakes.

WALKS. For walkers:

- The first 0.5 km (0.3 mile) loop of the 3.4 km (2.1 mile) Caribou Plain Trail is wheelchair- and stroller-accessible. The trail loops through bogs and Acadian forest.
- Kinnie Brook Trail leads 2.8 km (1.7 miles) to a rocky river valley.
- The 1.5 km (0.9 mile) Dickson Falls Trail loops to the waterfall.
- The 1.1 km (0.7 mile) Devil's Half Acre Trail loop explores Fundy's geology.
- The 1 km (0.6 mile) Shiphaven Trail explores the lumberjack and Atlantic salmon eras.

DAY-HIKES. For hikers:

- The 3.5 km (2.1 mile) Coastal Trail to Herring Cove features sea cliffs and offers vistas of the bay.
- Other hikes lead to waterfalls and through wooded river valleys.

BACKPACKING. Five of the park's trails have backcountry campsites for overnight or longer trips. Of interest:

- The Fundy Circuit, a 50 km (31 mile) three- to five-day backpacking route, links seven hiking trails through river valleys and along lakes, waterfalls and the coast.
- The trail network connects with the Dobson Hiking Trail, which leads from the northern park boundary to the city of Moncton; and with the Fundy Footpath, which extends from the park's western boundary along the coast of the Bay of Fundy. (Both trails are described separately in this chapter.)

Supplies ▶ Camping supplies are available in the town of Alma.

More Information:
Fundy National Park
PO Box 40
Alma, NB E0A 1B0
Telephone: (506) 887-6000
Fax: (506) 887-6008
Website: http://www.parkscanada.gc.ca/
E-mail: fundy_info@pch.gc.ca

3. Fundy Footpath
Rugged footpath through coastal wilderness

Bay of Fundy coastal wilderness is explored by the rugged 26 km (16 mile) Fundy Footpath west of Fundy National Park. It goes from the Goose River at Fundy Park's southwestern boundary to Dustan Brook, a tributary of the Salmon River. Along the route are spectacular views of the Bay of Fundy, deep V-shaped river gorges, and dark forests with ancient trees. For 200 years tall pines from this forest have been used for ship masts.

Fog is common. The entire route takes an average of four days. Tides can change quickly.

Guidebook ▶ *A Hiking Guide to New Brunswick.* (See end of chapter.)

More Information:
Fundy National Park
PO Box 40
Alma, NB E0A 1B0
Telephone: (506) 887-6000
Fax: (506) 887-6008
Website: http://www.parkscanada.gc.ca/
E-mail: fundy_info@pch.gc.ca

Topographical maps and tide charts: Geographic Information Corporation (506) 856-3303

Weather: Environment Canada (506) 851-6610

4. Kouchibouguac National Park
Sand dunes, secluded beaches along the Northumberland Strait

Situated on 26 km (16 miles) of the shoreline of the Northumberland Strait, this 238 square km (92 square mile) park has sand dunes formed by the sea and wind, secluded beaches, salt marshes, bogs, swamps, and an Acadian mixed forest.

Wildlife, Birds and Fish ▶ Among the mammals that live in the park are moose, deer, black bear, bobcat, red fox, raccoon, porcupine, beaver, otter and snowshoe hare.

The protected ponds, rivers, lagoons and bays of Kouchibouguac Park are resting places for waterfowl during their spring and fall migrations and more than 200 species of birds have been recorded. The shoreline has a large population of sandpipers, plovers, terns, gulls and kingfishers. The swamps, fields and woodlands are inhabited by crows, ravens, hawks, ospreys, ruffed grouse, woodcocks, woodpeckers and sparrows.

Bass, eel, smelt, trout, flounder, clams, crabs and lobster may be found in Kouchibouguac's waters.

WALKS. Kouchibouguac's walks include:

- The 3.4 km (2.1 mile) Claire-Fontaine Trail, which follows the banks of Rankin Brook.
- The 5.1 km (3.1 mile) Conservation Trail, which passes marshes and creeks abundant in birdlife.

DAY-HIKES. For hikers:

*   The 11 km (6.8 mile) Major Kollock Creek Trail traverses the mixed Acadian forest, cedar swamps, small bogs and open fields.

BACKPACKING. For backpackers:

*   The 14 km (8.6 mile) Kouchibouguac River Trail follows the banks of the "river of the long tides" to Kelly's Beach, with its many coves. A primitive campsite is along the trail.

Guidebook ▶ *A Hiking Guide to New Brunswick.* (See end of chapter.)

More Information:
Kouchibouguac National Park
Kent County, NB E0A 2A0
Telephone: (506) 876-2443
Fax: (506) 876-4802
Website: http://www.parkscanada.gc.ca/
E-mail: atlantic_parksinfo@pch.gc.ca

5. Mount Carleton Provincial Park
Highest peak in the Maritimes; exit from the Trans Canada Highway at Perth-Andover and take Highway 109 toward Plaster Rock, then left on Highway 385 to the park

Situated in northern New Brunswick, Mount Carleton Provincial Park offers rugged terrain and a variety of forest types, wildflowers, birds and mammals. Mount Carleton, which reaches 820 metres (2,693 feet), is the highest peak in the Maritime Provinces. The park's eight trails total 45 km (28 miles). Mount Carleton is also on the route of the International Appalachian Trail. (Described separately in this chapter and in Chapter 17, Quebec.)

WALKS. For walkers:

- The 2 km (1.2 mile) Pine Point Trail follows the edge of the point of land in Lac Nepisiquit.
- The 1.8 km (1.1 mile) Williams Falls Trail, a loop, extends to the waterfalls.

DAY-HIKES. For hikers:

- The 6 km (3.7 mile) Mount Bailey Trail leads to a point for viewing the area.
- The 9.6 km (5.9 mile) Mount Carleton Trail, a loop route, extends to the summit.

BACKPACKING. For backpackers:

- Campsites are located off the Mount Carleton Trail.

Guidebook ▶ *A Hiking Guide to New Brunswick.* (See end of chapter.)

More Information:
Mount Carleton Provincial Park
PO Box 180
Saint Jacques, NB E0L 1K0
Telephone: (506) 551-1377

6. Anchorage Provincial Park—Grand Manan Island
Largest of the Bay of Fundy Isles; situated off the southwest coast of New Brunswick near the Maine border

Grand Manan Island is 35 km (22 miles) long and 10 km (6 miles) wide at the widest point. It's reached by a daily ferry service from Blacks Harbour to North Head on Grand Manan. The eastern side of the island has several villages and long, sandy beaches. The uninhabited western side, where the island's famous dulse is harvested, is characterized by craggy 90 metre (300 foot) cliffs.

The climate on the island is unpredictable, and hikers should be prepared for cool weather and periods of fog.

Wildlife and Birds ▶ Deer and rabbit can be seen. More than 240 species of birds, including the sea-diving puffin, make Grand Manan their home.

WALKS/DAY-HIKES. Grand Manan has 16 hiking trails, both along the coast and through the interior:

- At the southern end, a scenic trail along the cliffs provides excellent coastline views—from the South West Head Lighthouse to Bradford's Cove Pond.
- From Dark Harbour on the western side, a longer trail follows the coastline to Big Pond, then crosses the island's interior to a highway on the eastern side.
- Many old logging roads may be hiked. Anchorage Provincial Park, which occupies 1.4 square km (0.5 square miles) on the island, has two fresh-water lakes, plus four trails that total 6 km (4 miles).

Guidebook ▶ *A Hiking Guide to New Brunswick.* (See end of chapter.)

More Information:
Anchorage Provincial Park
Seal Cove
Grand Manan Island, NB E0G 3B0
Telephone: (506) 662-7022

Grand Manan Tourism Association
PO Box 193
North Head, NB E0G 2M0
Website: http://personal.nbnet.nb.ca/gmtouris
E-mail: gmtouris@nbnet.nb.ca

Daily ferry service from Blacks Harbour to North Head:
Coastal Transportation Limited
PO Box 26
Saint John, NB E2L 3X1
Telephone: (506) 657-3306)

7. Campobello Island

Famous former summer home of U.S. President Franklin D.
Roosevelt

Campobello Island, at the southwestern corner of New Brunswick, is
part of the Roosevelt-Campobello International Park. Adjacent to the
park is Herring Cove Provincial Park, which has short trails.

WALKS. It's possible to follow much of Roosevelt Park's shoreline. In
addition, the park has 13.5 km (8.5 miles) of walking trails:

* The 1.2 km (0.8 mile) Fox Farm Trail to Upper Duck Pond goes
  along a small estuary.
* The 3 km (1.9 mile) Liberty Point to Raccoon Beach goes along hills
  and through gullies, with views of rocky headlands and cliffs.

Guidebook ▶ *A Hiking Guide to New Brunswick*. (See end of chapter.)

More Information:
Tourism Officer
Herring Cove Provincial Park
Welshpool
Campobello Island, NB L0G 3H0
Telephone: (506) 752-2396

8. International Appalachian Trail
Footpath through northern Appalachian Mountains

On mainland North America, the Appalachian Mountains extend north from Maine through New Brunswick and Quebec to Cap Gaspé at the Gaspé Peninsula's eastern tip on the Atlantic Ocean. The 1,000 km (600 mile) International Appalachian Trail links the Appalachian Trail at Mount Katahdin, Maine, to Cap Gaspé.

The New Brunswick section of the trail begins at the Maine border crossing at Fort Fairfield. It heads to the village of Perth-Andover, along the Tobique River and through the village of Plaster Rock to Mount Carleton Provincial Park. From here, it heads to the villages of Saint Quentin and Kedgwick and then follows the Restigouche River to Matapedia and the Quebec provincial boundary.

More Information:
New Brunswick Trail Council Inc.
Main St.
Fredericton, NB E3A 1E1
Telephone: (506) 459-1931
Toll-free telephone: 1-800-526-7070
Fax: (506) 458-5639
Website: http://www.internationalat.org/
E-mail: nbtrails@nbnet.nb.ca

Trans Canada Trail and Sentier NB Trail

The Trans Canada Trail will cross southwestern New Brunswick following part of the Sentier NB Trail. (*Sentier* is French for "trail.") Both trails are multi-use routes for hiking, cycling, horseback riding, cross-country skiing and snowmobiling. Some sections will be accessible for wheelchairs and strollers.

More Information:
New Brunswick Trails Council, Inc.
235 Main St.
Fredericton, NB E3A 1E1
Telephone: (506) 459-1931
Toll-free telephone: 1-800-526-7070
Fax: (506) 458-5639
Website: http://www.gov.nb.ca/dnre/trail/nbtrails.htm
E-mail: nbtrails@nbnet.nb.ca

Guidebook Sources

A Hiking Guide to New Brunswick. Marianne Eiselt and H.A. Eiselt. Fredericton, NB (Goose Lane Editions, 469 King St., Fredericton, NB E3B 1E5).

19

Nova Scotia

Shaped like a lobster, a native delicacy, Nova Scotia is 55,487 square km (21,425 square miles). The province is almost completely surrounded by water—the Bay of Fundy on the south and the Northumberland Strait and the Gulf of St. Lawrence on the north—and has 7,446 km (4,625 miles) of coastline. The Isthmus of Chignecto, less than 32 km (20 miles) wide at its narrowest point, joins Nova Scotia with the continental land mass. Cape Breton Island, linked to the mainland by Canso Causeway over the Strait of Canso, is well known for its spectacular scenery of rugged Atlantic coastline with a mountainous background. The northern part of the island is a wild, wooded plateau about 360 metres (1,200 feet) high. There are numerous trails along the scenic coastline and in the province's interior.

Nova Scotia has a moderate climate. The prevailing winds from the west and northwest are modified by the ocean. Sea breezes from the Bay

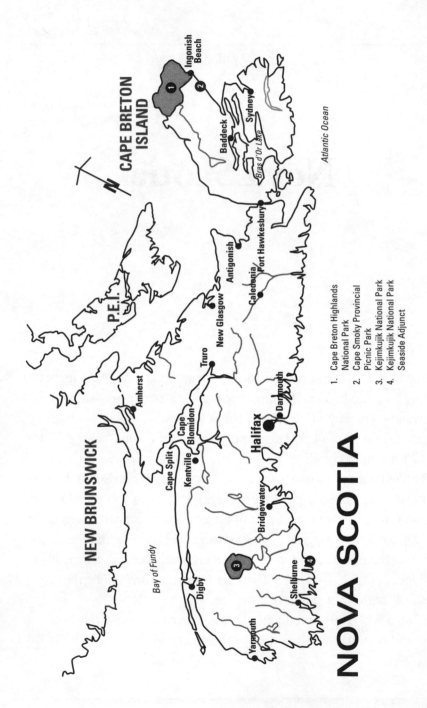

NOVA SCOTIA

NEW BRUNSWICK

CAPE BRETON ISLAND

P.E.I.

Atlantic Ocean

Bras d'Or Lake

Bay of Fundy

Ingonish Beach

Sydney

Baddeck

Port Hawkesbury

Antigonish

Caledonia

New Glasgow

Truro

Amherst

Cape Split

Cape Blomidon

Kentville

Halifax

Dartmouth

Bridgewater

Digby

Shelburne

Yarmouth

1. Cape Breton Highlands
    National Park
2. Cape Smoky Provincial
    Picnic Park
3. Kejimkujik National Park
4. Kejimkujik National Park
    Seaside Adjunct

of Fundy or the Atlantic Ocean keep summer daily temperatures averaging around 21°C (70°F). In summer, banks of fog drift inland—an average of 38 days during June, July and August—but rarely remain all day.

Average annual precipitation is 89 cm (35 inches). Spring arrives late in Nova Scotia but the autumn season is long.

Nova Scotia Tourist Information
Nova Scotia Tourism
PO Box 456
Halifax, NS B3J 2R5
Telephone: (902) 425-5781
Toll-free telephone (North America): 1-800-565-0000)
TDD: (902) 492-4833
Fax: (902) 420-1286
Website: http://www.gov.ns.ca/tourism.htm
E-mail: nsvisit@fox.nstn.ca

Hostels
Hostelling International—Nova Scotia
Sport Nova Scotia Centre
5516 Spring Garden Rd.
PO Box 3010 South
Halifax, NS B3J 3G6
Telephone/Fax: (902) 422-3863
Website: http://www.goldeye.com/Hostel/
E-mail: hostellingintl@ns.sympatico.ca

Ferry Information:
Depending where you're coming from, a ferry can shorten the drive to Nova Scotia.

Ferry service from Bar Harbour, ME, to Yarmouth, NS:
Bay Ferries
58 Water St.
Yarmouth, NS B5A 1K9
Telephone: (902) 742-6800
Toll-free telephone: 1-888-249-SAIL (7245)
Website: http://www.nfl-bay.com/mme-ns1.htm

Ferry service from Saint John, NB, to Digby, NS:
Bay Ferries
PO Box 418
Digby, NS B0V 1A0
Telephone: (902) 245-2116
Toll-free telephone: 1-888-249-SAIL (7245)
Website: http://www.nfl-bay.com/nb-ns.htm

Cape Breton Island

1. Cape Breton Highlands National Park
Coastal headlands and cliffs rising from the sea

Bounded on the east by the Atlantic Ocean and on the west by the Gulf of St. Lawrence, Cape Breton Highlands National Park is on the Appalachian Highlands. These reach 532 metres (1,747 feet), the highest point in Nova Scotia. The coastal cliffs on the western shore rise from sea level to 300 metres (1,000 feet), in contrast to the gentle hills on the eastern shore. The picturesque 950 square km (367 square mile) park offers wooded hills, tundralike highland bogs, treeless barrens, headlands and rocky and sandy beaches.

The park's trail system is more than 100 km (60 miles) in length.

Forest Cover ► The hills are covered with a thick Acadian forest of coniferous and deciduous trees. Balsam fir predominates at higher altitudes. Scrub growth and subarctic plants such as reindeer lichen grow on the central plateau.

Wildlife, Birds and Fish ▶ Deer, moose, fox, lynx, beaver, marten and black bear are indigenous to the area. More than 185 bird species, including sea birds such as gannets, puffins, terns and a variety of ducks and geese, may be observed. Atlantic salmon swim in the pools found on the park's western side; brook trout inhabit the many streams.

WALKS. Among the park's variety of trails:

- The 1.9 km (1.2 mile) Le Buttereau oceanside trail explores an area where pioneer Acadians first tilled the soil.
- The wheelchair- and stroller-accessible 0.6 km (0.4 mile) Bog Boardwalk Trail goes through a highland plateau bog.
- The 0.8 km (0.5 mile) Lone Shieling Trail explores the area's Scottish history and features a sheep-crofter's hut.
- The 4 km (2.5 mile) Middle Head Trail provides vistas of Ingonish Bay and Cape Smoky, with views of seabirds and whales.

DAY-HIKES. For hikers:

- The 9.6 km (6 mile) L'Acadien Trail loop leads to the top of Burnt Mountain, with panoramic views of the Acadian coast.
- The 7 km (4.3 mile) Skyline Trail loop is a headland cliff offering vistas of the Cabot Trail, the Gulf of St. Lawrence, and pilot whales, bald eagles and boreal birds.
- The 11 km (6.6 mile) return Coastal Trail follows the ocean shoreline.

BACKPACKING. For backpackers:

- The 16 km (10 mile) return Fishing Cove Trail leads along the Fishing Cove River to the ocean cove and a wilderness campsite. Explore the beach from here, and swim in either fresh or salt water.

Supplies ▸ Food supplies are available near the park.

Guidebooks ▸ Descriptions and maps of some of the park's trails are included in *Hiking Trails of Cape Breton Highlands National Park*, *Hiking Trails of Cape Breton and A Nature* and *Hiking Guide to Cape Breton's Cabot Trail*. (See end of chapter.)

More Information:
Cape Breton Highlands National Park
Ingonish Beach, NS B0C 1L0
Telephone: (902) 224-3403
Fax: (902) 285-2866
TDD: (902) 285-2691
Website: http://www.parkscanada.gc.ca/
E-mail: atlantic_parksinfo@pch.gc.ca

2. Cape Smoky Provincial Picnic Park
At Top of Smoky on the Cabot Trail

From here you have spectacular views of the coast. Situated opposite the Cabot Trail's highest point, 10 km (6 miles) south of Cape Breton Highlands National Park, Cape Smoky Park is in the center of an area that burned in 1968 when a smoldering campfire caused a large forest fire. The forest is now regenerating.

DAY-HIKE. For hikers:

• The 10 km (6 mile) return Cape Smoky Trail leads along 275 metre (900 foot) granite cliffs, with their many coastal lookouts.

Guidebooks ▸ *Hiking Trails of Cape Breton* and *A Nature and Hiking Guide to Cape Breton's Cabot Trail*. (See end of chapter.)

More Information:
Department of Natural Resources
Box 610
Baddeck, NS B0E 1B0
Telephone: (902) 295-2554
Website: http://parks.gov.ns.ca/

Nova Scotia Mainland

3. Kejimkujik National Park
Gently rolling landscape, and many lakes with islands and bays of inland Nova Scotia

Lakes, rivers and forests characteristic of inland Nova Scotia make up this 381 square km (147 square mile) park. Kejimkujik, a Mi'kmaq Indian word meaning "place that swells," refers to the largest of the park's many lakes.

Forest Cover ▶ The park's mixed forest consists of maple, oak, birch and white pine in the drier areas, and red spruce and balsam fir in the wetter areas.

Birds and Fish ▶ Among the birds that may be seen are the magnolia warbler, veery, pileated woodpecker and barred owl. American bittern and common yellowthroat nest in the large treeless bogs bordering many lakes. Rare birds, including the osprey and hooded merganser, nest in secluded areas. Brook trout, yellow perch and white perch swim in the park's waters.

WALKS. Among the park's 14 walking trails:

- The 3 km (1.8 mile) one-way Jakes Landing to Merrymakedge Beach Trail travels through a hemlock forest; includes a 0.9 km (0.5 mile) wheelchair- and stroller-accessible section along the shore of Kejimkujik Lake.

- The wheelchair- and stroller-accessible 0.3 km (0.2 mile) Mersey Meadow Trail features signs that identify the predators living in this habitat.
- The 2.2 km (1.4 mile) Beech Grove loop trail goes through a variety of forests along a drumlin—a hill formed by glaciers. A cassette tape provides information about the route's woodlands and wildlife.
- The 1 km (0.6 mile) Flowing Waters loop goes along the Mersey River.
- The 3 km (1.8 mile) Peter Point Trail goes through a good area for birdwatching and into forests of red maples, hemlock and old-growth sugar maples.

DAY-HIKES/BACKPACKING. For a longer day-hike, select part of one of the following backpacking routes, which range from two to six days. These routes explore a variety of forests, cross waterways and extend along lakes:

- Kejimkujik's longest hike is the 65 km (40 mile) Liberty Lake route. It stretches from Big Dam Lake to the Mersey River Bridge, a four- to five-day trip.
- The 20 km (12 mile) Big Dam Lake/Frozen Ocean Lake hike takes you on the first 10 km (6 miles) of the Liberty Lake route and returns by the same route.
- The 26 km (16 mile) Channel Lake is an overnight loop trail.

Supplies ▶ Supplies may be purchased in Caledonia, Maitland Bridge and other nearby communities.

Guidebook ▶ Several of the park's trails are described in *Hiking Trails of Nova Scotia*. (See end of chapter.)

More Information:
Kejimkujik National Park
PO Box 236
Maitland Bridge, NS B0T 1K0
Telephone: (902) 682-2772
Fax: (902) 682-3367
Website: http://www.parkscanada.gc.ca/
E-mail: Kejimkujik_Info@pch.gc.ca

4. Kejimkujik National Park Seaside Adjunct
White sand beaches and secluded caves

The 22 square km (8.5 square mile) Seaside Adjunct of Kejimkujik National Park straddles the tip of the Port Mouton Peninsula between Port Joli Bay and Port Mouton Bay, about 100 km (60 miles) from the inland portion of the park. The adjunct encompasses two white sand beaches, secluded coves, lagoons and exposed headlands. No facilities are available in this wilderness area, and overnight camping is not permitted.

Forest Cover ▶ The adjunct is made up of mixed forest and tundralike vegetation, including heath plants such as cranberry and bog rosemary.

Wildlife, Birds and Marine Life ▶ The park is home to mammals common to Nova Scotia, including white-tailed deer, snowshoe hare, raccoon and porcupine. From the shore you can see harbor seals, eider ducks, cormorants, sandpipers, yellowlegs and piping plovers.

WALKS. Although there are no trails in the seaside adjunct, hikers can walk along the coastal headlands and enjoy views of the rocky shore. Two rough trails—at times wet—provide the only access into the area:

- From Southwest Port Mouton, an old gravel road leads 8 km (5 miles) to the shore on Black Point.
- From the community of St. Catherine's River, a boardwalk extends 3 km (1.8 mile) and provides access to the western part of the adjunct.

Guidebook ▸ *Hiking Trails of Nova Scotia.* (See end of chapter.)

More Information:
Kejimkujik National Park
PO Box 236
Maitland Bridge, NS B0T 1K0
Telephone: (902) 682-2772
Fax: (902) 682-3367
Website: http://www.parkscanada.gc.ca/
E-mail: Kejimkujik_Info@pch.gc.ca

Trans Canada Trail—Nova Scotia
In Nova Scotia, the multi-use Trans Canada Trail will link with New-foundland at the ferry in North Sydney. The trail will go through Cape Breton Island and pass through Guysborough and Pictou County, where it will connect with the Northumberland Ferry to Prince Edward Island. It will then go through Colchester County and Cumberland County to Amherst, where it will link with New Brunswick. At Truro, a trail will link with Halifax. Approximately 700 km (420 miles) of the Trans Canada Trail will be in Nova Scotia.

More Information:
Nova Scotia Trails Federation
PO Box 3010 South
Halifax, NS B3J 3G6
Telephone: (902) 425-5450
Fax: (902) 425-5606
Website: www.trailtc.ns.ca
E-mail: sportns@fox.nstn.ca

Guidebook Sources

Hiking Trails of Cape Breton. Hostelling International—Nova Scotia. A guide to trails in Cape Breton Highlands National Park, Cape Smoky Provincial Park and other parts of Cape Breton Island. Fredericton, NB: Goose Lane Editions (469 King St., Fredericton, NB E3B 1E5).

Hiking Trails of Cape Breton Highlands National Park. Details 28 hiking trails in the park. Cheticamp, NS: Les Amis du Plein Air (Box 472, Cheticamp, NS B0E 1H0).

Hiking Trails of Nova Scotia. Hostelling International—Nova Scotia. A guide to many of the trails in and outside of Kejimkujik National Park Fredericton, NB (Goose Lane Editions, 469 King St., Fredericton, NB E3B 1E5).

A Nature and Hiking Guide to Cape Breton's Cabot Trail. David Lawley. Halifax, NS: Nimbus Publishing (PO Box 9301, Station A, Halifax, NS B3K 5N5, Telephone: (902) 455-4286 or 1-800-NIMBUS-9 (646-2879).

Trails of Halifax Regional Municipality: An Ambler's Guide to 25 City and Country Trails. Michael Hayes. Fredericton, NB: Goose Lane Editions (469 King St., Fredericton, NB E3B 1E5).

20

Prince Edward Island

Prince Edward Island, the "Garden of the Gulf," is a gentle place of rolling farmland and small woodlots bounded by hundreds of kilometres of sandy beaches. Only a few beach areas are crowded with tourists, leaving hikers to enjoy the rest in solitude. The crescent-shaped island has a total area of 5,654 square km (2,184 square miles), making it Canada's smallest province, and is separated from the mainland on three sides by the Northumberland Strait.

PEI's beaches are washed by warm Gulf waters because the island is sheltered from the Atlantic by Nova Scotia and Newfoundland and is not affected by the cold northern currents. (The same sheltering effect also leaves the island free of fog.)

The terrain is low and rolling. The highest point on the island, the Caledonia Triangulation Station at the southeast end, is only 152 metres (500 feet) above sea level. The soil contains little rock and is a

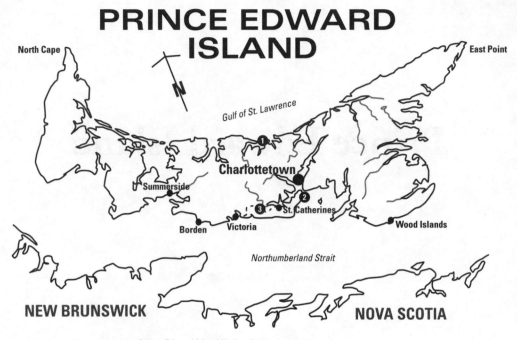

PRINCE EDWARD ISLAND

North Cape

East Point

Gulf of St. Lawrence

Charlottetown

Summerside

St. Catherines

Borden   Victoria

Wood Islands

Northumberland Strait

NEW BRUNSWICK

NOVA SCOTIA

1. Prince Edward Island National Park
2. Strathgartney Provincial Park
3. Bonshaw Hills Trail

distinctive red color. The irregular coastline has large bays and inlets, high cliffs and long sandy beaches with rocky coves.

PEI has a temperate climate; extreme and sudden changes in temperature are rare. Summer days are generally warm, thanks to an average high of 22.6°C (73°F). Nights are cool due to sea breezes. Overnight condensation usually keeps vegetation damp until about 10 am. Average annual precipitation is 110.5 cm (43.5 inches). The cooler autumn temperatures are also pleasant for hiking.

Confederation Bridge is the link between Cape Jourinmain, New Brunswick, and Borden-Carleton in PEI. The 12.9 km (8 mile) bridge is open 24 hours a day and takes about 10 minutes to drive across. It replaced the ferry service that formerly operated here.

Prince Edward Island Tourist Information
Tourism PEI
Box 940
Charlottetown, PEI C1A 7M5
Toll-free telephone: 1-888-PEI-PLAY (888-734-7529)
Telephone (outside North America): (902) 629-2400 or
(902) 368-4444
Fax: (902) 629-2428
Website: www.peiplay.com
E-mail: tourpei@gov.pe.ca

Hostels
Hostelling International—Prince Edward Island
PO Box 1718
Charlottetown, PEI C1A 7N4
Telephone: (902) 894-9696 in summer, 1-800-663-5777 in winter
Fax: (902) 628-6424
Website: http://www.hostellingintl.ca/database/PrinceEdwardIsland/

Hiking Trails:
Website: http://www.gov.pe.ca/infopei/Sports_and_Recreation/Trails/
Hiking/index.php3

Ferry Service (from Caribou, NS, to Wood Islands, PEI):
NFL Ferries
94 Water St.
PO Box 634
Charlottetown, PE C1A 7L3
Telephone: (902) 566-3838
Toll-free telephone: 1-888-249-SAIL (7245)
Fax: (902) 566-1550
Website: www.nfl-bay.com

Confederation Bridge:
Strait Crossing Bridge Limited
104 Abegweit Blvd.
PO Box 2032
Borden-Carleton, PE C0B 1X0
Telephone: (902) 437-7300
Toll-free telephone: 1-888-437-6565
Fax: (902) 437-7321
Website: www.confederationbridge.com
E-mail: info@confederationbridge.com

Wildlife, Birds and Fish ▶ Small wildlife, such as beaver, mink, muskrat, fox, weasel, squirrel and raccoon, is abundant on the island. Bird species include hawk, owl, falcon, black duck, Canada goose and teal. Anglers may fish the island's streams for brook trout, rainbow trout and Atlantic salmon.

1. Prince Edward Island National Park
Red sandstone cliffs, sand dunes, marshes, ponds, and saltwater beaches on the Gulf of St. Lawrence shore

Saltwater beaches on the Gulf of St. Lawrence dominate Prince Edward Island National Park's 32 square km (12 square miles). The magnificent white sand dunes contrast with the clear blue ocean. In July and August, water temperatures average 20°C (70°F), giving PEI beaches some of the warmest salt water north of the Carolinas in the United States.

WALKS/DAY-HIKES. The park's trails range from 1 to 8 km (0.6 to 5 miles):

• The 2.1 km (1.3 mile) Bubbling Spring Trail in the Dalvay Stanhope area loops through spruce woods and features a bird lookout over Long Pond.

- The 1 km (0.6 mile) Reeds and Rushes Trail is on a floating boardwalk over Dalvay Pond in the Dalvay Stanhope area.

- In the Green Gables House area in the Cavendish section are the 1 km (0.6 mile) Balsam Hollow Trail along the Babbling Brook (made famous in *Anne of Green Gables*); the 1.6 km (1 mile) Haunted Wood Trail through L.M. Montgomery's childhood environment, which inspired her writing; and the 5.5 to 8 km (3.4 to 5 mile) Homestead Trail through farmland and along the shore of London Bay.

More Information:
Prince Edward Island National Park
2 Palmers Lane
Charlottetown, PE CIA 5Z6
Telephone: (902) 566-7050
Fax: (902) 566-7226
Reservations (North America): 1-800-414-6765
Website: http://www.parkscanada.gc.ca/
E-mail: atlantic_parksinfo@pch.gc.ca

2. Strathgartney Provincial Park
Beech, sugar maples and yellow birches; a 20-minute drive from Charlottetown

Strathgartney Park, situated in the central Queens County Hills, offers scenic views of the West River.

Forest Cover ▶ A forest of beech, sugar maples and yellow birches is encompassed in the park.

WALK. For walkers:

* The 1.5 km (0.9 mile) Strathgartney Nature Trail traverses the park and neighboring Strathgartney Homestead in the central Queens County Hills. There are scenic views of the West River.

More Information:
Department of Fisheries and Tourism
Parks Division West
RR 3
O'Leary, PE C0B 1V0
Telephone: (902) 675-7476 (mid-June to early September);
(902) 859-8790 (year-round)
Website: http://www.gov.pe.ca/infopei/Sports_and_Recreation/
Trails/Hiking/index.php3

3. Bonshaw Hills Trail
Extends from outside Saint Catherines to Victoria

The Bonshaw Hills Trail extends for 30 km (18 miles) from the West River Bridge near the town of St. Catherines, to the beach at the town of Victoria. From the bridge, the trail follows the West River and crosses woodlots including a stand of white pine and hemlock near Appin Road. The route goes through old fields, on country roads and along the beach at Victoria. There are scenic views near Strathgartney and Hampton. The distances between road crossings range from 0.5 to 8 km (0.25 to 5 miles). Camping is available at Strathgartney Provincial Park, 3 km (2 miles) off the trail on Highway 1.

More Information:
Tourism PEI
Box 940
Charlottetown, PE C1A 7M5
Toll-free telephone: 1-888-PEI-PLAY (1-888-734-7529)
Telephone (outside North America): (902) 629-2400, or
(902) 368-4444
Website: http://www.gov.pe.ca/infopei/Sports_and_Recreation/Trails/
Hiking/index.php3

Confederation Trail/Trans Canada Trail—Prince Edward Island
Stretching across the island

From Tignish in the west to Elmira in the east, the 350 km (217 mile) Confederation Trail is on the right-of-way of the PEI Railway opened in 1875. Suited for hiking and bicycling and accessible for wheelchairs and strollers, the Confederation Trail crosses the island's terrain—fields, woodlots, wetlands, rivers and streams. It goes through villages with historic railway stations, and offers views of mussel buoys and fishing boats. The route is marked on the PEI Highway Map.

More Information:
Island Trails
PO Box 265
Charlottetown, PE C1A 7K4
Telephone: (902) 894-7535
Fax: (902) 628-6331
Website: http://www.tctrail.ca/pei.htm

National Office, Trans Canada Trail
43 Westminster Ave. North
Montreal West, QC H4X 1Y8
Telephone:1-800-465-3636
 Fax: (514) 485-4541
Website: www.tctrail.ca
E-mail: info@tctrail.ca

Guidebook Sources

Nature Trails of Prince Edward Island. J. Dan McAskill and Kate Mac-Quarrie. Charlottetown, PE: Ragweed The Island Publisher (PO Box 2023, Charlottetown, PE C1A 7N7, Telephone: (902) 566-5750, E-mail: books@ragweed.com).

21

Newfoundland

Newfoundland may well have been the first part of North America to be seen by Europeans. The Vikings certainly knew of it a thousand years ago, and European settlements date back 400 years. But most of its shores are still as rugged as they were when the first Viking splashed ashore. The interior still teems with caribou and bear, and the rivers still flash with trout and salmon.

The island of Newfoundland, with an area of 112,293 square km (43,359 square miles) is a continuation of the Appalachian Mountain chain. The Long Range Mountains on the northern peninsula rise abruptly from the west coast. Gros Morne Mountain, the island's second highest peak, reaches 795 metres (2,651 feet). Newfoundland's rugged southern and eastern coasts are laced with islets, filigree bays and coves.

NEWFOUNDLAND

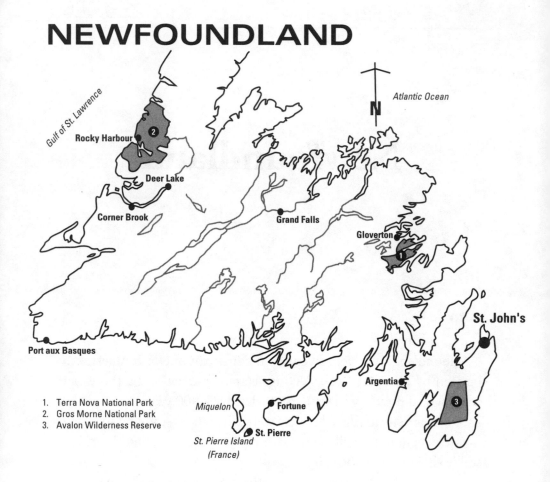

1. Terra Nova National Park
2. Gros Morne National Park
3. Avalon Wilderness Reserve

The island of Newfoundland lies directly in the path of storms moving northeastward up the Atlantic coast, and during the winter it experiences heavy snowfall. In early summer floating ice moves southward, producing fog and cool weather on the island. Newfoundland experiences frequent high winds, and precipitation on the east coast is heavy. St. John's experiences rain or snow an average of 201 days per year and averages a total of 137 cm (54 inches) annually.

Ferry service from North Sydney, Nova Scotia, to Port-aux-Basques, Newfoundland, is operated by Marine Atlantic; reservations are required and can be made in several ways (see below).

Newfoundland Tourist Information
Department of Tourism
Box 8700
St. John's, NF A1B 4J6
Telephone: (709) 729-2429 or call toll-free 1-800-563-NFLD (6353)
Website: http://www.gov.nf.ca/tourism/

Hostels
Website: www.hostels.com/ca.nf.html

Ferry Service:
Service operates from North Sydney, NS, to Port-aux-Basques, NF; reservations are required.

Marine Atlantic Ferry Service
PO Box 250
North Sydney, NS B2A 3M3
Toll-free telephone (Ontario and Quebec): 1-800-565-9411
Toll-free telephone (Newfoundland and Labrador): 1-800-563-7701
Toll-free telephone (New Brunswick, Nova Scotia and Prince Edward Island): 1-800-565-9470
Telelephone (rest of Canada): (902) 794-7203
Toll-free telephone (Maine): 1-800-432-7344
Toll-free telephone (rest of U.S.): 1-800-341-7981
Website: www.marine-atlantic.ca

1. Terra Nova National Park
Rocky fiords and a deeply indented coastline; located on the Trans Canada Highway, Terra Nova Park is 78 km (48 miles) southeast of the town of Gander.

Canada's most easterly national park, Terra Nova is located on the Appalachian Mountain Range and is 400 square km (155 square miles) of deep valleys, rocky fiords, rolling crested hills, spongy peat bogs, inland ponds and deeply indented shoreline. The cold Labrador current gives the area cool, wet summers. Icebergs, plus a variety of whales and seals, can occasionally be seen off the coast during the summer.

The park has more than 100 km (60 miles) of hiking trails.

Wildlife, Birds and Fish ▶ Moose, introduced to the island by man in 1878, are sighted frequently. Beavers, otters, snowshoe hares and black bears may also be observed.

Seabirds observed in the park include great black-beaked gulls, common terns, herring gulls and black guillemots. Land birds that may appear at the ponds include thrushes, sparrows, warblers, woodpeckers and willow ptarmigans.

Fishing for brook trout and Arctic char in the ponds, streams and lakes is excellent. Saltwater fish in the area include cod, mackerel, herring, lumpfish and capelin. Blue mussels, barnacles and periwinkles may be found on coastal rocks; crabs and lobsters thrive in deeper water.

WALKS. Among the park's more than 10 walking trails:

- The 5 km (3 mile) return Green Head Cove Trail is an easy walk along the coast of Southwest Arm where you may observe shorebirds, ducks and ospreys feeding.
- The Malady Head path leads 2 km (1.2 miles) to a lookout 200 metres (650 feet) above the sea, with views of the Arm and Alexander Bay.
- The 4 km (2.5 mile) Louil Hill loop trail leads to panoramic views of the park's northern end and Alexander Bay.
- The 8 km (5 mile) Buckley Cove Trail crosses forest and extends along the inner Newman Sound coastline past a small beach.

DAY-HIKES/BACKPACKING. For hikers and backpackers:

- On the 10 km (6 mile) return trail to Dunphy's Pond, the park's largest lake, are ruffed and spruce grouse, crossbills and great horned and boreal owls. A wilderness campsite is near Dunphy's Pond. From the trail are views of Clode Sound and the southern portion of the park.

- The 35 km (22 mile) Outport Trail extends along the coast from Big Brook, through the forest to the abandoned settlement at Minchin Cove, and to South Broad Cove, where there are primitive campsites.

Supplies ▶ Supplies may be purchased from the grocery store near Newman Sound, inside the park.

Guidebook ▶ A *Hiking Guide to the National Parks and Historic Sites of Newfoundland.* (See end of chapter.)

More Information:
Terra Nova National Park
Glovertown, NF A0G 2L0
Telephone: (709) 533-2801
Fax: (709) 533-2706
Website: http://www.parkscanada.gc.ca/
E-mail: atlantic_parksinfo@pch.gc.ca

2. Gros Morne National Park
Huge fiords with cliffs rising above the water; from Deer Lake on the Trans Canada Highway, take Route 430 for 50 km (31 miles) to Gros Morne Park

The tallest and most spectacular portion of the Long Range Mountains, Gros Morne Park lies on 1,805 square km (700 square miles) of Newfoundland's west coast on the Gulf of St. Lawrence. Gros Morne Mountain, at 806 metres (2,644 feet), is the second highest mountain in the province. The coastal Long Range Mountains are cut by huge fiords, with cliffs rising 650 metres (2,132 feet) above the water. The shoreline includes almost every type of beach, from fine sandy ones to those covered with large boulders. The coastal tidal pools support crabs, starfish, chitons, mussels, barnacles, periwinkles, hermit crabs, sea urchins and sea anemones.

The terrain is varied, and the park has more than 100 km (60 miles) of hiking trails through isolated areas of the coast and into the Long Range Mountains.

Forest Cover ▶ The barren top of the Long Range Mountains has a severe climate, producing a tundralike vegetation. Dense forests of balsam fir, black spruce, larch, white birch, mountain ash and red maple cover the lower slopes of the mountains. The Serpentine Tablelands south of Bonne Bay present a barren landscape that contrasts with the well-vegetated hills nearby. Because the park is located on the coast, hikers should expect some rain.

Wildlife, Birds, Fish and Marine Life ▶ Moose, caribou, black bear, arctic hare and red fox are some of the wildlife that inhabit the park.

One may observe birds characteristic of the upland plateau, such as eider duck, common and arctic terns, dovekies, herring gulls, great black-backed gulls and ptarmigans. Also seen are many southern forest birds, including the blue jay, black warbler and white warbler.

Anglers fish for salmon and brook trout in the park's fresh water and, in saltwater areas, for mackerel and cod. Several species of whales, porpoises and seals may be seen off the coast.

WALKS. These include:

- The wheelchair- and stroller-accessible Western Brook Pond Trail, a popular 3 km (2 mile) route across coastal bogs and low limestone ridges to the Western Brook Pond. There's a boat tour, and a beach near Stag Brook.
- The boardwalk on the 2 km (1.2 mile) Berry Head Pond Trail circles the pond and is wheelchair- and stroller-accessible.

- The 2 km (1.2 mile) Old Mail Road Trail leads to the Slants River.
- The 1-km (0.6-mile) Broom Point Trail goes through a tuckamore forest to a coastal meadow.

DAY-HIKES. For hikers:

- The 9 km (5.5 mile) return Green Gardens Trail leads to the coast, where sea stacks, volcanic pillow lavas, a sea cave (accessible at low tide) and secluded coves with waterfalls may be explored. Hikers can walk along the beach and through clifftop meadows.
- The Bakers Brook Falls Trail, a 10 km (6 mile) return hike, leads to the wide waterfalls.
- The 6 km (3.7 mile) each-way Lomond River Trail goes alongside the river.

BACKPACKING. For backpackers:

- The 16 km (10 mile) return Gros Morne Mountain Trail begins south of Rocky Harbor and crosses boreal forest, bog, alpine tundra and rock barrens to the summit of Gros Morne Mountain, which has views of Bonne Bay, the Tableland and the Long Range Mountains. A primitive campsite is located near the top of the mountain.
- In the Long Range Mountains—although there are no marked trails —hikers with map and compass may explore this spectacular area of deeply glaciated canyons and freshwater fiords situated 600 to 800 metres (2,000 to 2,600 feet) above sea level. The Long Range Traverse, a 36 km (22 mile) route through the Long Range Mountains, may be reached from Western Pond Brook or via the Gros Morne Mountain Trail.
- The 20 km (12 mile) North Rim Traverse, also not marked, is a route several kilometres north of the rim of the fiord

Guidebook ▶ *Best Hiking Trails in Western Newfoundland* and *A Hiking Guide to the National Parks and Historic Sites of Newfoundland* describe the park's trails. (See end of chapter.)

More Information:
Gros Morne National Park
PO Box 130, Rocky Harbour, NF A0K 4N0
Telephone: (709) 458-2417   Toll-free: 1-800-213-7275
Fax: (709) 458-2059   TDD: (709)772-4564
Website: http://www.parkscanada.gc.ca/
E-mail: grosmorne_info@pch.gc.ca

3. Avalon Wilderness Reserve

Precambrian barrens on the Avalon Peninsula; covered with tuck-amore, ship laurel, and Labrador tea

The Avalon Wilderness is situated on 1,070 square km (413 square miles) of the Avalon Peninsula in eastern Newfoundland. The barrens are covered with tuckamore, ship laurel, and Labrador tea. Canada's most southerly herd of caribou are seen here as well.

WALK. For walkers, there is:

• The 5 km (3 mile) Riverhead Trail, leading over barrens and bogs and into a caribou calving area.

DAY-HIKE. For hikers:

• The 10 km (6 mile) Biscay Bay Trail takes hikers along the Biscay River to Seven Islands. Caribou can usually be seen here.

BACKPACKING. For backpackers:

• The Daniel's Point to Holyrood Pond Trail is a two-day hike across the reserve's southwest corner.
• Extended trips are possible through the largely barren area. Hikers may encounter problems with boggy terrain in some areas; in others, it is nearly impossible to walk through the tuckamore.

More Information:
Parks and Natural Areas Division
PO Box 8700, St. John's, NF A1B 4J6
Telephone: (709) 576-2431 Toll-free: 1-800-866-2267
Website: http://www.gov.nf.ca/parks&reserves/

Newfoundland T'Railway—Trans Canada Trail
Along an old railbed across Newfoundland

The Newfoundland part of the Trans Canada Trail includes 883 km (530 miles) of the former CN Railway line from St. John's to Port aux Basques. Highlights include the 24 km (15 mile) Wreckhouse Trail near Port aux Basques. The trail, near Port Aux Basques, runs through coastal and mountain scenery and areas where many train wrecks happened as a result of high winds.

More Information:
Newfoundland T'Railway Council
PO Box 306, Gander, NF A1V 1W7
Telephone: (709) 256-8833 Fax: (709) 651-3849
Website: www.tctrail.ca/newfoundland.htm
E-mail: trailway@thezone.net

Guidebook Sources

Best Hiking Trails in Western Newfoundland. Keith Nicol. St. John's, NF: Breakwater Books (Box 2188, St. John's, NF, A1C 6E6).

A Hiking Guide to the National Parks and Historic Sites of Newfoundland. Barbara Maryniak. Fredericton, NB: Goose Lanes Editions (469 King St., Fredericton, NB, E3B 1E5).

Index